WESTERN IMAGININGS

The Intellectual Contest to Define Wahhabism

ROHAN DAVIS

The American University in Cairo Press
Cairo New York

The American University in Cairo Press
113 Sharia Kasr el Aini, Cairo, Egypt
420 Fifth Avenue, New York, NY 10018
www.aucpress.com

Exclusive distribution outside Egypt and North America by I.B.Tauris & Co Ltd., 6 Salem Road, London, W2 4BU

Dar el Kutub No. 13704/17
ISBN 978 977 416 864 2

Dar el Kutub Cataloging-in-Publication Data

Davis, Rohan
Western Imaginings: The Intellectual Contest to Define Wahhabism / Rohan Davis.—Cairo: The American University in Cairo Press, 2018.
p. cm.
ISBN 978 977 416 864 2
1. Wahhabism
2. Islamic fundamentalism
3. Muhammad Ibn Abd al-Wahhab, 1704–1792
297.814

1 2 3 4 5 22 21 20 19 18

Designed by Amy Sidhom
Printed in the United States of America

For my parents, Janice and Phil
And thank you Rob, I'm eternally grateful

Contents

Introduction

We shall not cease from exploration
And the end of all our exploring
Will be to arrive where we started
And know the place for the first time.
—T.S. Eliot, *The Four Quartets*

Like so many other authors, my researching and writing this book was inspired and motivated by an experience that had a profound effect on me. In 2008 I was in Stockholm, Sweden, staying in a small student apartment in the south of the city. It soon became clear to me that if I wanted to have something close to an authentic Swedish experience, then I needed to speak and understand some of the Swedish language. So I enrolled in a beginner-level Swedish language course, two classes a week. The classes had few students, and they were relaxed and enjoyable. The most interesting aspect of this experience was the friendships I made with other students while talking during coffee breaks and after class. It was a chance encounter with one young man in particular that would forever change how I would understand the world and which would inspire the years of researching and writing this book.

My new friend was from Palestine. We got to know each other during lunch and coffee breaks, and each week we shared more about life in our home countries. His story was particularly interesting because it gave me an insight into what it was like for Palestinians living under Israeli occupation. He told me about how the Israel Defense Forces had forcibly removed him and his family from their homes, and with no place to live, they fled to a Jordanian refugee camp. He lived in the camp for a few years until his application for asylum was eventually accepted by the Swedish government.

With the help of the Swedish refugee services, he was resettled in Kiruna, one of Sweden's most northern, darkest, and coldest cities. The small city is located north of the Arctic Circle, meaning it experiences both the midnight sun and the polar night throughout the year. Even for Swedes, Kiruna is especially cold, and it could not be any more different to the parched Palestinian landscape. Following the end of his employment in a factory, my new friend moved to suburban Stockholm where he lived with three other Middle Eastern refugees. Unable to speak Swedish fluently, he wanted to both communicate with the people of his adopted nation and have better employment opportunities. This inspired him to join the Swedish language class.

Up until this point in time I had never shown great interest in the situation in Palestine. When I thought about the ongoing conflict, far away from the suburbs of Melbourne, Australia, where I grew up, all I could recount was the narrative that tended to dominate the Western media: the Palestinians were by and large terrorists whose desire to violently attack Israelis was in part motivated by their radical Islamic beliefs. While we hear a lot more stories now about the dire situation in places like the West Bank and Gaza, my thoughts about the ongoing conflict were dominated by media reports about what they referred to as pro-Palestinian terrorist groups.

This narrative was however completely contradicted by what my new Palestinian friend was telling me. He was neither a terrorist nor a hater of Jews. He abhorred violence and did not want retribution against those responsible for displacing him, his family, his friends, and neighbors from their land. He wanted to spend his time doing what he loved—playing soccer, drinking coffee, and smoking. He called smoking his dirty habit, which he began during his time in the refugee camp to help him relieve stress, suppress his hunger, and pass the time. Like most people he also dreamed of falling in love and having a family. Most importantly, my conversations with him revealed to me another viewpoint about the ongoing Israeli–Palestinian conflict.

The stories I was told by the mass media about the conflict simply did not match up with what this man was describing, so I went online, searching for alternative news sites. The more I read, the more I became aware of the many competing narratives and categories writers were using when representing the alleged terrorist threat posed by Palestinians. One of the categories used by some writers that piqued my interest was something they were calling Wahhabism.

More research helped reveal to me that this was a term that became increasingly popular among Western scholars and commentators following the 9/11 terrorist attacks in New York and Washington. Prior to these attacks few Western scholars and commentators wrote about this phenomenon, and of those who did it was usually in relation to the role it played in the forming of the modern Saudi state. Articles about Wahhabism rarely appeared in popular US newspapers and magazines, and it was largely ignored by the plethora of US-based think tanks and foreign policy organizations now churning out documents about this primarily religious phenomenon. The 9/11 terrorist attacks were a turning point, as commentators began using the term when describing the influence it supposedly had on the Saudi Arabian hijackers. Furthermore, Western scholars and commentators began linking this Saudi state-sanctioned religion to Islamic radicalism and violent extremism throughout the world. The more reading I did, the less convinced I was of the apparent relationship between Wahhabism and Palestinian violence, which many US-based right-wing, conservative, and pro-Israeli commentators were claiming. My Palestinian friend had certainly never used the term. That experience planted a seed that has since grown to become this book.

This book is my modest attempt at understanding how the phenomenon Wahhabism has been represented by authors writing in a post–9/11 world characterized by anxiety about terrorism between and inside states. I am particularly concerned with how intellectuals belonging to the liberal and neoconservative traditions represent Wahhabism, and the different truth claims they rely on to support these representations. This book is also designed to understand some of the ways in which different ethical, political, and religious motivations are informing these representations.

I have set out a number of questions to help focus my book. They are: How have scholars represented Wahhabism? What kinds of problems are there with these interpretative exercises? What kinds of problems can we find in the sociology of intellectuals that warrant this kind of enquiry? How do liberal and neoconservative intellectuals in particular represent Wahhabism? And how are we to understand and make sense of these representations?

At this point it is important to briefly set out why I am focusing on *representations* of Wahhabism and not what is referred to as Wahhabism. There are numerous considerations that are shaping my inquiry. Though this proposition needs and gets some more elaboration later in the book, I want to highlight the basic difficulty of engaging with Wahhabism itself. There are good grounds for doubting that the phenomenon of Wahhabism has some natural or objective reality that can be immediately grasped as if it were a physical object. While we cannot see, feel, or touch the different social and intellectual processes constituting Wahhabism, we can examine its various representations. Additionally, it is hard to study a phenomenon in the social world for which we do not have a standard or widely agreed upon conceptualization or definition. Wahhabism, as I explain, is a contested category.

Let me start here with the proposition that Wahhabism does not have a natural or objective reality. This view owes a good deal to the critique of a long-standing tradition running through the history of Western philosophy after Aristotle and Augustine that treated language and its categories as if they were labels easily applied to real things. This view holds that a real thing exists in some external reality and corresponds with the concept in human thought to which the linguistic word refers. This tradition was subverted by what we can refer to as the linguistic turn, which is associated with philosophers like Ludwig Wittgenstein and Richard Rorty, and with the deconstructionist turn announced by Ferdinand de Saussure and later by Jacques Derrida. Critiquing this tradition, Saussure explains that this approach

> assumes that ideas already exist independently of words; it does not tell us whether a name is vocal or psychological in nature. . . . [F]inally, it lets us assume that the linking of a name and a thing is a very simple operation—an assumption that is anything but true. But this rather naive approach can bring us near the truth by showing us that the linguistic unit is a double entity, one formed by the associating of two terms.[1]

It was Saussure who pointed out that it is impossible for definitions of concepts to exist independently of or outside a specific language system. Concepts like Wahhabism cannot exist without humans naming and attaching meaning to it. Authors like Gustav Bergmann have built on these ideas, emphasizing the key role language plays in constituting the representations of reality that we can then work with.[2] This is why my book focuses on representations, and because they are a major focal point, it matters that we have an understanding of what I mean when speaking about representations of Wahhabism and how they work.

The term 'representation' means 'to bring to mind by description' and 'to symbolize, serve as a sign or symbol of, serve as the type or embodiment of.' It comes from Old French *representer* meaning 'present, show, portray' and from the Latin term *repraesentare* meaning 'make present, set in view, show, exhibit, display.' We can trace the study of representations to classical Greece when Plato and Aristotle considered literature to be an important form of representation. In fact, Aristotle believed the arts to be valuable forms of representation, seeing them as a distinctly human activity. According to Aristotle, "From childhood, men have an instinct for representation, and in this respect man differs from the other animals, that he is far more imitative and learns his lessons by representing things."[3]

Since then, representations have been the focus of study for modern philosophers like Ernst Cassirer.[4] These studies have tended to understand man to be *homo symbolicum*, or a representational animal, treating him as a creature whose distinctive character is the creation and manipulation of signs, which are understood as things that stand for or take the place of something else.[5] As I will detail later, representations are also important elements of political theory. Political theorists have focused on them since at least the eighteenth century, when Edmund Burke sought to deal with the reccurring question about the relation between aesthetic or semiotic representation (things that stand for other things) and political representation (people who act for others).[6]

W.J.T. Mitchell offers a useful way of thinking about representations. He says we should think of a representation as a triangular relation of something or someone, by something or someone, and to someone. It is only the third part that must be a person. In light of this, Wahhabism can be understood as a representation of something, by an author and to an audience. Aristotle wrote that representations differ from one another according to object, manner, and means.[7] The object is that which is represented, the manner is the way in which it is represented, and the means is the material used. In this study the object is Wahhabism, the manner is the ways in which intellectuals use language to represent it, and the document, for example, the newspaper article, magazine story, or online publication, is the means.

Authors are also able to use language in different ways to help achieve their desired outcomes. They can use particular rhetorical techniques like analogies, metaphorical language, similes, and neologisms. They can also construct violent accounts in such ways that help persuade the reader to either condemn or condone particular acts of violence. Another focus of this book is understanding how intellectuals use these particular rhetorical techniques to help achieve their intended aims.

It is also important that we have a deeper understanding of the relation between the representational material and that which it represents. Semioticians typically differentiate between three kinds of representational relationships: icon, symbol, and index.[8] It is the symbolic representation that is pertinent to this book. Symbols tend to be based on arbitrary stipulation rather than their resemblance to the thing signified. Authors representing Wahhabism use text to stand in for what they believe Wahhabism to be, and then many of us as (uncritical) readers agree to regard it in this way. Representation in language is symbolic in that letters, words, and texts can represent states of affairs without actually resembling the situation. We are, as Ludwig Wittgenstein famously pointed out, simply playing language games.[9]

Ian Hacking is among the authors to have raised some important questions when it comes to studying representations.[10] He encourages us to consider whether we are explicitly or implicitly denying the existence of the natural world and if we are ignoring the possibility that some representations of the world are better than others. When I say that Wahhabism is an observer-dependent phenomenon represented by an author to an audience, what I mean is that the experience of Wahhabism in the social world comes into existence when categories are created for it, and these categories are shaped by authors with differing prejudices operating in different social and cultural contexts. As we will see, the variability in representations of Wahhabism across time and space (between intellectuals belonging to different traditions) helps illustrate this. Pursuing this line of reasoning provides for powerful insights into the cultural fabric pertaining to the construction of Wahhabism.

It is important that I state that I am neither denying that an observer-independent reality exists in the natural world nor am I asserting that everything is socially constructed. In terms of my ontological and epistemological approach I accept that a reality does exist and my interest is in how people make sense of it. My work does not decide which representations of Wahhabism are more truthful or better; rather I offer a critique of the different truth claims authors rely on when representing Wahhabism. Just as is the case with Hacking's work on 'making up people,' in which he argues that creating classifications like 'fugue' creates new ways to be a person, the ideas motivating my study of representations are that authors' conceptions of the phenomenon of Wahhabism shape both the ways in which we respond to it and treat the people and groups we ascribe as belonging to it.[11]

Representations have indeed been the source of much scholarly debate, especially in the field of literature, and have drawn the attention of preeminent thinkers like Plato. He accepted the common view that literature is a representation of life and for that reason he believed it should be banished from the state. He understood representations as substitutes for the things themselves or, even more worryingly, as false or illusory substitutes having the ability to inspire antisocial emotions among people.[12] The only representations allowed to exist in Plato's republic of rational virtue were those carefully picked and controlled by the state.[13] If we look at the situation in the world today we can see that many states think and act in the same way; however, the emergence of new social media continues to challenge this control.

Wahhabism means very different things to different people, which is a point that has been accepted by some better studies and which will become clearer throughout this book.[14] Wahhabism is in effect a deeply contested category, and I now want to introduce the reader to this contest that is taking place.

Wahhabism: A Contested Category

Wahhabism is conventionally and popularly understood to be a conservative version of Islam originating in Saudi Arabia, where it has a substantial following.[15] Muhammad Ibn Abd al-Wahhab is considered to be the founder of this tradition, which played a decisive role in creating the modern Saudi state in 1932.[16] The widely accepted story as recounted by Western commentators in particular is that Abd al-Wahhab, a scholar from the Najd region in what is now Saudi Arabia, was intent on promoting his understanding of monotheism to a self-identifying Muslim populace he believed to be polytheists worshiping a corrupted version of Islam.[17] Born somewhere between the late seventeenth and early eighteenth centuries, Abd al-Wahhab is said to have traveled to Muslim lands beyond his native Najd in the early 1800s, where he witnessed what he understood to be a laxity of conduct with regards to the practice of Islam.[18] W.F. Smalley noted that Abd al-Wahhab "returned home, a prophet with a message . . . that the world had gone mad. It had become polytheistic. . . . Islam had wandered far from the principals of Mohammed."[19] It is said that Abd al-Wahhab was particularly incensed by Muslims using the rosary, dressing in expensive attire, smoking tobacco, drinking alcohol, visiting shrines of dead Muslims, and debating the nature of God.[20]

Returning to his homeland a few years later with the aim of reforming Islam as it was practiced in the Najd region, Abd al-Wahhab's ideas made him unwelcome in his home city and he fled to the nearby city of Deraiyah, where he teamed up with a local leader, Muhammad Ibn Saud (from the now (in)famous Sa'ud family), who had his own political ambitions. The deal between the two, recounted by many Western scholars, was that they would unite the warring towns, villages, and tribes in the region under a government where Abd al-Wahhab could enforce his strict interpretation of Islam and Ibn Saud would be appointed the political ruler.[21]

Ultimately they were able to achieve their desire for religious and political control through both ideological subversion and military might, the latter supplied by fierce local Bedouin warriors commonly referred to as the Ikhwan.[22] While their rebellion against the Ottoman rule in Arabia was put down in 1818, the Wahhabi rebellions of the nineteenth and twentieth centuries ultimately proved successful in uniting the tribes of Najd and forming what would become the modern Saudi state.[23] It is said that the Ikhwan were seduced by this new religious identity they believed would allow the Bedouin in the region to unite and fight under the common banner of Islam, rather than continually fighting each other.[24] Their violent energies were channeled away from killing each other and instead focused on people in neighboring lands who did not share the religious vision promoted by Abd al-Wahhab. Joseph Kostiner explains that "according to the typical portrait, the Ikhwan were bold fighters, fanatical and absolutely devoted to their country and to the spread of Wahhabi tenets."[25] The modern Saudi state is therefore considered to be a fusing between the religious beliefs of an ideologue, a leader wanting to exert his control over a people, and a group of warriors inspired by both.

Today Wahhabism is generally described as a relatively small but very influential branch within Islam in general and Sunni Islam in particular, advocating a return to what its proponents claim to be the true principles of Islam.[26] Wahhabism is often identified for its ongoing efforts to purify what is seen as the modern, corrupted version of Islam, with the movement advocating for a return to basic principles, rules, and teachings of the version of Islam that existed during the time of the Prophet Muhammad and the first three generations of Muslims (often referred to as the pious ancestors, or the *salaf*).[27]

The doctrine of monotheism (*tawhid*) is widely considered to be the hallmark of both Abd al-Wahhab's teaching and the Wahhabi movement he inspired.[28] Proponents of Wahhabism are said to believe that a failure to adhere to and uphold *tawhid* is the key reason for a collapsing in social order, tyranny, corruption, oppression, injustice, and degeneration.[29] Proponents of Wahhabism are therefore widely known for condemning any practices or activities violating or that could violate this belief.[30] Commentators often remark that Wahhabism holds that dedication to *tawhid* must be absolute and any kind of worship or veneration of objects, or superstitious, animist, or other kinds of religious worship, are not tolerated.[31] It is said that other interpretations of Islam like Sufism, Shi'ism, and other versions of Sunni Islam are viewed by proponents of Wahhabism to be as unacceptable as the non-Islamic religions. Wahhabism's puritanical and iconoclastic philosophies are often blamed for its conflict with other Muslim groups.[32]

Here it is also worthwhile to have a basic understanding of how scholars have distinguished between the different versions of Sunni Islam. Wahhabism is commonly understood by those studying the evolution of the movement to have derived from an offshoot of the Hanbali school of law, considered to be the most conservative and smallest in terms of followers of the four schools of Islamic thought/religious jurisprudence (also called *madhhab* in Arabic) within Sunni Islam (the others are Shafi'i, Hanafi, and Maliki).[33] The Hanbali school largely derives its religious law (known as sharia law) from the Qur'an, the Hadith (the words and customs of the Prophet), and the views of the Prophet's companions (known as the *sahaba*). Unlike the Hanafi and Maliki schools, the Hanbali school does not accept community customs or jurist discretion as a basis for Islamic law in the absence of the Qur'an's and the Hadith's failure to provide clear answers to arising issues. Wahhabism's unwavering commitment to the basic principles, rules, and teachings of the version of Islam practiced during the time of the Prophet Muhammad and the *salaf* is the major reason why it is typically considered the most austere version of Sunni Islam.[34]

Followers of Wahhabism are, however, likely to reject the categorization as an offshoot of the Hanbali school, which views (what outsiders would call) Muslims as belonging to one of two groups: followers of the *salaf* or followers of the *khalaf* (those who come after the *salaf*), the latter of which are not typically considered by followers of Wahhabism to be real Muslims.[35] Some commentators have suggested that those following the way of the *salaf* will often label themselves as Salafis, while many outsiders, particularly those wanting to denigrate the movement, will insultingly label them as followers of Wahhabism.[36] The term Wahhabism is considered by some to be derogatory because of its suggesting that these Muslims are followers of the scholar Muhammad Ibn Abd al-Wahhab and Wahhabism as enforced by the Saudi Arabian state, as opposed to followers of the *salaf*. My choosing to use the term Wahhabism in this book is for practical reasons. It is how most laypeople identify this tradition and is the term used by the overwhelming majority of writers, commentators, and scholars, particularly those in the West. I am aware of the negative associations often attached to the term and can only hope that readers, particularly those within Saudi Arabia, understand there is no malicious intent inspiring and motivating my use of the term.

Modern Saudi Arabian society is widely understood to be the quintessential society ordered according to Wahhabi religious doctrine.[37] Wahhabism is typically seen as providing the theological basis for modern Saudi societal practices such as gender segregation, prohibition of alcohol, and the ban on women from driving.[38] Wahhabism is not, however, said to be confined to Saudi Arabia, with Western commentators in particular often writing about the different states and groups of people promoting this belief system.[39] Outside of Saudi Arabia, Qatar is the country most often described as enforcing Wahhabi religious doctrine, often attributed to the Saudi royal family's ongoing support for Qatar's ruling al-Thani family since the nineteenth century.[40] Outsiders however tend to view the Wahhabism enforced by the Qatari state as a lot less rigid than in Saudi Arabia.[41]

Beyond these basic understandings, Wahhabism is a heavily contested category. This quality is captured in the Wikipedia entry on the Wahhabi movement. As is so often the case with Wikipedia, the entry draws on a rich assortment of sources of varying degrees of credibility, tendentiously describing it as

> a reactionary religious movement or offshoot branch of Islam variously described as "orthodox", "ultraconservative", "austere", "fundamentalist", "puritanical" (or "puritan"), an Islamic "reform movement" to restore "pure monotheistic worship", or an "extremist movement."[42]

In the West, Wahhabism has been frequently singled out for attention as the source of modern Islamic terrorism. The US 9/11 Commission Report claimed that Islamist terrorism had found its inspiration in a long tradition of extreme intolerance flowing through the founders of Wahhabism, the Muslim Brotherhood, and prominent Salafi thinkers.[43] In Europe the directorate-general for External Policies of the European Parliament issued a report in 2013 warning, "the risks posed by Salafist/Wahhabi terrorism go far beyond the geographical scope of the Muslim world. The attacks on New York, Washington D.C., London and Madrid remind us of this." [44]

Equally, and given long-standing and close ties between a succession of US administrations and the Saudi government, it has mattered that Saudi officials have long insisted that Islam is tolerant and peaceful. They have repeatedly denied allegations that their government exports religious extremism or supports extremist political movements.[45] Likewise, careful scholarship by authors like Trevor Stanley suggest Islamic terrorism cannot be adequately explained as the export of Saudi Wahhabism, as many have claimed.[46]

This contest to define Wahhabism also involves Islamic scholars living in the West. Differing representations offered by Islamic scholars like Khaled Abou El Fadl and Stephen Schwartz are a microcosm of a much larger intellectual debate taking place in a range of scholarly and intellectual forums.[47] Both these authors are inspired and motivated by different religious and political interests. El Fadl claims to represent the majority of Muslims he believes to be moderate, peace-loving, and who, like many in the West, value human rights, embrace modernity, and respect women. According to his self-proclaimed moderate Islamic approach, Wahhabism is a corrupted version of Islam existing on the lunatic fringe of the wider Islamic faith.

Schwartz is strongly motivated by a desire to promote his Sufi Islamic beliefs. Drawing on his personal experiences with Sufism in the Balkan region throughout the 1990s, Schwartz claims Sufism can provide the much-needed voice of reason at a time when radical Islamists like the Wahhabis, with the support of the Saudi state, are engaging in terrorism and violence. Like El Fadl, Schwartz understands Wahhabism to be a corrupted and perverse version of Islam; however, this is because it does not align with his own Sufi beliefs, as opposed to the modern and progressive interpretation of Islam that El Fadl claims to follow.

As both intellectuals are offering different particular Islamic views, both are clearly inspired by differing political and religious interests. It is therefore unsurprising that they also rely on different kinds of evidence to support their claims. In terms made famous by Benedict Anderson, both El Fadl and Schwartz are constructing slightly different Imagined communities.[48] These differences in approach and reasoning only increase as we consider other scholarly representations of Wahhabism.

The Role of Intellectuals

There are important reasons why we should pay close attention to the work of intellectuals in general and the way intellectuals represent Wahhabism in particular. The long and rich scholarly tradition known as the sociology of intellectuals acknowledges that it matters what intellectuals are saying and writing.[49] Intellectuals writing in newspapers, scholarly journals, online, and in magazines produce a lot of what we think we know and understand to be Wahhabism. Many scholars have acknowledged it is these intellectuals who are producing knowledge in the social world in the form of representations that are informing our judgments and decisions, particularly with regards to foreign policy.[50] If we want to understand and make sense of some of the information influencing the modern political debate and policy- and decision-making processes regarding Wahhabism, then we must pay some attention to the ways in which intellectuals are representing this phenomenon.

The contest to define Wahhabism involves intellectuals, commentators, and polemicists from different intellectual and political traditions and frameworks, using different rhetorical techniques, making different claims to truth, and motivated by different ethical, political, and religious considerations. The sites of this contest are numerous and include the scholarly literature, mass media publications like newspapers and magazine articles, and the blogosphere as well. The significance of this intellectual battle becomes readily apparent when we consider the effects intellectuals' representations of a phenomenon like Wahhabism can have on politicians, public opinion, and policymaking, particularly when these are occurring in a political and social context characterized by heightened anxiety about Islamic terrorism.

We currently have a situation where a rise in spin has been accompanied by an increased demand on the part of policymakers and governments that are increasingly reliant on evidence when making policy.[51] Both the use of spin and the appeal to evidence rely on Enlightenment assumptions and approaches to securing the conditions of truth: public administrators rely on the rigorous collection of evidence to evaluate their legislative programs and policies, while governments rely on the scientific study of the effects of public relations campaigns.[52]

This conjunction has meant that since 2001 we have seen many Western governments rely on the creative presentation of facts or spin as evidence to manipulate public opinion and mobilize support for policies, particularly those involving military invasions of sovereign nations like Afghanistan and Iraq and supporting security and intelligence-gathering measures aimed at protecting Western interests from Islamic terrorism. Certain Western governments intent on pursuing their own political aims and goals have proven to be disingenuous and deceptive and have manipulated and fabricated facts to support their policies. The quintessential example is the intelligence failure inspiring the US-led coalition's invasion of Iraq in March 2003. The US and British governments claimed to have evidence that Saddam Hussein's regime possessed weapons of mass destruction that threatened the security of the West.[53] We now know this was not the case. The result is that we currently have a situation Hannah Arendt first commented on when writing about the politics of the Cold War in the 1960s, in which even factual truths have become open to manipulation.[54]

What is interesting to me and what helps animate and legitimate this book is the role Western intellectuals representing Wahhabism are playing in the modern political context. I am especially interested in their roles as representatives of particular interest groups keen to promote their beliefs and values. I share this interest with many prominent scholars who have dedicated a lot of time and energy to making sense of the role of intellectuals in the modern political context. This has become known as the sociology of intellectuals tradition.

This tradition began with groundbreaking work done by Karl Mannheim.[55] We have since seen an evolving tradition of inquiry and debate between intellectuals as diverse as Antonio Gramsci, Jean-Paul Sartre, Raymond Aron, Edward Shils, J.P. Nettl, Peter Berger, Michel Foucault, Jürgen Habermas, Judith Butler, Noam Chomsky, Michael Walzer, and Edward Said, all of whom have attempted to say what defines an intellectual and offered guidance on how we are to best understand their social significance.[56] Some of these writers like Foucault and Said have understood intellectuals as living on the margins or even outside of society, a circumstance warranted by their eternal pursuit of truth and of speaking truth to power.[57] Others like Habermas have treated intellectuals as critical to the maintenance of a public sphere and to the health of a democratic order.[58] There are also scholars like Gramsci who treat intellectuals as social animals bound to interest groups that use various ideological apparatuses like the media to help impose and legitimate particular values and beliefs on a society.[59] The debates about the role of intellectuals that I reprise at length in the next chapter help shape some of the issues I explore in the book.

The public sphere is also an important concept I refer to numerous times and warrants closer attention. The representations of Wahhabism provided by the intellectuals studied in this book appear in places like mainstream American newspapers, magazines, books, and online. We can categorize these different mediums as belonging to what we call a public sphere. Often when we think about the nature of the public sphere, we think of a community or public acting in a particular space. It is sometimes assumed civil dialogue flourishes in this kind of setting so long as it is free from domination and exclusion. This kind of approach however fails to recognize that communication in public rarely involves widespread and equal participation. We must appreciate the fragmented nature of these spaces, in which there are few who receive attention and many who give it. We must also understand that these spaces are largely comprised of audiences that are generally watching, reading, or observing what is happening.

Jürgen Habermas is often credited as providing the quintessential notion of the public sphere.[60] Habermas conceptualizes a public sphere as a place in which critical debate takes place and lists a number of conditions that must be met in order for a space to be categorized as a public sphere: there must be the ability to form a public opinion; all citizens must be granted access; citizens must be free of political and economic controls, therefore allowing them to speak about matters of general interest; and there must be debate about the general rules governing relations. Habermas's normative account has been extremely influential and is an interesting philosophical idea; however, there are more pragmatic conceptualizations like the one offered by Ari Adut that provide a better and more useful way of understanding this concept.[61]

Adut's conceptualization of the public sphere fits perfectly with how we can understand representations as working. The idea of access is integral to Adut's conceptualization, and he describes three ways people are able to attain this. One is to be physically present in the space, for example, when people meet and talk in the street. The second has to do with representational access, meaning that one's name, image, or words can appear in spaces like newspapers or magazines. Thirdly, we can have sensory access when the contents of the space are made available to our senses.

The term public sphere implies general access; however, the reality is quite different. Many public spaces have obstacles preventing most of us from being seen or having our opinions heard. This is especially the case when dealing with spaces that tend to receive a lot of publicity. Generally speaking, the more publicity a space receives, the harder it is to be heard or seen. Mainstream US newspapers like the *New York Times* and *Wall Street Journal* are good examples, as a select few contributors are able to publicize their opinions. When dealing with spaces that receive relatively high amounts of publicity, physical access becomes very hard and representational access is highly valued. Nearly anyone can submit an opinion piece to these newspapers, but very few will ever have their articles printed.

Conversely, forums on websites that encourage inclusivity like 4chan provide examples of spaces that receive relatively less publicity but are easier for people to access. Despite this, few would deny that newspapers like the *New York Times* form an important part of what we conceptualize as the public sphere. As a space it does not grant general access but it does provide many with sensory access. The public sphere as conceptualized by Adut is thus a generic term denoting all virtual or real spaces, the contents of which obtain general visibility or audibility. Key here is the term 'virtual,' which points to the important role played by online platforms. The internet as the new public sphere or as a key part of the public sphere continues to be a focus of much scholarly enquiry as more users go online to get information.[62] The integral role played by social media in the recent Arab Spring shows just how important the online world has become.

At this point it is also necessary to clarify whom we categorize as an intellectual and explain the basis for these claims. There has been and continues to be a lot of discussion about who is and who is not an intellectual. As we see with authors like Gramsci, Mannheim, Foucault, and Said, the conceptualizing of who or what is an intellectual is often tied to the role and responsibilities these authors believe intellectuals should adopt and adhere to. We are wise to reject the narrow and arguably prescriptive conception of the intellectual offered by authors like Said and Foucault, where the intellectual is someone existing on the margins of society.[63] More apt is the inclusive approach like that promoted by Gramsci. In this book, an intellectual is understood to be anyone who uses ideological apparatuses like the print and mass media and digital technologies to produce and disseminate representations of Wahhabism.

Whereas those adopting a more narrow definition of the intellectual may distinguish between a commentator, understood as someone who expresses a written opinion on a subject in the public sphere, and an intellectual, a relatively more inclusive approach means a commentator is treated as an intellectual. While Gramsci's ideas are hugely influential, it should be noted that the conceptualization of the intellectual used in this book is not Marxist, in that there is no reliance on any determinist assumptions about the work of the intellectual in relation to their class origins or affiliation. We can however associate our understanding of an intellectual to a particular group, including those writers promoting liberal and neoconservative values and beliefs.

I am also interested in the broader question about the role intellectuals play in creating what Anderson calls Imagined communities and what Said calls Imagined geographies.[64] These scholars, in addition to those like Eric Hobsbawm, Anthony Smith, Ronald Suny, and Michael Kennedy, are among those to recognize the important roles intellectuals play as catalysts in a variety of nationalist ideologies and movements.[65] Animating and legitimating this book is the desire to understand and make sense of the role intellectuals representing Wahhabism play in socially constructing a community that is imagined by the people who perceive themselves as part of that group, and the way intellectuals use text to create a perception of space that has helped inspire the global war on terror. It is in this sense that intellectuals play crucial roles in shaping the politics of modern societies.

The Nature of the Political

The nature of the political is a second wider intellectual problem at stake. How we are to understand politics, including how we define it and what we think the aims and goals of politics are, has been the focus of much scholarly debate. Early twentieth-century authors like Carl Schmitt and Max Weber offered challenging accounts of the political, controverting the then-conventional liberal framework. Weber and especially Schmitt questioned why this tradition had too readily assumed the legal, rational, and ethical norms undergirding the legitimacy of liberal democracies, a position that had long been accorded a hegemonic conceptual status in the West.[66] In more recent times authors like Bernard Crick and Simon Critchley have contributed to a different kind of critique of the liberal tradition.[67] For Crick and Critchley, politics is about helping to end injustice and wrongs suffered by the Other.[68] Like these scholars, it is important to understand that intellectuals representing Wahhabism make different assumptions that influence their representations. This matters when we begin to consider the influential role these representations can play in the policymaking process.

The relation between intellectuals' representations of Wahhabism and the policy- and decision-making process is the third key intellectual problem animating and legitimating this book. Bacchi provides an important and revisionist account of policy as a product of processes that lead to a particular way of representing political or policy problems. Her work is important because it helps show how policy works, how we are governed, and how the practice of policymaking implicitly constitutes us as subjects. Bacchi highlights the integral role intellectuals play in this process as it is them who are framing, choosing to highlight or ignore, particular aspects of problems in their representations that are informing the policy-making process.[69]

This raises some very important questions when we think that these intellectuals' representations of Wahhabism have the ability to influence foreign policy in an age where Western liberal governments are obsessed with the (real or imagined) threat posed by radical Islam. This circumstance requires that we ask, what are the bases for these representations? What are intellectuals choosing to emphasize and ignore, and why? What particular claims to truth are intellectuals relying on to support their assessments of the situation?

This takes me to my fourth and final problematic animating and legitimating this book, which is making sense of and dealing with the relation between truth and politics. This issue has been raised by a number of writers, including Hannah Arendt. Arendt writes that we live in an age of mass manipulation where even the status of factual truth is likely to be challenged.[70] We have, as Stephen Toulmin and John Caputo more recently pointed out, moved beyond a conception of truth framed in terms of timeless and universal propositions, without needing to give up on the idea of truth itself.[71] This entails that we still find ways of dealing with different claims to truth, particularly those that are religious and political in origin or substance.

Unable to make certain assumptions about truth that would then require defending a particular view and testing the veridicity of particular representations of Wahhabism against this view, I instead deal with the role prejudice plays in truth claims. I follow Arendt's advice and deal with the relation between truth and politics by identifying and unpacking the prejudices attached to and inspiring these truth claims.[72] This speaks to the much larger problem of how we should treat truth claims in the political sphere, which has major implications for things like foreign policy-making.

In this book I have decided to focus on intellectuals belonging to two traditions, namely liberalism and neoconservatism. I have identified these traditions because they are among the most prominent traditions in the political theory and international relations fields and because they have arguably had the most influence on governments in the modern political world. Neoconservatives, for example, played a major role in the George W. Bush presidency (2001–08), an administration determined to both wage and lead the global war on terror project that continues to dominate the international political context.[73] Liberalism has long provided a large framework of political vocabulary and ideas, which have informed Western governments and international and local activists keen on transforming totalitarian Middle Eastern regimes into liberal democratic states.[74]

To access the work of intellectuals from these traditions, I have chosen to analyze texts from a variety of sources, including books, journal articles, mainstream US newspapers, online magazines, and think tanks. Part of my reasoning for deciding to focus on US newspapers when analyzing texts written by neoconservatives is that neoconservatism tends to be US-centric.[75] Its effects are certainly global, especially when neoconservatives have positions of influence within the US government like they did during the George W. Bush administration; however, its intellectuals write articles primarily aimed at an American populace responsible for electing its political representatives.

There are a number of reasons why I have selected a range of articles appearing in scholarly literature, newspapers, online magazines, and from think tanks. First, these different forms can be conceptualized as providing key parts of what we can call a public sphere. This means that they are sites where information can be translated from an intellectual to a wider audience. For example, large numbers of people read newspaper articles written by liberal and neoconservative intellectuals appearing in the *New York Times*, *Wall Street Journal*, *Washington Times*, *Washington Post*, and *USA Today*.[76]

I have also chosen to include some lesser-known and less popular sources. Sometimes this has been a deliberate choice and other times it has been a necessity. An example of the former is my decision to include an analysis of neoconservative intellectuals' representations of Wahhabism appearing in the online magazine *The Weekly Standard*. This publication is widely regarded as one of the most prominent neoconservative publications.

At this point I should also talk about some of the major theories and frameworks influencing my work. I have drawn on the dialectical tradition Bertell Ollman has done a lot to resurrect and clarify.[77] This tradition, as Ollman and Smith argue, is a way of thinking about and using a set of categories that captures the real changes and interactions happening in the social world. It offers a way of investigating social reality and presenting what we find to others. A dialectical imagination encourages us to think less about things and more about relations and processes that are constantly affecting one another. It emphasizes the evolving nature of things and the relational nature of the social world. This approach has two key elements that are influencing my work, namely a philosophy of internal relations and a process of abstraction.[78]

To help show how this process of abstraction works, I will highlight the major role played by several important elements in constituting representations of Wahhabism. These elements are what Gerald Holton calls themata and what Kurt Danziger calls generative metaphors.[79] Holton defines themata as those presuppositions that often exist for long periods of history and which are not derivable "from either observation or analytic ratiocination."[80] Danziger describes generative metaphors as metaphorical descriptions that have been used over long periods of time and which have come to be thought of "as expressing some kind of literal truth."[81] I will describe both of these in greater detail later. At this point I want to point out that my ability to make sense of liberal and neoconservative representations of Wahhabism relies in part on my ability to abstract the roles both of these processes play when considering how intellectuals make sense of the world and the representing process.

This dialectical framing is particularly congruent with a critical discourse analysis approach I draw on when analyzing some of the different rhetorical techniques employed by liberal and neoconservative intellectuals. Since foundational work by key figures like Ruth Wodak, Norman Fairclough, and Clive Holes, this kind of approach has helped us to focus on the different ways social and political domination are reproduced in text and talk.[82] As a result of this work critical discourse analysis has become a well-known interdisciplinary approach to the study of discourse as a social practice and seems especially appropriate when engaging the work of intellectuals, whose practice is essentially discursive in nature. That critical discourse analysts treat language as a social practice means it is especially helpful in highlighting the dialectical nature of language as a constitutive medium that is made in and makes the world. This approach appreciates in particular the relational character of power and the often opaque nature of the relations between discourse and society. It also recognizes that these relations play integral roles in securing the interests of those in power.

Intellectuals have a plethora of rhetorical techniques available to them when constructing their representations of Wahhabism. Generally speaking, the more skilled and versed intellectuals are in applying their trade, the more rhetorical techniques they will have in their arsenal and the more complex their rhetorical techniques will be. All research faces limitations, and one of those I have encountered is that I am not able to analyze all of the different rhetorical techniques employed by intellectuals. Such a task would likely result in thousands of pages of textual analysis that would no doubt bore readers. I have chosen to focus on five specific elements of discourse, namely metaphors, similes, analogies, neologisms, and the structuring of accounts of violence. The general case for focusing on metaphors, similes, and analogies as crucial elements of discursive practice has been made by George Lakoff, Mark Turner, and Mark Johnson in a series of groundbreaking works, and more recently by Douglas Hofstadter and Emmanuel Sander.[83] Philosophers like Mary Midgley have also acknowledged the way these central features of language are integral to the mythmaking process.[84]

I have chosen to focus on neologisms primarily because many neoconservative intellectuals have chosen to deploy them when representing the apparent threat posed by Wahhabism. I think of how prominent neoconservative intellectuals like Frank Gaffney Jr., who uses the neologisms "Islamofascist" and "Islamofascism" when representing the apparent threat posed by Wahhabism.[85] I have also adapted Karen Cerulo's cognitive approach to establishing the ways the architecture of narratives of violence work to mobilize a range of ethical and emotional responses on the part of readers.[86] This is valuable because it allows me to abstract and make sense of intellectuals' claims relating Wahhabism to violence. The fact that Wahhabism received very little, if any, attention from Western scholars pre-9/11 and pre-global war on terror suggests its relation to violence is significant to some of the intellectuals representing it in the modern political context. Focusing on the structuring of violent accounts also helps to reveal some of the more subtle rhetorical techniques writers use in their attempts to persuade their audience. While many readers may have an understanding of what metaphors, similes, and analogies are and how they work, very few may be aware of the cognitive structuring of violent accounts.

Finally, I want to outline the structure of the argument in the book. In Chapter One I provide a cursory review of some of the scholarly literature dedicated to Wahhabism, teasing out some of the dilemmas that inspired this book. This involves looking at some of the truth claims scholars rely on when representing Wahhabism, examining how some scholars construct Imagined communities and Imagined geographies, and dealing with the problem of translation.

In Chapter Two I take a more concentrated look at the role of the intellectual. This involves taking a close look at the sociology of intellectuals tradition and establishing some of the key issues it has set loose. I also talk about making sense of truth, which helps us to deal with the different truth claims intellectuals rely on when representing Wahhabism, and the key role prejudice plays in influencing how we make sense of the social world.

In Chapter Three I describe some of the key theories influencing how I go about deconstructing and making sense of liberal and neoconservative intellectuals' representations of Wahhabism. I describe the dialectical imagination I have adopted, what fuzzy categories are and how they work, and how I make use of Max Weber's ideal type. I also describe the critical discourse analysis approach I have adopted and the epistemological assumptions it carries with it.

In Chapter Four I begin the interpretative and analytic process and deal with how liberal intellectuals have gone about representing Wahhabism. In Chapter Five I describe what generative metaphors and themata are and how they work, and then make sense of the different representations of Wahhabism. In Chapter Six I continue the interpretative, analytical, and sense-making process by looking at the different ways neoconservative intellectuals have gone about representing Wahhabism. In the Conclusion I explicate and clarify the wider significance of the book, particularly in the context of the sociology of intellectuals and the policy- and decision-making processes.

1
Wahhabism as a Contested Category

For last year's words belong to last year's language
And next year's words await another voice.
—T.S. Eliot, *Four Quartets*

Wahhabism is both conventionally and popularly understood to be an extremely conservative, fundamentalist, or radical version of Islam. Historians agree that it has its origins in Saudi Arabia in the eighteenth century and that its founder was Muhammad Ibn Abd al-Wahhab. Abd al-Wahhab is said to have developed a version of Islam he insisted was a rigorous and conservative interpretation of the Qur'an. The general consensus is that Wahhabism played a decisive role in creating the Saudi state in 1932, where Wahhabism is credited as having a substantial following today.[1] Beyond this, Wahhabism is a hotly contested category and this contest begins with those who are said to be followers of this version of Islam. Those who are labeled followers of Wahhabism tend to reject this term, instead referring to themselves as Muslims or Salafists. The contest continues when dealing with the relation between Wahhabism and modern Islamic terrorism, particularly with regards to the apparent influence it is said to have on well-known terrorist groups like al-Qaeda.

At this stage I want to present some of the major ways scholars influenced by a variety of political and religious beliefs, aims, and goals have represented Wahhabism. I will continue to expand on this contest throughout the book, particularly when I take a closer look at how intellectuals from the liberal and neoconservative traditions have represented Wahhabism. Now I want to demonstrate that there is little consensus among those writers and researchers dealing with Wahhabism with what might be thought to be the kind of scholarly regard for careful, nuanced inquiry found in academic centers devoted to the study of religions, contemporary political science, or international relations. While some would see this as the basis for resolving the controversies and issues this survey highlights, by appealing to some empirical or theoretical benchmarks of objectivity or accuracy, I continue to hold that this is impossible given that Wahhabism is an observer-dependent phenomenon with no objective reality. The following analyses provide for a great starting point for why we need to pay more attention to the issues of how and why intellectuals represent a phenomenon like Wahhabism in different ways.

I have taken exemplars of some of the ways scholars have dealt with Wahhabism. These representations appear in books in libraries and online and in academic journals, and are often regurgitated or referred to by writers, bloggers, and government officials around the world. These representations are also influencing students, other scholars, and researchers. My analysis begins with a group of scholars emphasizing the negative and dangerous aspects of Wahhabism, which is certainly the dominant representation, and then turns to those offering softer and less threatening portraits. In both cases there are important issues involved in translating Wahhabism that I explore in greater detail toward the end of the chapter. While these issues of translation are important for those seeking to make sense of the contest to define Wahhabism, they also have a much wider application.

Intellectuals, Imagined Geographies, and Imagined Communities: Wahhabism as a Threat

Benedict Anderson's famous account of the role played by intellectuals in constructing Imagined communities and Edward Said's Imagined geographies are pertinent ideas when considering how intellectuals like Dore Gold, Bernard Lewis, and David Commins represent Wahhabism.[2] Each, albeit in different ways, draws on an historical account of a relationship between spaces and people to arrive at distinctly negative portraits of Wahhabism. Ron Eyerman's claims that intellectuals are often projecting their own "needs and fantasies" and their "deep-seated needs and interests" are certainly relevant here.[3]

Anderson makes the point that all "communities larger than primordial villages of face-to-face contact . . . are imagined."[4] Imagined communities are not unreal by virtue of being imagined, but instead constitute a network of socially consequential relationships with the same degree of reality as members of communities enjoying face-to-face relations. We may not see everyone that is a part of our Imagined community; however, our ability to communicate helps us to know they exist. Intellectuals play key roles in this communication process. Anderson points to the crucial role print media plays in creating these communities, highlighting the first European nation-states as quintessential examples. Said's ideas about Imagined geographies are similar to Anderson's.

Said uses this term when referring to perceived spaces created by intellectuals through the use of particular images, texts, and discourses.[5] His ideas are based on his analysis of the ways in which those in the West have created Imagined geographies of the Orient. He claims that Western culture's modern understanding of the Orient is based on a selective imagination conjured up through intellectual representations, including academic Oriental studies and travel writings. Said claims that intellectuals' representations have feminized the Orient by portraying it as open and virgin space with no concept of organized rule or government. The intellectual's ability to create these Imagined geographies serves as a powerful tool that can be used to control and subordinate the Other. The Other is a term I use throughout the book and it refers to that which is alien and divergent from that which is given, such as a norm, identity, or the self. Its binary is the Same. The constitutive Other often denotes a different, incomprehensible self outside of one's own. It is a concept that is key to Said's work on Orientalism.

Dore Gold's popular representation of Wahhabism is a good example of an intellectual creating an Imagined community. His representation is worth considering given his book, *Hatred's Kingdom: How Saudi Arabia Supports the New Global Terrorism*, appeared on the *New York Times* bestseller list.[6] Published soon after the 9/11 terrorist attacks, it is unsurprising that his book was so popular given the widespread anger and the need of many to find answers or assign blame for the rise in Islamic terrorism and its focus on Western targets. It should also be noted that the US-born Gold is a prominent intellectual that has served as Israel's ambassador to the United Nations, as an advisor to Israeli Prime Ministers Ariel Sharon and Benjamin Netanyahu, and is president of the Jerusalem Center for Public Affairs. He also testified as an expert before the US Senate Committee on Governmental Affairs, claiming Saudi Arabia provides ideological and financial support for Islamic terrorist groups and organizations.[7]

Gold is one of the authors whose representations I first read when researching the Israeli–Palestinian conflict following my discussions with my Palestinian friend in Stockholm. His views and his book are widely cited. He is one of those authors who uses representations of Wahhabism, which he understands as responsible for inspiring and promoting Islamic terrorism, when writing about this conflict. Gold creates an Imagined community in which the West, particularly the United States and Israel, belong, and Palestinians and other supposed terrorist groups and organizations do not. Additionally, he creates an Imagined community of Jewish Israelis in the state of Israel (which he sees as encompassing what many others would deem Palestinian land), of which Palestinians are not a part. A firm supporter of Israel's actions in the Occupied Territories, Gold uses representations of Wahhabism in an attempt to explain Palestinian aggression toward Israel.

Assuming the land in question belongs to Israel and rejecting Palestinian claims, Gold has a rationale for looking for alternative explanations for what he sees as a long history of pro-Palestinian terrorism directed against Israel. Dismissing claims that pro-Palestinian groups could be motivated by political and/or economic aims and goals, for example, wanting a functional economy and Palestinian statehood, Gold finds that religion, specifically radical Islam and more specifically Wahhabism, is to blame for inspiring and motivating anti-Israeli violence. Gold's blaming of religion in general is evident in the following extract:

> The United States and its allies can win the most spectacular military victories in Afghanistan; they can freeze terrorists' bank accounts and cut off their supplies of weaponry; they can eliminate terrorist masterminds. But even taken together, such triumphs are not enough to remove the terrorist threat, for they do not get at the source of the problem. Terrorism, on the scale of the September 11 attacks, does not occur in a vacuum. People do not just decide spontaneously that they are going to hijack an aircraft, crash it into a building, and commit mass murder (and take their own lives) because of some political grievance or sense of economic deprivation. No, there is another critical component of terrorism that has generally been overlooked in the West: the ideological motivation to slaughter thousands of innocent people.[8]

Contrary to what Gold claims, history shows us that political grievances have certainly motivated many hijackings and other forms of violence. As a firm supporter of Israel, Gold does his best to convince readers that Palestinian violence is religiously motivated and that many pro-Palestinian groups are getting their inspiration from the radical Wahhabi ideology exported from Saudi Arabia.

David Commins, who is a prominent scholar and whose book, *The Wahhabi Mission and Saudi Arabia*, appears on bookshelves around the world, also provides a representation of Wahhabism worth closely considering.[9] A professor of history, Commins provides a good example of an intellectual using Wahhabism to create an Imagined geography. Throughout his book Commins represents Wahhabism as a religion for backward, uncivilized, and antimodern people. Commins claims Saudi Arabia, which is beholden to its Wahhabi religious beliefs, is struggling to resist (Western-led) forces of change, namely liberalization/democratization. Saudi students studying abroad in Western nations are returning home with Western ideas about government and society. However, the kingdom's steadfast adherence to Wahhabism is preventing it from embracing these changes. Displaying the kind of Orientalism Said first pointed to, Commins shares the premise with many political liberals and neoliberals that Western-inspired economic and social globalization is a natural and progressive process that Saudi Arabia should embrace. Commins in part blames the kingdom's Wahhabi religious beliefs for resisting these changes. Representations like these help inspire and motivate Western policy- and decision-makers, should they ever decide to invade Saudi Arabia 'for its own good' and in the name of progress.

Renowned British-American historian Bernard Lewis, who is well known for his associations with neoconservatives and is a former advisor to the George W. Bush administration, also constructs the Middle East as a backward and antimodern space in need of progress. Echoing the foreign policy initiatives of the recent Bush administration and adopting the role of an intellectual conceptualized by authors like Edward Shils, Lewis's representation suggests that Western nations have the responsibility of bringing modernity to traditional societies. Lewis blames what he terms the Islamic revivalist/awakening movement, of which Wahhabism is a key part, for the Middle East's failure to become more democratic and free. Again we see an ethnocentric intellectual creating an unflattering imagined space of the Middle East encouraging Western intervention.

Understanding Wahhabism through a Feminist Lens

Moving away from the prominent views of influential, older white Western men for just a moment, it also worth considering some alternative representations of Wahhabism appearing in scholarly articles. Margaret Gonzalez-Perez provides an interesting representation through the lens of the Western feminist intellectual tradition.[10] Understanding that her role as an intellectual is to draw attention to the injustices and wrongs perpetrated against women, she writes about the experiences of female suicide bombers, specifically those used by al-Qaeda, Palestinian Islamic Jihad, and Hamas, all of which she categorizes as terrorist organizations. Gonzalez-Perez claims these terrorist organizations are using radical, violent, jihadist and un-Islamic interpretations of Islam to help persuade women to carry out suicide bombings. She blames Wahhabism, the writings of thirteenth-century Islamic theologian Ibn Taymiya, and key twentieth-century Islamic ideologues like Sayyid Qutb for providing these terrorist organizations with perverted interpretations of Islam.

Gonzalez-Perez's representation is interesting because she assumes that Palestinian Islamic Jihad, Hamas, and al-Qaeda are terrorist organizations of the same kind. Gonzalez-Perez's categorization of Hamas as a terrorist organization in particular is very interesting. While Dore Gold and many other pro-Israeli scholars and neoconservative intellectuals would certainly agree with this assessment, there are those who would reject this categorization and instead understand Hamas as primarily a resistance and welfare organization. For example, Khaled Hroub in *Hamas: A Beginner's Guide* makes the point that Hamas has been the victim of persistent and prevailing negative misconceptions, reducing it to a mere terrorist group.[11] The real Hamas, argues Hroub, is a Palestinian resistance movement and an educational and social welfare organization. Only a small part of the Hamas organization, namely its military wing Izzedin al-Qassam, is dedicated to violently resisting the Israeli occupation. It is also worth reading Zaki Chehab's description of Hamas's social welfare intiatives in his book *Inside Hamas: The Untold Story of Militants, Martyrs and Spies.*[12]

Gonzalez-Perez obviously has very different political views from supporters of the Palestinian resistance. If she did treat Hamas as part of the Palestinian resistance instead of categorizing it as a terrorist organization akin to al-Qaeda and Palestinian Islamic Jihad, then it is possible that she would not have drawn the same conclusions regarding the role played by Wahhabism in influencing these 'terrorists.' Rather than looking for a religious rationale, Gonzalez-Perez might otherwise be searching for political and economic reasons for Hamas's use of female suicide bombers. The important point to be made here is that one's political prejudices have implications for how one understands and represents Wahhabism.

It is also significant that Gonzalez-Perez's representation relies on an assumption that particular interpretations of Islamic texts, like those she claims belong to the Wahhabi religious doctrine, are un-Islamic and that those interpreting these texts are not real Muslims. This is a premise popular among those providing negative portraits of Wahhabism. In reaching these conclusions, Gonzalez-Perez assumes there is an objective and truthful interpretation of Islam that does not promote violence and strictly prohibits suicide bombing. She writes:

> The female suicide bombers of nominally Muslim groups like Hamas, the PIJ [Palestinian Islamic Jihad], and Al Qaeda are no more Islamic

> than the Hindu Tamil women bombers of Sri Lanka or the communist female suicide bombers of the Kurdish Workers' Party in Turkey. They are not Islamic martyrs nor any other manifestation of orthodox religious faith.[13]

To help bolster her case, Gonzalez-Perez provides an extensive list of authors she believes provide truthful and objective interpretations of Islam. She also adds her own interpretation of Islamic texts that she categorizes as objective and truthful. Gonzalez-Perez writes:

> Within Islam, the rules of engagement and conduct of war have been established by over one thousand years of scholarly interpretation and precedent. According to the Qur'an and Islamic tradition, warfare is the domain of the state and can only be authorized by the executive of an established government [37: 124]. . . . Mainstream scholars are unequivocal, "The rules of Islam are clear. Individuals cannot declare war. A group or organization cannot declare war. War is declared by the state. War cannot be declared without a president or an army. . . . Otherwise, it is an act of terror" [22: 2].[14]

Gonzalez-Perez's representation raises many of the key issues pertinent to this book, particularly whether there can ever be an objective interpretation of religious texts and social phenomena like Wahhabism, and the key role political prejudices plays in the sense-making process. The issues regarding the objective interpretation of texts is something I want to explore more in the next section when I examine the work of scholars making sense of Saudi school textbooks.

Saudi School Textbooks and the Problem of Translation

There is a group of Western scholars that includes Eleanor Abdella Doumato and Michaela Prokop whose representations of Wahhabism are based on their translations of Saudi Arabian school texts written in Arabic.[15] They see these as having been influenced by Wahhabi religious ideology. Doumato and Prokop have studied these texts, searching for evidence of anti-Western sentiments and extremist ideas with the aim of establishing whether or not there is a relation between the kingdom's school curriculum and modern Islamic terrorism. Saudi school texts have been the focus of much criticism. For example, in his witness testimony to the US Senate's enquiry into terrorism financing (the same hearing in which Dore Gold testified), executive director of the Investigative Project, Steven Emerson, criticized passages he found in Saudi school texts that were distributed in the United States with "the full imprimatur of the Kingdom of Saudi Arabia."[16] He stated:

> I refer to the curricular used in grades 4 through 11, but let me just cite a quote from the 7th grade class Book 5. The book says, "'What is learned from the Hadith?' and teaches, 'The curse of Allah be upon the Jews and the Christians.'" Grades 8 through 11 continue to emphasize the notion and piousness of the jihad, and in grade 11 it warns against taking the Jews and Christians as friends or protectors of Muslims.
>
> I think this, unfortunately, helps develop a whole generational mind-set that leads to terrorism, noting that terrorism is really the culmination of indoctrination and recruitment. Much of that indoctrination is entirely legal, with terrorism being the violent, illegal expression ultimately and representing the culmination of the indoctrination and recruitment.[17]

Those at the Middle East Media Research Institute (MEMRI) have long made it their mission to 'reveal' to the world the hate and violence promoted in Saudi textbooks. Since the 9/11 terrorist attacks, MEMRI has consistently published "special dispatches" claiming that Saudi textbooks are portraying Jews as animals and eternal enemies of Muslims.[18] MEMRI claims Saudi textbooks are inciting violence towards Jews and are encouraging its readers to understand the Israeli–Palestinian conflict as a microcosm of an overarching war between Muslims and Jews.[19] MEMRI TV has also documented the global spreading of these Wahhabi-infused textbooks, showing for example teachers using Saudi Education Ministry textbooks in remote villages in Africa.[20]

Since 9/11 MEMRI has gained public prominence for its news and analysis of events in the Muslim world. It distributes its reports and translations to members of the US Congress, policymakers, journalists, and academics and its articles have been routinely cited in the US mainstream media, including the *New York Times* and *Washington Post*. MEMRI claims to be independent, nonpartisan, and not-for-profit. Critics have accused it of having a pro-Israeli bias, deliberately misleading readers, especially with regards to translations of Arabic texts, and highlighted its links to the neoconservative movement.[21]

Neither Doumato nor Prokop, whose representations of Wahhabism rely on translating Saudi textbooks, are Marxist intellectuals. However, their studies certainly parallel arguments made by prominent Marxist scholars like Louis Althusser and Antonio Gramsci that education is a key ideological apparatus able to be used to impose particular beliefs and values on a society.[22] Doumato's understanding of Wahhabism is primarily based on her interpretation and analysis of religious texts produced by the Saudi state and prescribed for Saudi students in grades 9 through 12. She finds that these texts have the ability to promote hostility against non-Muslims, encourage exclusivity among Muslims, and inspire violent jihad. Doumato writes:

> Hostile messages there are, but the *mood* of these texts is less hostile than overwhelmingly defensive. . . . They claw with self-doubt, conjuring up enemies, real and perceived, who are not only at the gates but inside themselves. Looking at the texts alone, the message in the religion curriculum is that "we Muslims are under siege, and it is the duty of every single one of us to man the barricades."[23] [emphasis added]

Like Doumato, Prokop's representation of Wahhabism in part relies on her English translation of Arabic religious texts used in the Saudi education system, which she claims are "heavily influenced by the Wahhabi ideology."[24] Prokop's analysis is focused on school textbooks for secondary school grades 1 through 3. She posits that there *could* be a link between Wahhabism and violence. She also claims these texts occasionally promote intolerance and sometimes incite hatred. However, they are often coupled with contradictory messages about peace and tolerance between people of different faiths. Prokop writes:

> The content of the official textbooks is heavily influenced by the Wahhabi ideology. Teaching about the 'others'—other cultures, ideologies and religions, or adherents of other Muslim schools of jurisprudence or sects—reflects the Wahhabi view of a world divided into the believers and preservers of the true faith and the kuffar, the unbelievers. The teachings about other religions, particularly those pertaining to the 'People of the Book', Christians and Jews, are contradictory. While some passages denounce Christians and Jews clearly as unbelievers, people whom one should not greet with salutations of peace or take as friends, or against whom jihad should be waged, other passages stress the peaceful nature of Islam.[25]

Both Doumato and Prokop rely on translations from Arabic texts. Before accepting their representations of Wahhabism on face value, it is important to note that the translation process is far from an exact science and that both authors are unable to achieve equivalence in their translations. Martin Müller points out that translation is too often treated as a process in which a translator assumes a neutral relay role producing an objective outcome.[26] This is an issue affecting many social science researchers subscribing to Enlightenment and religious ideas of truth when making sense of phenomena in the social world. As John Caputo points out, we no longer live in an age where one story can explain everything that happens in the social world.[27]

Müller has these ideas about truth and objectivity in mind when he writes that "if we are to take seriously the problems of representation and speaking for/with others," then "we are called on to problematize translation as a political act."[28] Recognizing translation as a political act is integral to recognizing the antagonisms and struggles for meaning taking place in a foreign language. We must remember the observer-dependent roles intellectuals play when representing social phenomena like Wahhabism when we consider Müller's claim that "increased attention to the political implications of translation also spells out the case for broaching the translating geographer as an active agent who molds the production of meaning."[29]

These concerns about translation have preoccupied many scholars, including Müller, H.P. Phillips, Pamela Shurmer-Smith, Gustavo Esteva,

Madhu Suri Prakash, Bogusia Temple, and Alys Young, all of whom identify equivalence as a key issue.[30] Phillips notes that achieving equivalence in translation is an intractable problem given "almost any utterance in any language carries with it a set of assumptions, feelings, and values that the speaker may or may not be aware of" and that the transferring of meaning from one language into another can only ever be partial and never complete.[31] Different languages structure the world in different ways and translations are never able to completely convey the richness of connotations. Müller points out that this is especially the case when translating "god words."[32]

There are a number of problems shadowing Doumato's representation. First is the problem of establishing the basis for her claim to have an objective or literalist way of translating texts. This seems especially problematic when it comes to capturing the "mood" (as Doumato claims to do) of the texts.[33] Many scholars could analyze the same texts and provide very different interpretations, especially when it comes to capturing something so diffuse as mood. Second, we can neither assume that Saudi students will uncritically accept what is presented to them in the school texts nor can we be sure they will act on these hostile ideas. Each student is influenced by their own ways of making sense of the world into which they have been thrown. Indeed, Doumato acknowledges that students can receive conflicting information from a wide variety of sources: "In thinking about what students learn we also have to think about how or whether lessons taught in schools are reinforced outside of school, in the public media, in the mosque, or in the family."[34]

Like Althusser, Gramsci, and Doumato, Prokop recognizes school education is only one element of a society's ideological apparatus that can be used to promote and impose a particular value and belief system. Prokop writes:

> Formal education is only one element in shaping an individual's perspective and religious inclinations. The perception of Saudi students is also shaped to an equal if not greater degree by informal teachings in mosques, in homes and through the new media. The mosque is particularly important for the older generation since adult illiteracy

> rates remain high. Additionally, the so-called 'hidden curriculum'—contextual factors, such as teacher personality, prevailing classroom dynamics, social background or place of residence—also determine how the message is received and interpreted.[35]

With so many qualifications it is hard to be convinced that Prokop's analysis clearly demonstrates a link between the Saudi school curriculum and violence and terrorism. In this case, the truth claim rests on a premise that there are secure, technical, and methodical paths to be taken so as to arrive at the truth. We must also keep these considerations in mind when reading intellectuals providing less critical, softer, or positive portraits of Wahhabism. I will now turn my attention to focusing on some of these kinds of representations.

Wahhabism Is Not So Bad After All

There are many scholars who have made a case for a quite different representation of Wahhabism. Juan Cole is one such scholar, defending it against the common claim that it is responsible for inspiring modern Islamic terrorism.[36] Cole claims that a portrait of Wahhabism as an ideological source of Islamist terrorism has been used as part of the intellectual arsenal deployed by Western governments to help achieve their imperialistic aims and goals in the Middle East. Cole writes:

> It is sometimes implied that the Saudi effort to spread Wahhabism has the effect of spreading terrorism and anti-Americanism. That outcome would be difficult to demonstrate. . . . Further, it is not at all clear that puritanism or Wahhabism, while it may produce negative attitudes toward consumerism and libertinism, predispose people to commit terrorism, as some pundits have alleged. Most suicide bombings in the past thirty years have not been carried out by Wahhabis or persons influenced by them, but rather by individuals fighting what they see as the foreign military occupation of their country. . . . Connecting a religious tradition to terrorism would require more evidence than a few instances of guilt by association.[37]

Cole clearly understands his role as an intellectual is to help dispel myths and misinformation promoted by Western "terrorism experts," "right-wing pundits," and "American hawks," who he believes are racist, ignorant, and eager to wage war. Cole writes:

> As I've glared at the self-appointed "terrorism experts" who have paraded across my television screen since 2001, I've become more and more alarmed at the dangerous falsehoods many of them purvey. Most of them have no knowledge of the languages or cultures of the Middle East, or any history of residence there. The message of the right-wing pundits and pastors and politicians is that Muslims form a menace to the West unless they are subdued and dominated. In that sense, the military occupation of Iraq that began in 2003 exemplifies the mind-set of American hawks.[38]

Cole is dismissive of many of the ignorant and deliberately misleading claims made by Western commentators about Wahhabism, including the commonly asserted claim that it "predisposes people to commit terrorism."[39] As evidence, Cole highlights the fact that the majority of suicide bombings in the last thirty years have been motivated by anti-imperial and anticolonial ideas rather than by Wahhabi religious ideology. Referring to incidents like the pro-Palestinian suicide bombings in Israel, Cole's claims rely on the assumption that conflicts like those between Israeli and Palestinian forces are anticolonial and anti-imperialist in nature rather than acts of terrorism. This view is diametrically opposed to those offered by Gonzalez-Perez and Gold and helps highlight the relation between one's political prejudices particularly with regards to the Israeli–Palestinian conflict and representations of Wahhabism. Since Cole sees the Palestinian as primarily anticolonial and anti-imperial in nature and not religiously inspired, he is not inclined to search for a religious rationale for the violence, meaning he does not consider the possibility that Wahhabism is responsible for inspiring and motivating Palestinian violence.

Cole's role as an intellectual aligns more with conceptualizations offered by authors like Chomsky, who maintains that an intellectual's role is to speak truth to power rather than promoting particular class and group interests.[40] While Cole's representation absolves Wahhabism of any blame, it would not be categorized as a positive portrait. These are hard to come by when trawling bookshelves in public libraries, universities, and colleges in the Western world. Natana DeLong-Bas's book, *Wahhabi Islam: From Revival and Reform to Global Jihad*, is certainly the exception to the rule and I will take a closer look at this shortly. Positive portraits are a little easier to find when searching academic journals online. However, the obvious problem is these representations do not have the ability to reach the same number of people given that the negative portraits have the backing of many of the leading Western publishers. Nonetheless, Muhammad Al-Atawneh's article, "Wahhabi Self-Examination Post-9/11: Rethinking the 'Other', 'Otherness' and Tolerance," is certainly worth considering given the stark contrast between his views and the more mainstream and popular views published in popular books and US newspapers.[41]

Muhammad Al-Atawneh is a Muslim intellectual whose article about Wahhabism appears to be in response to the common charge that Saudi Arabia is responsible for promoting this radical version of Islam. Writing in 2011, Al-Atawneh claims Saudi Arabia and the Wahhabi religious establishment after the 9/11 terrorist attacks made the necessary policy changes ensuring that Wahhabism does not in any way promote violence, intolerance, or extremism among Saudi Arabians. He wants to challenge the notion that Saudi Arabia is in any way complicit in Islamic terrorism, referring to a number of policy initiatives and government actions as evidence of the kingdom's commitment to tolerance, harmony, and an embracing of the Other.

Unlike Gold, Lewis, and Gonzalez-Perez, Al-Atawneh challenges the idea that Wahhabism is radical per se. He wants us to distinguish between its radical and conventional interpretations. Al-Atawneh fervently rejects the idea that the Saudi Kingdom is engaged in the kind of politics typically associated with the political realist tradition where the international political arena is conceptualized as a battleground of competing interests, where the state does everything in its power to secure its own interests.[42] Instead he sees the Saudi Kingdom as dedicated to a version of politics geared at helping end injustices and wrongs. This approach resonates with recent conceptualizations of the political provided by authors like Critchley and Crick.[43] Instead of blaming the Saudi and Wahhabi establishments for inspiring the radical interpretation of Wahhabism that is responsible for some recent Islamic terrorism, Al-Atawneh puts the blame on rogue elements. He writes that most "of the post-9/11 criticism appears to be lodged against extremist groups, described by Saudi officials as those who have 'gone astray' (*firqa dalla*)."[44]

On first appearances, one could easily understand Al-Atawneh as an apologist for the Saudi state. Indeed, though we need to approach such claims with a certain ironic detachment, Al-Atawneh is exactly the kind of intellectual that authors like Chomsky are extremely critical of. According to Chomskian logic, Al-Atawneh should instead be "seek[ing] the truth lying hidden behind the veil of distortion and misrepresentation, ideology and class interest, through which the events of current history are presented to us."[45] If we were to imagine the representations of Wahhabism as existing on a spectrum, Al-Atawneh and Gold's representations would certainly feature at opposite ends. Unfortunately for Al-Atawneh and supporters of the Saudi state, Al-Atawneh's article appears in an online scholarly journal, while Gold's book appeared on the *New York Times* bestseller list.

The question of truth claims is again on display in work by Natana DeLong-Bas.[46] Her work is the closest thing we can see as a defense of Wahhabism sitting on bookshelves at libraries, bookstores, and places of higher education throughout the Western world. She offers a spirited defense of the faith, claiming Wahhabism actually promotes peace, encourages tolerance, and advocates women's rights. Wahhabism is not, according to DeLong-Bas, in any way responsible for inspiring modern Islamic terrorism. She writes:

> Ibn Abd al-Wahhab's emphasis on the importance of Islamic values and the intent behind words and actions, as opposed to concern for ritual perfection, has opened the door for reforms in Islamic law, the status of women and minorities, and the peaceful spread of Islam and the Islamic mission in the contemporary era.[47]

Her account is one of the most prominent—and widely criticized—representations of Wahhabism in the post-9/11 period.[48] Her critics have among other things accused her of being an apologist for extremist Islam. Well-known Saudi and Wahhabism critic Stephen Schwartz, whose articles appear in a variety of right-wing and neoconservative publications, has claimed that DeLong-Bas has "reached a depth of mendacity about radical Islam it is hard to imagine her exceeding."[49] She has also drawn the ire of pro-Israeli writers like Caroline Glick who wrote:

> DeLong-Bas told the newspaper [London pan-Arab daily *al-Sharq al-Awsat*] that she does "not find any evidence that would make me agree that Osama bin Laden was behind the attack on the Twin Towers of the World Trade Center. All we heard from him was praise and acclaim for those who carried out the operation."
>
> This was not the first time the Brandeis faculty member acted as an apologist for jihadists. Indeed she seems to be making a career out of it. According to a *FrontPageMag.com* expose of her career, in 2004 she published *Wahhabi Islam: From Revival to Global Jihad*, a work partially funded by Saudi Arabia that defends the extremist Wahabi strain of Islam that has formed the basis of the belief system of men like Osama Bin Laden and the September 11 hijackers.[50]

DeLong-Bas is not a Muslim, suggesting she is not likely to be motivated or inspired by Islamic religious beliefs in the same way authors like Haneef James Oliver are.[51] DeLong-Bas's representation of Wahhabism is not first and foremost a defense of Saudi interests as authors like Glick and Schwartz would have you believe. Instead, it rests on a certain claim to truth. DeLong-Bas believes she offers a truthful interpretation of Wahhabi doctrine primarily based on the writings of its founder Abd al-Wahhab. Her claims to truth rest on what she believes to be an objective interpretation of sacred Wahhabi Islamic texts, involving comparing and contrasting these Wahhabi Islamic texts and the beliefs and doctrines of modern Islamic terrorists. This is not the only major issue with her representation. Her case also depends on an appeal to the legitimacy of her translation and interpretation of Wahhabi texts from the eighteenth century and on her capacity to compare these to what she understands to be the beliefs of the modern Wahhabi movement.

There is of course a major problem here: much of this exercise depends on an assumption that we are doing something meaningful when we compare and interpret the original texts of a new belief system with much later or contemporary expressions of that belief system. It is highly doubtful that the modern nature of what we understand to be Wahhabism can be established in this way, and we use the term 'genetic fallacy' to describe authors who make this kind of error in reasoning. To commit a genetic fallacy is to make conclusions about a movement based on its origins as opposed to considering the contemporary expression of ideas and beliefs and doing so on their own merits and in their current context. DeLong-Bas's interpretation fails to fully appreciate the constantly evolving nature of the Wahhabi movement. She fails to understand that Wahhabism in the twenty-first century is not an exact replica of how it appeared during eighteenth-century Arabia. We live in a different time and in a vastly different political context.

Next I want to consider the contribution made by Haneef James Oliver in his book *The Wahhabi Myth: Dispelling Prevalent Fallacies and the Fictitious Link with Bin Laden*.[52] I have included Oliver's book because of its unique approach. Oliver seeks to defend his faith by providing what he believes is an objective understanding of sacred Islamic texts. Oliver is a self-proclaimed Salafi (he rejects the use of the term Wahhabism, labeling it a misnomer) inspired by what he believes to be God's word and a desire to convince people that terrorists like Bin Laden are not Salafists or true Muslims. He makes his intentions very clear from the outset:

> My objective in doing so is not to deceitfully defend anyone or anything unworthy of a defence, *as Islaam commands that a Muslim speak a word of truth*, even if it be against him or herself, or followers of the same faith. Rather, it is my objective to deal only with those issues which have been unjustly brought against Islaam and Salaiyyah (Salafism) in particular, as opposed to defending the actions of the contemporary "Islaamic" groups and movements, which have only aided those who wish to harm the Islaamic Nation.

> . . . [I]t is my objective to give the reader another perspective on some of these issues which they might never have been exposed to before. I have made every effort to avoid producing another book which is filled with opinion while lacking in *textual proofs*. Instead I have tried to produce a book in which Muslims and non-Muslims alike will be able to reflect upon the directives of the Qur'aan and the narrations (ahaadeetha) of the Prophet Muhammad for themselves.[53] [emphasis added]

As we can see, Oliver believes his role is to "speak a word of truth" which he believes can be supported by "textual proofs." There are a number of issues with these claims. One is that the legitimacy of his claims rests on our accepting that his interpretation of Salafism/Wahhabism provides the one big story about human history. Two, like some of the other scholarship I have dealt with earlier, Oliver's representation of Wahhabism relies on his interpretation of Qur'anic texts originally written in Arabic and translated into English.[54] To briefly reiterate the important point I made earlier, it is impossible for an author to achieve equivalence and we can understand the translator's role as a subjective act influenced by their prejudices. Oliver's book is self-published and it is very easy to see why, as it lacks the intellectual rigor typically demanded by reputable publishing organizations.

Oliver's work is indicative of an author who lacks nuance when seeking to understand the Wahhabi movement. I have, however, come across one study in which the author does treat the phenomenon of Wahhabism with the kind of scholarly regard we should expect of those working in higher education and policy organizations. Quintan Wiktorowicz seeks to make sense of what he also terms the Salafi movement, and like Oliver he prefers this term rather than 'Wahhabi,' which he also calls a misnomer.[55] Wiktorowicz claims we can distinguish between different groups within the wider Salafi tradition according to how they interpret Islamic religious texts. Pertinent is his example regarding the differences in reasoning on the use of weapons of mass destruction. Wiktorowicz writes that many jihadists today cite the Prophet Muhammad's sanctioning the use of a catapult during war as providing religious justification for their own use of weapons of mass destruction:

> In drawing analogies, jihadis argue that the catapult was the WMD of the Prophet's lifetime and that his example legitimates the use of WMD today. *This conclusion is not rooted in an objective reading of the religious sources*: it is *entirely dependent* on whether one views the catapult as the historical equivalent of nuclear, biological, and chemical weapons. *Human reasoning thus plays a critical role.*[56] [emphasis added]

Wiktorowicz makes a very important point that very few scholars representing Wahhabism acknowledge, that "human reasoning . . . plays a critical role" when it comes to making sense of things in the social world like religious texts and different events. Hans-Georg Gadamer and Hannah Arendt have both emphasized the crucial roles human reasoning and prejudice play in how we make sense of the world.[57] The works of Gadamer and Arendt remind us that translating is a not an exact science with an objective outcome, but is instead a subjective and political act. It is clear that Oliver's translation of Arabic religious texts into English is influenced by, among other things, a desire to defend his understanding of the Islamic faith.

This contest to make sense of Wahhabism occurring between the different scholars I have drawn on in this chapter is a microcosm of a much wider debate occurring between intellectuals relying on very different analytical and theoretical frameworks and influenced by different interests, commitments, and what scholars like Gadamer have called prejudices.[58] My cursory review of some of the scholarly literature dedicated to making sense of Wahhabism helps highlight a number of important issues warranting and legitimating this research. My review helps show that a scholar's interests and truth claims have major implications for how they make sense of and represent Wahhabism. I have shown how an intellectual's desire to promote the interests of a particular group or intellectual tradition can result in very different representations of Wahhabism, ranging from Wahhabism as responsible for promoting and inspiring modern Islamic terrorism to Wahhabism as a religious belief system that promotes peace, harmony, and tolerance. In the next two chapters I want to take a closer look at some of the issues I have raised during this chapter, specifically the role and responsibilities of the intellectual, making sense of truth, and the crucial role prejudice plays in influencing how we make sense of the social world.

2
On Intellectuals, Prejudice, and Understanding the Social World

Quis custodiet ipsos custodes?
—Juvenal, *Satires*

Socrates often wandered through the marketplace in Athens asking people whether they had any knowledge to reveal to him. His practice of the Socratic dialogue and use of Socratic irony (*elencthia*) implied that few of his fellow-citizens knew what they were talking about.[1] Soon after he had been condemned to death by his fellow Athenian citizens, he told them, in what has since become one of the best-known philosophical phrases in the Western philosophical tradition, "the unexamined life is not worth living."[2] Socrates's point was the more you lead such a life, the more equipped you are to live a good life.

Everything we know about Socrates as one of the first public intellectuals in the Western intellectual tradition tells us that he set loose several permanent puzzles for philosophy. One of the enduring puzzles was how we are to both examine our life and establish the veridicity or truth of the knowledge we claim to possess. This problem continues to haunt the sociology of intellectuals and provides something of the big puzzle sitting behind this book. Yet in this respect a nonremediable problem attends any such exercise. It does so in terms that echo the ominous question, who guards the guardians? When we ask, how are we to make sense of the sense-makers? This is a central question in the evolution of the sociology of intellectuals.

In the twentieth century, Karl Mannheim did more than most to establish the modern contours of the sociology of intellectuals.[3] Mannheim wrote between two world wars, when older and longstanding cultural values were being shaken profoundly and many of his fellow intellectuals were making dire predictions about the future of civilization. Mannheim understood his work in Socratic terms as a search for knowledge that would play a crucial role in helping construct an equal society with a tolerant citizenry. Mannheim argued that citizens developed their freedom through self-reflection and by understanding their cultural origins.[4] This was not however meant to be an easy or effortless task undertaken by the individual. Mannheim pointed to the all-important role of the intellectual and to the intersection between the reflective practice of the intellectual and those decision-makers like politicians and policymakers who deal with day-to-day politics.

Mannheim began his seminal work *Ideology and Utopia: An Introduction to the Sociology of Knowledge* by addressing the problem of how men think.[5] He distinguished between everyday thinking and the kind that is done by philosophers, mathematicians, and physicists in special circumstances. Mannheim designed a critical method he believed intellectuals could draw on to help create a better society. This method acknowledged both the specificities of historical context and the need to achieve a certain objectivity that would enable us to see the world as uncontaminated by ideology, which he understood as the kind of knowledge shaped by social interests or partisan politics.[6]

At the same time Mannheim saw the intellectual as charged with the responsibility of developing utopian ideals without retreating into a contemplative state completely removed from political life. However, Mannheim struggled to say how this would be possible. He argued that intellectuals necessarily enjoy a certain amount of freedom, because they are free-floating and the keepers of cultural standards, which allows them to operate freely from the constraints of ideology. Mannheim also offers important insights about dealing with competing value systems.

Developing a sociology of knowledge was Mannheim's method for arbitrating this competition. He argues that intellectuals capable of operating outside particular value and belief systems or ideologies could use this method to discover how and why particular individuals and groups see the world as they do. Mannheim writes:

> . . . [T]he sociology of knowledge regards the cognitive act in connection with the models to which it aspires in its existential as well as its meaningful quality, not as insights into 'eternal' truths arising from a purely theoretical, contemplative urge . . . but as an instrument for dealing with life-situations at the disposal of a certain kind of vital being under certain conditions of life.[7]

Mannheim's prescriptions are not designed to be "blueprints: it is neither a list of abstract desiderata for the philosopher nor a detailed program for the administrator."[8] Indeed, his work might be best understood as suggestions put forward with the intent of promoting discussion about the major political concerns of the moment. Whatever the success or failure of Mannheim's own program, his thinking about the intellectual helped inspired the subsequent development of the sociology of intellectuals. His work poses important questions that have continued to be asked throughout the twentieth and twenty-first centuries and which are still relevant today. His work raises difficult questions about the relationship between political partisanship and truth telling, the responsibilities of the intellectual, the relevant ethical and political motivations of intellectual practice, and the standards by which we should judge intellectuals' claims to truth. Mannheim's ideas about the roles of the intellectuals have sparked a robust debate helping inspire and legitimate this book.

Mannheim's ideas also point to the wider issue of sense-making with regards to the social world. The social world is distinguishable from what we typically refer to as the natural world where we can come to know reality by using scientific measures. Our major tasks as researchers when dealing with the natural world is to design and implement particular research methods that help us to understand its different elements and how they fit into the whole. Our roles as researchers are very different when dealing with things in the social world. Our understanding of it is observer-dependent. Unlike the natural world there is no *objectivity* in the social world. Instead it is characterized by what is usually referred to as *subjectivity*, or what writers like Alfred Schutz and Charles Taylor have insisted is a better way of denominating this, namely intersubjectivity.[9]

This shift away from the notion of subjectivity is meant to highlight the role played by shared systems of belief, symbolic schema, and the various social practices we rely on to understand and live in our world. Writers as diverse as Ludwig Wittgenstein, Rudolf Carnap, and Nelson Goodman have pointed out that a variety of social and symbolic systems, including language, play a crucial role in both understanding and structuring the social world.[10] Ferdinand de Saussure was among the first to highlight that it is our linguistic system that enables us to define concepts that we understand as existing in the social world.[11] Things like Wahhabism only exist because of our decision to use and manipulate symbolic systems.

Intellectuals produce a lot of what we think we know about the social world, and hold privileged positions in society as the writers of scholarly articles, books, and newspaper and magazine articles. Their interpretations of concepts like Wahhabism are widely distributed and read by the general public and policy- and decision-makers, who may have never previously thought about this phenomenon. That is to say that we tend to rely on intellectuals' representations to make sense of things like Wahhabism that we assume exist out there in the social world. This becomes extremely important when we consider that policy- and decision-makers can draw on these representations when making policies that have the ability to cause great harm and destruction, and that the public's support for such policies can also rely on the same representations.

To borrow a concept from Gilles Deleuze that has since been expanded by authors like Thomas Osborne, we can best understand intellectuals as mediators of ideas in today's knowledge society.[12] Both authors emphasize the important role intellectuals play in communicating ideas about the social world to their audience. For Deleuze, the modern intellectual as a mediator is a creative catalyst of ideas. Osborne writes, "the mediator is interested above all in *ideas* . . . which are going to make a difference . . . in some later event."[13] However, the major issue with Osborne's conception is that he considers the intellectual as a mediator to be "value-neutral," unconcerned with "the 'big ideas' of the epoch of 'grand narratives.'"[14]

The important question I want to address, and which is at odds with the account offered by Osborne, is whether intellectuals are indeed value-neutral mediators communicating ideas about what is happening in the social world to their audience or whether there is something else going on? Additionally, we also need to establish whether Osborne's claim that many intellectuals are not concerned with the big ideas and grand narratives of our time is adequate. As will become clearer throughout this book, a case can certainly be made that intellectuals representing Wahhabism are indeed concerned with promoting the big ideas and grand narratives associated with popular intellectual traditions like neoconservatism and liberalism. It is equally likely that many intellectuals are also unknowingly or unconsciously promoting key beliefs that resonate with or get their authority and appeal from these prominent intellectual traditions.

In both instances the outcome is often the same, a particular sense of order is imposed on the social world and is created and recreated in particular ways. Contrary to Osborne's claim, it is crucial to consider the intellectuals' ideas within the political context in which they have been formed and appear. We only need to look at the fact that Wahhabism was largely ignored pre-9/11 to see that the relatively new interest in it is related to the post-9/11 period in which many Western governments and intellectuals are living during a time of heightened anxiety about radical Islamism and are fixated with the Western-led global war on terror.

Given the important roles intellectuals play in this knowledge-producing process, it matters that we pay close attention to the particular truth claims intellectuals make when justifying their interpretations and think about how we are best to understand this process. As has proven to be the case in recent times, if we are going to make policies informed and supported by these truth claims, it matters that we fully understand them. If Western nations are going to invade sovereign Islamic nations in the Middle East with the aim of promoting democracy, or bomb civilians and terrorists in the name of security then we must have an understanding of the claims supporting and justifying these kinds of actions. This understanding requires intense scrutiny that involves the careful deconstructing of representations.

I dedicate this chapter to setting out the rationale for my book. I argue that a review of the relevant literature points to a number of key problems or questions that have been the focus of considerable scholarly debate. These problems or questions provide the overarching intellectual and analytical problematic for my inquiry into the ways certain groups of intellectuals represent Wahhabism. First, it is clear there is an ongoing debate about the motivation and identity of intellectuals. I show how scholars have sought to make sense of the different motivations and inspirations influencing intellectuals. I aim to answer the question, what is it that leads some to become intellectuals? Related to this idea is how we define an intellectual. Here I ask, is the function of critique fundamental to the identity of intellectuals? Secondly, there is a discussion about the particular practices in which intellectuals play a special role. How important is the proposition that intellectuals set about constituting our world? This leads me to consider their role in constructing what Anderson called 'Imagined communities' and Said called 'Imagined geographies.'[15] Among the many issues about the relationship of intellectuals to conceptions of truth, I deal with the role prejudice plays in the ways intellectuals make sense of and represent the social world. The need to do this is raised by Chomsky's provocative suggestion that it is the responsibility of intellectuals to speak the truth and to expose lies and Arendt's more nuanced account of the problem of how we are to think about the relation between truth and politics.[16] At stake here is how some intellectuals justify their claims as purveyors of truth.

On the Collective Identity and Attachment of Intellectuals

Scholars differ in their understandings with regards to what defines or constitutes an intellectual, what their roles are and should be, and to whom or what they owe their allegiance. Charles Kurzman and Lynn Owens offer a useful typology that distinguishes between three major approaches scholars adopt when considering these different issues. These are intellectuals as class-less, intellectuals as class-bound, and intellectuals as a class in themselves.[17] I prefer to think of and describe the second category of intellectuals as class, group, or movement-bound; for me, class-bound implies a Marxist or quasi-Marxist understanding, while class, group, or movement-bound can be used to describe intellectuals with any affiliation to an interest group. Understanding this debate is important because it informs our understanding of and helps us to distinguish between the different roles intellectuals adopt when representing Wahhabism. More specifically this helps us to understand the different factors inspiring and motivating intellectuals in their representations of Wahhabism: are they motivated and inspired by a desire to speak truth to power or by particular class and group interests?

First we will deal with the group Kurzman and Owens call the classless intellectuals. Prominent writers belonging to this long tradition include Karl Mannheim, Noam Chomsky, Talcott Parsons, Edward Shils, and Christopher Hitchens.[18] As the term suggests, these scholars maintain that intellectuals are nonpartisan and not attached or fixed to any particular group or class. Their critiques of the social world for their audience are inspired by utopian ideals, rather than personal glory or class interests. If we are to consider the roles these kinds of intellectuals play in representing Wahhabism, we can say they are motivated and inspired by bringing attention to perceived injustices and wrongs with the ultimate aim of creating a more harmonious society.

Mannheim saw intellectuals as "not too firmly situated in the social order," "socially unattached," and as a part of an "unanchored, *relatively* class-less stratum."[19] He believed intellectuals to be motivated and inspired by a desire to encourage mutual understanding between different sections and groups in society or as he puts it, "to create a form outside of the party schools in which the perspective of and the interest in the whole is safeguarded."[20] He believed intellectuals were entrusted with the responsibility of making sense of the current political situation for society and he saw nonintellectuals as those members of society who are firmly entrenched and participating in everyday activities. Mannheim believed that the common person, due to their relative lack of education, was incapable of having a deeper understanding of the different political forces operating and competing in society. He believed the common person absorbed a worldview as if by osmosis, "while the person who is not oriented toward the whole through his education, but rather participates directly in the social process of production, merely tends to absorb the Weltanschauung [worldview] of that particular group."[21]

Mannheim, however, was extremely worried that intellectuals in the twentieth century were not living up to their responsibilities and were instead promoting the interests of particular groups, to the detriment of wider society. Chomsky expresses a similar concern about intellectuals, especially Western intellectuals in the twenty-first century whose relative "political liberty, from access to information and freedom of expression" means they have the responsibility "to seek the truth lying hidden behind the veil of distortion and misrepresentation, ideology and class interest, through which the events of current history are presented to us."[22] Mannheim was worried that intellectuals were failing to transcend their class and instead joining or remaining in interest and class groups. He wrote that "the decline of a relatively free intelligentsia" during this period threatened "the comparative and critical approach which an atmosphere of multipolar viewpoints stimulates."[23] As we will see, Mannheim and Chomsky are right to worry. Many of the intellectuals representing Wahhabism in the twenty-first century remain tied to particular interest groups and favor the promoting of their interests instead of attempting to facilitate understanding between different groups in order to create a better society.

Talcott Parsons and Christopher Hitchens have adopted similar approaches. Parsons argued that intellectuals, rather than engaging in partisan politics, should aim at imposing universalistic standards as a way of promoting and creating a more inclusive and harmonious society.[24] Parsons also appreciated the observer-dependent role people in general play when making sense of phenomena in the social world. He saw intellectuals as responsible for dealing with the meaning of symbolic systems, arguing they should dedicate themselves to describing the symbolic interactions between competing groups. Parsons would certainly categorize my work in this book in describing and analyzing the symbolic interactions occurring between intellectuals from competing groups as intellectual in nature.

Hitchens also sees intellectuals as unattached to a specific class or group and believes bona fide intellectuals would never use the term when referring to themselves: "I cannot think of any—except [Alan] Wolfe who would have said on his or her own behalf, 'I am an intellectual.'"[25]

Hitchens claims it is important that we distinguish between the "true intellectuals" and the rival callings of "opinion maker" or "pundits," especially as the last two are intimately bound up with the world of television.[26] Hitchens's awareness of the major role television plays, which is largely ignored by Mannheim and Parsons, is understandable given his sociology of the intellectual has been provided in the modern political context. Hitchens maintains that a true intellectual does not promote the interests of a specific group or class; rather, he or she "attempt[s] to soar on the thermals of public opinion."[27] The intellectual is subversive and earns their living through the "battle of ideas."[28] They

> "care for language above all and guess its subtle relationship to truth; and who will be willing and able to nail a lie. If such a person should also have a sense of irony and a feeling for history, then, as the French say, 'tant mieux.'"[29]

While the intellectual does not necessarily have to speak truth to power, they should be skeptical of authority as well as claims about utopia, heaven, and hell. The intellectual must also be able "to survey the present through the optic of a historian, the past with the perspective of the living, and the culture and language of others with the equipment of an Internationalist."[30]

Shils's understanding of the intellectual is somewhat similar to the accounts offered by Mannheim, Parsons, and Hitchens, given he also sees intellectuals as free-floating and class-less. Basing his understanding of the intellectual on his experiences in postcolonial India, where he sees intellectuals as playing "a great historical role on the higher levels of administration," Shils expresses a deep regret that some of the intellectuals were motivated by personal glory.[31] According to Shils, the intellectual as a responsible critic should neither give in to such selfish and egoistic motivations nor get too involved in partisan politics or promote government interests. What distinguishes his account from those provided by Mannheim, Parsons, and Hitchens is that Shils believes intellectuals could play minor roles in government. Kurzman and Owens's typology encourages us to categorize Shils's conceptualization with those offered by Chomsky and Parsons; however, the major problem with this is that it overlooks Shils's support for intellectuals as key proponents of the political liberal tradition.

Shils's approach would be better understood as belonging to those approaches treating intellectuals as promoters of particular class or group interests. Shils understood intellectuals as playing key roles in bringing modernity to traditional societies. Displaying some of the ethnocentric tendencies held by many in the political liberal tradition, Shils advocated for the modernization of all backward nations and believed the United States provided the blueprint for an ideal society. "Modern means being western without the onus of following the West. It is the model for the West detached in some way from its geographical origins and locus."[32] Acutely aware of possible charges of racism, Shils chose to use the terms modernization and modern because he (wrongly) thought it steered away from implications of Western superiority suggested by the terms Christianization or Westernization.[33] This call for intellectuals to promote a particular belief system stands in contrast to the approaches adopted by authors like Mannheim, Parsons, and Chomsky, who champion speaking truth to power.

My initial account of these key authors helps to make an important point when considering the different approaches within the sociology of intellectuals tradition. It is important we understand the political contexts in which these conceptualizations are offered. While Shils was largely concerned with the decolonization of India, both Mannheim and Parsons wrote during a time in the twentieth century that was dominated by several global wars. Having experienced or learned about another global war only a few decades earlier, scholars studying the sociology of intellectuals were typically pessimistic about the future of humanity. Watching as many in the world chose their sides and proceeded to kill one another in the name of politics, many scholars including Mannheim and Parsons longed for a situation in which intellectuals could transcend these base instincts for the good of society and humanity. They wanted intellectuals to rise above politics and to be of service to all humanity.

A second approach used to understand the roles, motivations, and inspiration of intellectuals involves treating them as a class in themselves.

Prominent advocates of this approach have included Julien Benda, George Orwell, Vaclav Havel, and Leszek Kolakowski.[34] Like Mannheim, Shils, and Parsons, these writers understand intellectuals as existing separate from particular class and group interests. Proponents of this approach tend to see intellectuals primarily as servants of truth, philosophers, and educators, inspired and motivated by the utopian ideals of creating a better society. This idea became prominent among intellectuals in the early twentieth century when the Dreyfus Affair in France inspired an appeal to a conception of intellectuals as defenders of the truth. Robert Levy was among those who called for "Intellectuals of all countries, [to] unite!"

> Unite because the war, which decimated you, has reduced the survivors to the wages of misery; unite because, among other workers, your brothers, you [survivors] dare to speak of the material conditions of your miserable lives, which are brightened only by the will to learn or teach.[35]

The Dreyfus intellectuals, who included prominent figures like Emile Zola, Alan Montefiore, Octave Mirbeau, and Anatole France, did not see themselves as attached to a particular class of production but instead considered themselves to be their own class. Christopher Hitchens points out the term intellectual was also one of abuse used by critics of the pro-Dreyfus intellectuals who saw them as preferring "the urbane abstractions of "the intellect" to the verities of church and soil."[36]

Julien Benda, who was an early and prominent advocate for this approach, writes that intellectuals should be inspired by "non-material advantages" and not "the pursuit of practical aims."[37] He said they find "joy in the practice of an art or a science or metaphysical speculation . . . and hence in a certain manner say: 'My kingdom is not of this world.'"[38] Benda's seminal work *La Trahison des Clercs*, which along with Mannheim's work is considered to be one of the founding documents in the sociology of intellectuals, was essentially an attack on contemporary intellectuals who failed to live up to their responsibilities as anti-class and non-partisan. "The modern 'clerk' has entirely ceased to let the layman alone descend to the market place" and in doing so "betrayed their duty, which is precisely to set up a corporation whose sole cult is that of justice and truth."[39]

Benda's calls to truth makes him a part of a long tradition of scholars who hold that one of the intellectuals' chief responsibilities is to be, as is so eloquently stated by Ignazio Silone, in "the humble and courageous service of truth."[40] This tradition also includes George Orwell and Vaclav Havel, who saw intellectuals as disturbers of peace in constant pursuit of the truth, irrespective of whether or not this infuriated authorities. Havel writes:

> The intellectual should constantly disturb, should bear witness to the misery of the world, should be provocative by being independent, should rebel against all hidden and open pressure and manipulations, should be the chief doubter of systems, of power and its incantations, should be a witness to their mendacity.[41]

Orwell wrote during the mid-twentieth century, a time dominated by imperialism, fascism, and Stalinism. His claim to be identified as belonging to the Left has proved to be a rich source of disagreement. He favored an internationalist stand to nationalism and was critical of many in the intellectual class who championed man-made ideologies. Orwell was also a fierce critic of Catholic intellectuals who colluded with the Catholic Church to advance their religious agenda. However, it is his anti-imperialism that is the strongest and most consistent theme throughout his writings, and the bulk of his efforts were dedicated to championing the emancipation of the formerly colonized world. British involvement in India was a central concern to him given his and his family's personal experience with the British imperialist forces in the country. His anti-imperialist ideas are evident in both *The Lion and the Unicorn* and his introduction to Joyce Cary's *African Freedom*, where he demands a full and independent India free from British interference.[42] Orwell lived the life he believed a responsible critic should live, which meant always facing power, particularly when revealing its relationship to cruelty and force, and ensuring his or her opinions are given without dilution, particularly when appearing in the mass media.[43]

Orwell believed that one should always speak the truth and these efforts should be focused on the relationship between the dominated and dominator, and that one should never compromise oneself by associating with ideological and interest groups when doing so. Orwell's ideas about the role of the intellectual and the constant anti-imperialism that pervaded his writings are made clear in his refusal to speak on the platform of the League for European Freedom at a meeting protesting Communist brutality in Yugoslavia:

> Certainly what is said on your platforms is more truthful than the lying propaganda to be found in most of the press, but I cannot associate myself with an essentially Conservative body which claims to defend democracy in Europe but has nothing to say about British imperialism. It seems to me that one can only denounce the crimes now being committed in Poland, Jugoslaiva etc. if one is equally insistent on ending Britain's unwanted rule in India. I belong to the Left and must work inside it, much as I hate the Russian totalitarianism and its poisonous influence in this country.[44]

Similar conceptualizations are offered by Emile Zola, Leszek Kolakowski, and Edward Said, who used his famous Reith Lectures in 1993 to argue that the primary responsibility of the modern intellectual is to speak truth to power.[45] These scholars have also been labeled as belonging to a moralist tradition within a sociology of intellectuals and it is worth noting that critics of this tradition claim they offer a normative conception of intellectuals rather than one that is apparently empirically grounded.[46]

The third approach in Kurzman and Owens's typology deals with scholars who understand intellectuals as class-bound. To reiterate, I believe we can also describe these intellectuals as movement- and group-bound. This means their social class or interest group is the basis of their intellectual activity. When considering the role of the intellectual as a mediator, this approach advocates for mediations or representations of the social world by intellectuals that serve or help advance the interests of a particular group or class. This can be understood as a political approach that often relies on truth claims inspired and motivated by partisan politics, as opposed to more utopian ideals or speaking truth to power.

This approach was pioneered by Italian Marxist Antonio Gramsci, who argued that the role of intellectuals must be understood by locating them within the class system of modern societies. Gramsci began his analysis by asking, "are intellectuals an autonomous and independent social group, or does every social group have its own particular specialized category of intellectuals?"[47] Gramsci chose the second option, arguing that each social group creates within itself a set of organic intellectuals who provide it with "homogeneity and an awareness of its function" in the political, social, and economic fields.[48] Intellectuals can be categorized as such when they use society's ideological apparatuses like the media and the education system to help promote their groups or class interests in an attempt to make their way of thinking the cultural norm. Gramsci's key point was that intellectuals are not able to form their own class group but belong to or work for other social classes.

It is important to understand the political context in which Gramsci offered this conceptualization. This was during a time when the Italian Communist Party was a major player in Italy and the Communist Party in the Soviet Union was dominating the international workers' movements. Gramsci was himself a part of the Italian Communist Party, whose concern for the welfare and wellbeing of those belonging to the lower and middle classes inspired and motivated him to act politically. Gramsci's account of intellectuals can be understood as a call to the lower and middle classes to adopt activist roles in an attempt to revolutionize society with the ultimate aim of bettering their economic and social conditions. Scholars like William Domhoff, who have adopted a Gramscian/Marxist approach, typically identify and criticize scholars they believe represent the interests of the upper classes and are inspired in maintaining the (capitalist) status quo.[49]

Intellectuals and the Nation-State

Kurzman and Owens identify three key questions worth asking when considering the roles of intellectuals within the class- and interest-based approach: "under what conditions do intellectuals aspire to organicity; what does it mean for an intellectual to be 'organic' in a community; and can intellectuals construct the community in which they claim to be organic?"[50] The responses to these questions have been particularly pertinent for scholars dealing with nationalism. Whether or not intellectuals can construct the group to which they are said to have some kind of organic connection has been key to scholars wanting to understand another kind of organic connection, namely that between intellectuals and their identity with and membership in nation-states.

I have already anticipated some of my argument in the introduction by referring to the roles some intellectuals play in constructing Imagined communities and Imagined geographies when representing Wahhabism. As I discuss here, there is a long tradition of writers including Ron Eyerman, Eric Hobsbawm, Anthony Smith, Ronald Suny and Michael Kennedy, Benedict Anderson, Edward Said, and Derek Gregory who claim that intellectuals often have a connection with particular communities and that they play key roles in helping to create these communities.[51] This debate focuses on what inspires and motivates these intellectuals to act in this way and whether their constructing of particular spaces and communities has positive or negative implications for the situation on the ground.

Building on the ideas of Gramsci, Eyerman claims that we can think of those helping to construct particular groups as 'movement intellectuals' because they are a part of a particular class or other social movement, group, or intellectual tradition.[52] However, instead of groups producing their own intellectuals as Gramsci suggests, Eyerman maintains that movement intellectuals are producing organic groups. This role of the intellectual has been central to scholarly debates about nationalism. Eyerman is critical of intellectuals choosing to help create imagined groups, claiming this allows them to project "their own needs and fantasies"[53]—an important issue when it comes to considering neoconservative and liberal intellectuals' representations of Wahhabism.

Scholars like Benedict Anderson, Eric Hobsbawm, Michael Kennedy, Anthony Smith, and Ronald Suny have emphasized the key roles intellectuals play as catalysts and agents in helping constitute national ideologies and nationalist movements.[54] As I explained in Chapter 1, Anderson sees nations as socially constructed communities imagined by people who think of themselves as part of that group. Although we may not enjoy face-to-face relations with everybody in our Imagined community, our ability to communicate helps us to know they exist, and the mainstream media can play a crucial role in this process.

Many writers, especially more traditionally inclined Marxists, have been hostile to the kinds of nationalism fostered by intellectuals in terms rendered by Anderson as Imagined communities. They treat them as distractions that divert the lower and middle classes from understanding the real and true source of their subjugation and oppression. In spite of criticisms offered by authors like Eric Hobsbawm and Ernest Gellner, Anderson does not see nationalism as a negative thing. He remarked, "I am probably the only one writing about nationalism who doesn't think it ugly."[55] Anderson believes that there exists a valuable utopian element in nationalism that helps give people meaning, as it inspires comradeship and encourages feelings of belonging to a group much bigger than themselves. Unfortunately history tells us that any utopian element is generally outweighed by its use as a force to divide and encourage hatred and violence among people.

Also pertinent here are Said's ideas about Imagined geographies. To reiterate, Said uses this term when referring to perceived spaces created by intellectuals through the use of particular images, texts, and discourses. The intellectual's ability to create these is a powerful tool that can be utilized to help control and subordinate another group. Said's ideas have inspired scholars like Derek Gregory, who applies his theory to the modern post-9/11 political situation.[56] Gregory claims that the ideas motivating and inspiring the Western-led global war on terror against radical Islamists builds on the same Imagined geographies highlighted by Said. Aware of the ability of intellectuals' representations to influence the policy- and decision-making processes, Gregory emphasizes the crucial role intellectuals' representations of particular spaces in the Middle East have played in the making of Western foreign policy. This link between representing the problems and making policy is a key point also emphasized by scholars like Carol Bacchi.[57]

Gregory's study shows that Western culture has a tendency to represent the Islamic world as uncivilized, backward, and failing and that this has helped justify the recent Western military interventions in the Middle East, especially in Afghanistan and Iraq. He criticizes prominent Western commentators like Huntington, Lewis, and Zakaria (both Lewis and Zakaria are intellectuals whose representations of Wahhabism I analyze in this book) for promoting Orientalist frames when writing about the international political space. Gregory claims that the current Western-led global war on terror is a continuation of the European colonization process: "For what else is the war on terror other than the violent return of the colonial past, with its split geographies of 'us' and 'them,' 'civilization' and 'barbarism,' 'Good' and 'Evil'?"[58]

The works of Gregory, Anderson, Said, and Eyerman are especially pertinent to this book given my interest in studying the relations between intellectuals' representations of Wahhabism (including their role in creating Imagined communities and Imagined geographies) and the political, decision-, and policy-making processes. It must be noted that some scholars disagree on the flow of causality, that is to say, whether nationalist ideas are products of pre-existing communities with intellectuals playing the roles of midwives, or whether intellectuals create and impose nationalist ideas reconfiguring communities. While the roles intellectuals play in this process are pertinent, issues regarding causality are not. Unlike many of those scholars engaging in this debate, my view of how the world works is shaped in part by dialectics, a philosophy of internal relations and abstraction. In the next chapter, I describe how these concepts work in addition to looking at the key role prejudice plays in how we make sense of the social world. However, before moving along there is another major issue I want to address: how do we go about making sense of truth?

Making Sense of Truth

It was Julien Benda who strenuously argued that the intellectual's essential role is to be a servant of truth; their allegiance must be to truth and not to class or group interests.[59] Chomsky later joined Benda in his criticism of those intellectuals refusing to speak truth to power in favor of serving their material interests.[60] But what exactly do we mean when we use this term 'truth'? To what kind of 'truth' are these authors referring?

This question has been a major focus of many philosophers and scholars in the twentieth century and has inspired many ongoing discussions-cum-controversies between contending schools of philosophy. Though it simplifies matters somewhat, the case for a realist, naturalist, or objectivist account of truth has been made by writers like Bertrand Russell, Alfred Jules Ayer, Rudolf Carnap, William P. Alston, and Susan Haack who are working from within traditions like empiricism and logical positivism.[61] Ranged against these traditions, philosophers associated with pragmatism, critical theory, discourse theory, and poststructuralism have made the case for a constructivist, perspectivist, and contingent account of truth. These arguments and controversies have involved writers like Hans-Georg Gadamer, Martin Heidegger, Stephen Toulmin, Hannah Arendt, Richard Rorty, Jacques Derrida, and John Caputo.[62]

I want here only to briefly indicate the kinds of considerations influencing how I propose dealing with the issue of truth when analyzing intellectuals' representations of Wahhabism. My understanding is based on observations made by both Toulmin and Caputo that we live in a time that has moved beyond a conception of truth framed in terms of timeless and universal propositions.[63] Caputo writes that truth is perpetually on the go and that we are currently living in an age "marked by modern transportation systems in which we can travel almost anywhere, and modern information systems, through which almost anything can travel to us, [which] is much more pluralistic than life in the past."[64] Traveling is a key part of our modern lifestyle, and when we travel we are able to experience many different views of reality. This new way of being and thinking has threatened our once cherished modernist or Enlightenment ideas of truth. During that period in time we were committed to the idea that there was one big story that explained all the world's phenomena.

That one big story was science, and still there are many people working from the assumption that we can use a natural scientific approach to measure, explain, or predict social phenomena. The same one big story idea was also pervasive in the age dominated by religious thought immediately prior to the Enlightenment. During this period in history it was generally believed that all things could be understood in terms of God's plan. We have seen how dangerous this idea can be. There are still many people who continue to think in this way, seeing their lives as a part of some divine plan. The standard Judeo-Christian interpretation, for example, ends with the Messiah returning to the earth and saving the believers.

Caputo's key point is that we now live in an age defined by multiple and competing interpretations of the world. However, this does not mean we must go down the rabbit hole of the postmodern conception of truth, where everybody's conceptions of truth are equally valid, where nothing can be confirmed or denied, and where anything can be asserted in whatever style one chooses. This is tantamount to giving up on the idea of truth. Instead we must save truth and we can do this by following a line of thought that started with Heidegger and was developed by two of his successors, Gadamer and Arendt.

This is a tradition that can be traced back to the ideas of Martin Heidegger, expressed in his seminal work *Being and Time*.[65] Heidegger uses the concept *Dasein* to describe the process and responsibility people have for understanding and making sense of the world into which they have been thrown. The German word *Dasein* is usually translated as 'existence,' though a more exact translation would be 'being there.'[66] Heidegger uses this term to describe the specific human experience of being. Heidegger uses *Dasein* to help emphasize the responsibility we have as humans to be aware of and deal with a range of issues, including our mortality and the dilemma of living in relationships with others while at the same time being alone with one's self. It is a way of being that involves caring for the world in which one lives but at the same time remaining aware of the contingent element of that involvement, of the priority of the world over the self, and of the evolving nature of the self. Heidegger describes the opposite of *Dasein* as the forfeiting of meaning in favor of an escapist way of being.

Heidegger's ideas about one's own truth and making sense of one's existence inspired Hans-George Gadamer's formative work on prejudice.[67] Gadamer takes a step back and identifies the existence of anticipatory structures affecting the way we come to know and understand the world. When it comes to 'knowing,' the German language distinguishes between the verbs *kennen* and *wissen*. *Wissen* implies the knowing of a fact, while *kennen* implies knowing in the sense of being acquainted with and having a working knowledge of something.[68] The terms are often used in the field of epistemology when distinguishing between various settings of knowledge production and emphasizing their contextual aspects. Different fields of study are endowed with their own epistemic culture, prescribing what is and what is not adequate knowledge and how this knowledge can be obtained. The knowing of a fact or *wissen* typically applies to the natural world that is observer-independent. Here we are concerned with *kennen*, which deals with the social world, is observer-dependent, and is influenced by our *Vorurteile*.

Gadamer's hermeneutic conception of knowledge holds that every act of understanding presupposes a preunderstanding, the elements of which are one's *Vorurteile*, prejudgments or prejudices. These "absolutely fundamental anticipations, that is, anticipations common to us all," are what Gadamer calls "tradition."[69] This is an important point as we start to consider representations of Wahhabism provided by intellectuals belonging to the liberal and neoconservative intellectual traditions. Our prejudices are affected by things like the context in which we are currently living, born into, and raised, or as Heidegger phrases it, 'the place in the world into which we are thrown.'[70]

There is a tendency for people to hear or read the word 'prejudice' and think of it in negative terms. One often thinks of racial or homophobic prejudice, which are both certainly negative and hateful views. Rather than understanding all prejudices as bad, Gadamer maintains that prejudices can also be understood as good things. Gadamer is responsible for reviving the concept of prejudice, recognizing the fact there can be such things as legitimate prejudices.[71] What this means is that some opinions can be true in that they speak to the way things really are, and some opinions are false because they do not describe how things really are.

The key tasks when dealing with prejudices are not only to identify them so as to understand the ways in which intellectuals, for example, make sense of the world, which includes making and relying on particular truth claims, but to also consider how those prejudices speak to the way things really are. Gadamer writes that the fundamental epistemological question is not how can we remove prejudice or bias, a process that many social scientists mistakenly think can be done, but rather to find answers to the question, what makes prejudices legitimate? Or as Gadamer phrases it, "what distinguishes legitimate prejudices from the countless others which it is the undeniable task of critical reason to overcome?"[72]

This is precisely what Arendt recommends. She writes that this approach prohibits us from adopting a rationalist method when seeking to then dispel these prejudices. We as social scientists cannot develop scientific methods aimed at removing prejudice or bias from studies of phenomena in the social world because prejudice is an irremovable part of us. If we want to dispel these prejudices then we must find and expose them for what they are, which involves finding their *Wahrheitsgehalt*. "If one bypasses this step," writes Arendt, "entire battalions of enlightened speakers and entire libraries of pamphlets will achieve nothing."[73]

Arendt recognizes that we have moved beyond the idea that there is a timeless eternal truth in the social world and that we live in an age of mass manipulation where even the role of factual truth is challenged. She points to the official Russian view of its recent history in which Leon Trotsky has been erased as the quintessential example of this manipulation—such was the fate "of a man by the name of Trotsky, who appears in none of the Soviet Russian history books."[74] Despite this she maintains that we must still find a way of dealing with truth claims, especially those that are religious and political in nature, and which have the ability to influence the political and decision-making processes. She proposes that we shift our attention to the prejudices underscoring these truth claims. More specifically she recommends identifying and unpacking these prejudices with the aim of understanding what in them is true.

We now have an understanding of some of the different roles and responsibilities intellectuals can have and the crucial roles they can play as mediators of ideas in today's knowledge society. These ideas are important as we begin to consider the roles adopted by intellectuals belonging to the neoconservative and liberal intellectual traditions when representing Wahhabism. In this chapter we have also dealt with the issue of making sense of truth, which focuses on identifying and unpacking the prejudices associated with these truth claims. This also becomes important as we begin deconstructing neoconservative and liberal representations of Wahhabism and identifying the key prejudices influencing these. In the next chapter I take a closer look at the key theories and frameworks influencing the deconstruction, analytical, and interpretative processes.

3
Dialectics, Ideal Types, Fuzzy Categories, and Analyzing Language

Between the idea
And the reality
Between the motion
And the act
Falls the Shadow . . .
—T.S. Eliot, *The Hollow Men*

The representation of Wahhabism by two specific groups of Western intellectuals is the primary focus of my book, and up until this point in time I have made the case for why such a study is needed. In this chapter I describe the major theories and frameworks influencing how I go about this. Conventional approaches dictate that we can understand the relation between the phenomenon we choose to call Wahhabism and intellectuals' representations of it by assuming that there is some kind of causal relationship between the reality of Wahhabism and the way the representations are then constructed. Such an approach belongs to a philosophy of external relations that treats one thing as affecting another and understands things as existing independently, having a history and external communications with other things. It assumes an observer-independent view of the social world that we can somehow grasp, perhaps even measure, quantify, or provide causal and explanatory-predictive accounts of its processes and relations. My views are influenced by authors like Roslyn Bologh who is one of the many to offer a scathing critique of this naive realist and positivist view of the social world:

> [This approach] treats subjects and objects as separate and knowable in that separation, as if the sense of an object could be taken for granted as emanating from the object independently of any relation to the subject. In this way, the object as it is known, that is, the knowledge or meaning of the object, appears to be natural and eternal rather than social and grounded in an historically specific form of life.[1]

Because I am not so naive as to think that we can enjoy some kind of unmediated access to the social world that is separate from human experience, I find that I am able to understand and appreciate Karl Marx's dialectical imagination. A dialectical imagination encourages us to think less about things and more about relations and processes that are constantly affecting each other, emphasizing the evolving nature of things. Dialectics encourages us to focus on how relationships arise, develop, and fit into the larger context of which they are a part. It offers a much more complex and nuanced understanding of the social world that is sensitive to and aware of its relational nature. This approach has two key elements: the process of abstraction and the philosophy of internal relations. I dedicate the first part of this chapter to exploring these ideas. I then describe what fuzzy categories are and introduce the reader to Max Weber's ideas about the ideal type, which helps in understanding how I have gone about determining who is and who is not a liberal or neoconservative intellectual.

In the second part of the chapter I briefly describe the use of a critical discourse analysis paradigm, which I make use of when deconstructing liberal and neoconservative intellectuals' representations of Wahhabism. This involves focusing on a number of key features of language and discourse, including the use of metaphors, similes, analogies, and neologisms, as well as the structuring of accounts of violence. This method of analysis provides us with the information we need to then go about identifying and deconstructing the prejudices influencing the intellectuals in their representations of Wahhabism, which in turn allows us to make determinations regarding their roles as intellectuals, for example, are they acting as movement intellectuals as Eyerman suggests, or are they highlighting wrongs and injustices and speaking truth to power?

Dialectics

> If one were to attempt to define in a single word the focus, so to speak, of the whole correspondence [between Karl Marx and Friedrich Engels], the central point at which the whole body of ideas expressed and discussed converges—that word would be dialectics. The application of materialist dialectics to the reshaping of all political economy from its foundations up, its application to history, natural science, philosophy, and to the policy and tactics of the working class—that was what interested Marx and Engels most of all, that was where they contributed what was most essential and new, and that was what constituted the masterly advance they made in the history of revolutionary thought.[2]
>
> —V.I. Lenin, *The Marx-Engels Correspondence*, 1913

Bertell Ollman and Tony Smith point out that "with such excellent press . . . one might have thought that . . . dialectics would be well understood and that dialectical studies the norm rather than the exception."[3] This however is not the case. Dialectics is a way of thinking and a set of related categories capturing the real changes and interactions happening in the social world. It offers a method for investigating social reality, helping us to see and analyze relations and processes of which we are a part as they have unfolded, are currently unfolding, and have yet to unfold.[4]

The dialectical imagination takes the whole as a given. Interconnections and changes that make up the whole are inseparable from what anything is, internal to its being, and are essential to fully understanding it. A dialectical imagination encourages us to understand the world as consisting of processes in relations of mutual dependence rather than as existing independently. In the history of ideas this has been described as the philosophy of internal relations.[5] Ollman points out that the philosophy of internal relations can be traced as far back as the Greek philosopher Parmenides (515–460 BC), whose ideas first came into prominence in the early modern period in the work of Spinoza (1632–1677). Spinoza grounded his philosophy on

Aristotle's definition of 'substance' and infused it with his own religious ideas. Spinoza understood the world as made up of transient things that were the sum of interrelations. He used the term 'God' to describe this manifold system of interrelations constituting everything. A century or so later Hegel dealt with the philosophy of internal relations. Ollman notes that the distinctiveness of Hegel's treatment of this idea lies in the many means he used to keep our attention focused on the whole while also distinguishing between its parts. Hegel described things as determinations, moments, and phenomenon, suggesting the impartial and unfinished nature of things whose full analysis requires that it be thought of as including much more than is immediately apparent.[6] Informed by Hegel's ideas, this is precisely why I often choose to describe Wahhabism as a phenomenon throughout this book.

These ideas were again dealt with and further refined by Karl Marx, who rejected Hegel's claim that ideas somehow developed independently of humankind (Hegel called this the "absolute idea"[7]). Rejecting the religious flavor that writers like Spinoza and Hegel had developed, which saw humankind as ultimately passive and at the will of a higher force, Marx emphasized the role humans played in influencing and shaping the world. According to Marx, change becomes a matter of man transforming his existence. He is not a passive observer of development as Hegel maintained, rather he is the actor whose daily life brings about this change.[8] This resonates with understanding Wahhabism as an observer-dependent rather than observer-independent phenomenon. What we understand as Wahhabism and the different elements we assign it are not changing by themselves or at the will of a higher force, rather it is how we choose to think and talk about it that makes it change.

Key to the philosophy of internal relations is seeing the world as an interconnected whole rather than a conglomeration of loosely connected elements or things. No one thing can ever exist in isolation; everything in the social world is connected *and* in a constant state of flux. It is because of this interconnectedness that changes in one element will result in changes in other elements. This helps us to understand the constant change in operational definitions and intellectual traditions as well as the phenomenon called Wahhabism they are representing. Contexts are constantly changing. People's ideas and experiences are also constantly changing and their understanding of the social world and phenomena in it is therefore always in a constant state of flux.

At this point we still do not really know anything specific about these relations. After assuming there exists a complex whole, the next step in dialectics is to abstract patterns in which most change and interaction occur. Seeing the world as composed of an infinite number of sense-perceptible qualities whose interdependence makes them a whole, it was Joseph Dietzgen who asked, "where do I begin and where do I stop?"[9] Unlike Marx, we are not dealing with the entire social order dominated by the capitalist mode of production. This book is somewhat easier because we are dealing with intellectuals' representations of Wahhabism. Nonetheless, where do I begin and where do I stop? Or put another way, what elements do I choose to 'abstract' for closer analysis?

The term 'abstract,' which I borrow from Ollman, who borrows it from Marx, comes from the Latin term *abstrahere* meaning 'to pull from'—'to abstract' is to extract or pull out. Abstraction can be used as both a verb (abstracting) and as a noun (abstraction). This technique is useful because it allows us to focus on a particular element or a few elements within a complex whole. Ollman points out that the abstracting process is one of six key successive and repeating moments in the dialectical approach.[10] First is the ontological moment of having to deal with what the world really is, which is understanding the world as an infinite number of mutually dependent processes that coalesce to form a totality. The second is the epistemological moment that concerns how we organize our thinking in order to understand this kind of world. This involves opting for a philosophy of internal relations and abstracting dominant patterns where change interaction occurs. Third is the moment of inquiry where one uses categories that convey these patterns of internal relations as aids to investigation. Four is the moment of intellectual reconstruction where one puts together what has been found. Following that is the moment of exposition, which involves trying to describe the dialectical grasp of these findings to an audience. Last is the moment of praxis where one acts in the world, changing and testing what has been learned, which at the same time helps deepen one's understanding.

The epistemological moment, especially the abstraction process, is a particularly useful technique when it comes to constructing a Weberian ideal type for the neoconservative and liberal intellectual traditions and focusing on particular rhetorical techniques intellectuals use when representing Wahhabism. As I point out, in the moment of inquiry, the terms 'neoconservative,' 'liberal,' and 'Wahhabism' can be understood as categories we can use to describe patterns of internal relations. However, before I describe what an ideal type is and how it works so the reader has an understanding of how I have determined what does and does not constitute a liberal and neoconservative intellectual, it is important to recognize the inherent fuzzy nature of these and all other categories. The idea of fuzzy categories is especially congruent with the dialectical tradition, and because of its association with the role played by metaphors, which are also a major focus of this book, it is also congruent with the critical discourse analytic tradition.

On Fuzziness and Ideal Types

Humans divide the social world into categories to help with the sense-making process. Many of these categories have blurred edges and what Lotfi Zadeh describes as "grades of membership."[11] This is especially the case when dealing with concepts like Wahhabism in the field of social science. Many social science concepts, including Wahhabism, are contestable precisely because they do not have an exact definition. In the field of mathematics Zadeh's classical set theory offers a way of handling categories allowing for partial membership.[12] Inspired by Zadeh's work, researchers like Charles Ragin have since advocated using fuzzy sets in fields like sociology and political science.[13]

We tend to associate the term fuzzy with terms like 'unclear' and 'muddled'; however, it takes on a very different meaning when we think about the concepts of fuzzy set theory and fuzzy categories. Zadeh was among the first to use the term when describing the ability of categorical types to refer to varying degrees of membership.[14] A fuzzy set contrasts with a conventional set, where a thing is normally considered to be either definitively in or out. This is comparable to a binary variable with two values. A fuzzy set allows for membership between these two values.

Fuzzy sets are particularly useful for imprecise and complex categories like those we are dealing with in this book: Wahhabism, neoconservatism, and liberalism. Ragin points out that fuzzy sets give social scientists the ability to enliven, intensify, and extend the dialogue between ideas and the information studied:

> In short, with fuzzy sets researchers can analyze evidence in ways that directly reflect their theoretical arguments. . . . [F]uzzy sets have the potential to transform research that is oriented towards "discovery," toward gaining new insights about the world.[15]

Ragin draws attention to a number of advantages of using fuzzy sets when studying the social world.[16] Chief among these is encouraging social science researchers to give up the idea of homogenizing assumptions typically underscoring the quantitative analyses of social phenomena. This is an idea continuing to motivate and inspire researchers stuck on the Enlightenment idea that there is a big scientific story that can explain all the happenings of the social world. Instead, fuzzy sets encourage researchers to focus on and appreciate diversity. They attend to heterogeneity and difference, especially to differences in kind. They promote a configurational approach to analyzing social phenomena, meaning they encourage treating cases as specific configurations of aspects and features. This encourages the search for heterogeneity within a given population, conceives of difference in terms of kinds and types of cases, and allows for degrees of membership. As Ragin notes, "Thus, the incorporation of fuzzy sets allows for 'variation' without forsaking the core emphasis on types and kinds of cases."[17]

For a more practical understanding of the differences between how fuzzy set and the conventional approaches work, we can refer to Ragin's using of the concept Protestantism:

> Imagine that the conventional measure is based on a variety of indicators of Protestant behaviors, attitudes, and beliefs and that these different indicators strongly correlate with each other, justifying their combination into a single index of degree of Protestantism. Assume

> that this scale is both valid and reliable. But where on this scale is a full-fledged Protestant? Where on this scale is a full-fledged non-Protestant? Where on this scale is the cut-off value (or values) separating those who are more in the set of Protestants from those who are more in the set of non-Protestants?[18]

In this book we are dealing with intellectuals belonging to the neoconservative and liberal traditions. To help answer these kinds of questions Ragin raises of who belongs, who does not, and who partially belongs, one must possess and demonstrate substantive knowledge about these intellectual traditions. A solid grasp of their theoretical relevance and some kind of index of each is also required: "Without this infusion of theoretical and substantive knowledge the fine-grained measure of Protestantism remains vague and imprecise—*uncalibrated.*"[19] I do precisely this when constructing the liberal and neoconservative categories. I specify and justify my categorization process, making use of Max Weber's ideal type in the process.

Weber wrote that "an ideal type is formed by the one-sided accentuation of one or more points of view," according to which "concrete individual phenomena . . . are arranged into a unified analytical construct (*Gedankenbild*)."[20] He said that we can think of an ideal type as a "thought-picture" whose "conceptual purity . . . cannot be found empirically anywhere in reality."[21] Its purpose, as Susan Hekman explains, is to synthesize meaningful and characteristic aspects of individual phenomena in order to help explain the occurrence of social events.[22] While ideal types provide thought-pictures against which a particular phenomenon may be compared, that is not to say the particular phenomenon under investigation resembles the ideal type in every way. Weber understands social reality as more complex than any ideal type might be able to be used to investigate, meaning the ideal type can never totally resemble the object of investigation: "All knowledge of cultural reality . . . is always knowledge from particular points of view."[23] An ideal type accentuates, as opposed to copying, various features of a given social phenomenon for closer analysis.[24]

The Weberian ideal type is an extremely useful tool and makes studying social phenomena like neoconservative and liberal intellectuals' representations of Wahhabism a manageable task. However, we must acknowledge the various limitations and implications associated with such an approach. For example, Weber highlights the role an individual's prejudice plays in how he or she constructs the ideal type as well as the fact that all ideal types are necessarily partial and preliminary. Weber writes:

> Insofar as [an ideal type] traces a specific element of cultural life through the most diverse cultural contexts, it is making an historical interpretation from a specific point of view, and offering a partial picture, a preliminary contribution to a more complete historical knowledge of culture.[25]

We must appreciate the complexity of the social world, understanding that we can only expect so much from the abstraction process. In this book that means I only use a handful of key beliefs when it comes to identifying intellectuals as belonging to particular intellectual traditions. There are authors who provide long lists of different beliefs they believe characterize the neoconservative and liberal intellectual traditions. These lists can include many differences; however, they also tend to feature a number of similar core beliefs and it is these similarities that I have paid particular attention to when forming my ideal type. My ideal type when distinguishing liberal intellectuals representing Wahhabism consists of four interrelated key elements: a belief in liberty/freedom, a belief in individualism, a belief in secularism as a way of ordering society, and a belief in progress. My ideal type for discerning those intellectuals who are part of the neoconservative tradition consists of three key elements: a belief in the global promotion of democracy, a belief in the categorizing of nations and groups as either friends or enemies of the United States, and an unwavering support for the state of Israel. I explain each of these in greater detail throughout chapters Four and Five, where I undertake the deconstructing and sense-making processes.

I buttress this process with additional research that includes scrutinizing the intellectual's known political affiliations, the known networks they operate in, and the publications in which their articles appear. The neoconservative network in particular, consisting of think tanks, policy organizations, and online publications like *The Weekly Standard* and

FrontPageMag, is well known and has been the focus of many scholarly studies.[26] Coupling this with my ideal type makes my task of identifying neoconservative intellectuals an easy process.

At this point some readers familiar with the liberal and neoconservative traditions may identify different beliefs they think are core to these traditions. Compiling a shopping list of beliefs and then looking for traces for each of these in an intellectual's representation of Wahhabism is much too great a task for one book. It is also important to note that the beliefs that form my ideal type and which I abstract for closer analysis are also those that are popular among those representing Wahhabism specifically and not some other kind of social phenomenon. This process does however highlight what Weber describes as the inevitable breakdown of every ideal type. While my ideal type may reflect the prevailing ideas at *this moment in time* regarding what does and does not constitute the core beliefs of liberal and neoconservative traditions, the evolving nature of things, the fuzzy nature of categories, and a changing in context means these ideas are bound to change. As Weber points out, every ideal type will eventually break down in the face of the infinite multitude that is social reality.[27]

My selecting of particular rhetorical techniques for closer analysis is also an act of abstraction that is not without its limitations. Intellectuals have a plethora of rhetorical techniques available to them when representing Wahhabism, ranging from the ways in which they order their words and sentences to framing and creating particular images for the reader. Again, it is far too great a task for one book to analyze all of these rhetorical techniques. To make this task more manageable we can focus on a few of the popular techniques deployed by intellectuals. It is important to note that my selection of particular rhetorical techniques is a process that is also influenced by my own beliefs about the social world and the context in which I am currently living. As I have already stated the rhetorical techniques I choose to focus on are the use of metaphors, analogies, similes, neologisms, and the structuring of violent accounts. I will now offer a brief description of each for those who are unfamiliar with these different techniques; the structuring of violent accounts in particular is not well known.

Metaphors, Analogies, Similes, Neologisms, and the Cognitive Structuring of Violent Accounts

Metaphors and similes are two of the most basic and fundamental elements I abstract from intellectuals' representations of Wahhabism for closer analysis. Both are different kinds of analogies that play key roles in how we make sense of the world. This is a key point emphasized by Douglas Hofstadter and Emmanuel Sander in *Surfaces and Essences: Analogy as the Fuel and Fire of Thinking*. They describe our ability to make analogies as the "driving force behind all thought."[28] "Faced with a seething multitude of ill-defined situations . . . our poor besieged brain is constantly grappling with this unpredictable chaos," and our minds respond by constantly assimilating things we see and feel to mental categories constructed by long chains of previous analogies. [29] For example, when we see a tree we recognize and identify it as a tree by 'building a bridge' of similarity between this new tree and all the information accumulated about the trees we have seen before.

Hofstadter and Sander show how "concepts designated by a single word are constantly having their boundaries extended by analogies."[30] They define a concept as "an abstract pattern in the brain that stands for some regular, recurrent aspect of the world and to which any number of words . . . can be attached."[31] This is an example they use to help describe how the boundaries of a concept can constantly change for an individual. There is a young boy named Tim whose understanding of the term mother is shaped by his own experiences with her, ". . . but as new instances of the concept *mommy* are superimposed and start to blur in his memory, the mental mapping that Tim will automatically carry out . . . will start to be made . . . onto the nascent and growing concept of *mommy*."[32]

The important and pertinent point Hofstadter and Sander are making is that our mind's mental representation of a concept is always changing. Our understanding of the situations in which concepts are used are constantly blurring and creating new mental structures, and it is analogies that are driving these changes. "It's this idea of concepts extending themselves forever through a long series of spontaneous analogies."[33] This is important as we begin to consider how we make sense of the concept Wahhabism and the role mediators like intellectuals play in this process.

None of us can ever directly experience the concept Wahhabism. While we can grab and hold onto our mothers like Tim does, we cannot do the same for observer-dependent phenomena. We do however, as Hofstadter and Sander describe, make sense of both things in our minds in the same way. What is important are the messages our brains are receiving that are helping us to make sense of a phenomenon. When it comes to Wahhabism many of those messages we are receiving are coming from intellectuals writing about it in places like magazines, the blogosphere, and newspapers. As I described earlier, and to again borrow ideas from authors like Gilles Deleuze and Thomas Osborne, we can understand these intellectuals as mediators of ideas in today's knowledge society.[34] These intellectuals are also using particular rhetorical techniques with the aim of influencing our understanding. This includes using analogies, which, as Hofstadter and Sander point out, play crucial roles in how we make sense of concepts.

Again, it is important to understand that intellectuals have a vast array of rhetorical techniques at their disposal. When it comes to using analogous language, they can use exemplification, comparison, and allegory in attempts to influence our understanding of a phenomenon like Wahhabism. We can understand analogous language as a complex whole comprised of many different elements. Given the scope of this study, analyzing the entire whole is a daunting and unmanageable task and again, this is where the abstraction process is useful as we are able to focus on particular elements. In this study I have chosen to focus on metaphors, analogies, similes, and neologisms.

A metaphor describes a subject by claiming it is the same as another unrelated object. The important role they play in our cognition is emphasized by scholars like George Lakoff and Mark Johnson.[35] They describe how metaphors encourage us to understand one conceptual domain, which they call the 'target domain,' in terms of a dissimilar conceptual domain, which they call the 'source domain.' This activates a system of entailments understood as correspondences between selected elements of the two domains in metaphoric relation. The corresponding elements can be either entities or attributes that are common to the structure of both concepts and to the relational structure. We then use language to express these entailments.

Here it is important to distinguish between the terms 'metaphor' and 'metaphorical expression' given I use the two terms in the coming chapters when deconstructing representations of Wahhabism. Lakoff encourages us to use the term 'metaphor' to describe the cross-domain mapping that happens in the conceptual system, while 'metaphorical expression' is used to describe the surface realization in the form of linguistic expression of this cross-domain mapping.[36] As we will see, liberal and neoconservative intellectuals draw on metaphors and use metaphorical expressions in their writing.

In her book *The Myths We Live By*, Mary Midgley points out that metaphors play important roles in what she calls the 'mythmaking process.'[37] While the term is often understood as 'a widely held false belief or idea,' Midgley defines 'myths' as "imaginative patterns, networks of powerful symbols that suggest particular ways of interpreting the world."[38] Myths help to both constitute our world and shape its meaning, and they play formative roles in the liberal and neoconservative traditions. Myths provide these traditions with the imaginative patterns they need to make sense of and impose order and meaning on the world. We can understand 'myth' as an umbrella term that includes things like themata.

Similes are the second kind of analogous language I abstract from intellectuals' representations of Wahhabism for closer analysis. While metaphor asserts the identity of unlike things, simile asserts the similarity of things.[39] The standard view holds that simile is a figure of speech typically understood as an explicit comparison between things using the terms 'like' or 'as.'[40] In contrast, a metaphor makes implicit comparisons between things. The parallelism of simile means it is commonly understood as a paradigm of allegory.[41] Allegory here is understood as an extended metaphor. Like metaphor, allegory has its origins in myths and it continues to play an integral role in mythmaking today.[42]

Metaphors and similes use different sentence patterns. As Shibata et al. explain, "a metaphor is a figurative statement expressed by means of a copula sentence (An X is a Y) whereas a simile is a figurative statement using a hedge word such as 'like' or 'as' (An X is like a Y)."[43] However, the traditional view holds that they express almost the same figurative meaning and that a metaphor can be paraphrased as a simile.[44] It was

Aristotle who wrote, “the simile is also a metaphor, the difference is but slight.”[45] This approach understands metaphors as abbreviated similes; for example, the claim made by some neoconservatives that ‘the Wahhabi is a savage’ is treated as an abbreviation of ‘the Wahhabi is like a savage.’

Recent psycholinguistic studies have however shown that similes and metaphors are much more different than what we have traditionally thought. It has been pointed out that both promote different comprehension processes in the human brain, suggesting that metaphors are not in fact abbreviated similes.[46] Glucksberg and Keysar are proponents of this view, which has been called the class-inclusion model, maintaining that simile is best understood as a process of comparison using explicit marks and metaphor is best understood as a categorization process.[47] Shibata et al. write:

> In the sentence “My lawyer is like a shark”, “shark” refers to the marine creature, whereas in the sentence “My lawyer is a shark”, “shark” does not refer to the literal creature. In the latter case, the lawyer is categorized as a predator, and the shark is used to represent predators. Thus, the class-inclusion model argues that the comprehension processes used in understanding metaphor and simile differ.[48]

Further differences in how our brains make sense of metaphors and similes are also highlighted in studies conducted by Dan L. Chiappe and his colleagues.[49] It is now widely accepted that the two play distinct roles in the rhetorical, mythmaking, and cognitive processes. The implication for this study is that I should and am justified in adopting a more nuanced approach that treats the two as different elements, and which recognizes the important role both play in influencing how our brains make sense of all the information we are continually bombarded with.

While similes and metaphors are both different kinds of analogous language I focus on, I have also chosen to look at what is more broadly and commonly understood as analogy. Analogy is understood here as a comparison between two objects or systems of objects that highlight ways in which they are thought to be similar.[50] We can understand an analogous argument as a logical argument where the user demonstrates how things are alike by pointing out shared characteristics, with the aim of showing that if things are alike in some ways, then they can be alike in other ways as well.

Neologisms are the fourth element in the intellectuals' representations of Wahhabism I abstract for closer analysis. In *Fifty Years Among the New Words*, John Algeo writes:

> A community is known by the language it keeps, and its words chronicle the times. Every aspect of the life of a people is reflected in the words they use to talk about themselves and the world around them. As their world changes—through invention, discovery, revolution, evolution or personal transformation—so does their language. Like the growth rings of a tree, our vocabulary bears witness to our past.[51]

Algeo makes the point that vocabulary is a major indicator when tracking changes in culture and language and that new words or neologisms are useful tools for understanding how culture evolves. He comments on the great shifts in how we live and talk about the world. We are always introducing new words into our lexicon to describe new concepts, and at the same time old words are continually falling out of use as we assign them less cultural significance.

'Neologism' is the name we give these newly coined words, terms, or phrases that are not yet prevalent in mainstream language. The word comes from the Greek *neo-* meaning 'new' and *logos* meaning 'speech or utterance.' Authors like David Crystal, John Ayto, John Algeo, and Adele Algeo have all offered similar descriptions regarding the formation of neologisms.[52] These descriptions include the creating, borrowing, combining, shortening, blending, and shifting of words. We can see some of these processes at work when we look at neologisms like 'Islamofascism,' which is the combining of the words 'Islam' and 'fascism,' and the adding of an 'o.'

Neologisms like 'Islamofascism' encourage a new interpretation or understanding of something and are often attributable to a particular person, period, or event. This term, which I will later describe in greater detail when analyzing neoconservative intellectuals' representations of

Wahhabism, is understood to have first been used in 1990 by Scottish writer Malise Ruthven when writing for the *Independent* newspaper.[53] He used it to describe the ways in which traditional Arab dictatorships used religious appeals in order to stay in positions of power. Since then prominent intellectuals like Christopher Hitchens have used it when describing "fascism with an Islamic face."[54] As we will see, neoconservative intellectuals like Frank Gaffney have recently used it when describing Wahhabism, with the aim of likening it to twentieth-century European fascist movements.[55]

It should be acknowledged that different fields of study treat neologisms in different ways. What is particularly interesting is how the field of psychiatry, for example, has traditionally understood neologisms. *The American Heritage Medical Dictionary* states that neologisms are traditionally understood as newly coined words whose meaning may be known only to the patient using it. Because of this, neologisms have often been viewed as a symptom of psychosis.[56] This is interesting as we start to consider that the use of neologisms when representing Wahhabism is a practice most common to neoconservative intellectuals. Remembering it was the neoconservatives, especially those holding influential positions in the George W. Bush administration, who were mainly responsible for both constructing the largely phantasmagoric threat posed by Saddam Hussein and initiating and supporting the global war on terror. There are some who would see these acts as related to psychopathic or psychotic disorders. This assessment is given further weight by those who consider the religious and political beliefs held by many in the neoconservative movement to be delusional.

The final element I focus on when deconstructing representations of Wahhabism provided by neoconservative and liberal intellectuals is what Karen Cerulo has called the cognitive structuring of violent accounts. Cerulo's book, *Deciphering Violence: The Cognitive Structure of Right and Wrong*, is a detailed study focusing on the different ways authors, reporters, and artists depict violent acts and how audiences respond to these violent representations.[57] Authors can use a variety of techniques, including assigning the violent perpetrator certain characteristics like having a clear intention to commit violence, having instrumental aims, and belonging to a minority group. They can represent the violent act in particular ways, for example, physical rather than nonphysical violence, and they can represent the victim in particular ways, for example, as belonging to a dominant group in society and emphasizing their (female) gender. These characteristics are shown to elicit specific emotional responses in the audience, who then classifies the violent act in one of three ways: as normal, deviant, or ambiguous. This encourages readers to either see the violent acts as justified, warranted, and legitimate or unjustified, unwarranted, and illegitimate. For example, violence perpetrated 'in the spirit of the community,' meaning to protect or benefit others in the community, is likely to be viewed by the audience as normal, warranted, and justified. Religiously inspired violence committed by someone with an out-group status is likely to be viewed as deviant and unwarranted.

My abstracting of these elements from neoconservative and liberal intellectuals' representations of Wahhabism for closer analysis constitutes what Ollman would describe as my moment of inquiry. This analysis is also taking place from within a critical discourse analysis research paradigm that carries with it its own epistemological assumptions. It matters that we have an understanding of these.

Critical Discourse Analysis: Language Is Made in and Makes the World

Like those whose works I analyze in this book, I necessarily make and rely on epistemological assumptions when making sense of the social world. I am also cognizant of the fact that in order for my research to be both coherent and sound, there must be an alignment between my assumptions about the theory of knowledge and my dialectical imagination. It is because of these reasons that I have chosen to draw on the critical discourse analysis research paradigm. This kind of discursive approach goes beyond treating language as a mere mirror of a phenomenon existing in the social world. It treats discourse as playing a major role in the constructing of ideas, social processes, and phenomena constituting the social world.[58] As James Paul Gee explains, this kind of approach recognizes that "we fit our language to a situation or context that our language, in turn, helped to create in the first place."[59] Put another way, critical discourse analysis treats discourse as socially produced *and* socially constitutive.

As Gee's description suggests, this kind of approach perfectly aligns with a dialectical imagination. This is because a critical discourse analysis paradigm appreciates the dialectical nature of language and because it treats language as a social practice. That is to say, it appreciates that language is both made in and makes the world. Prominent discursive theorist Norman Fairclough also make this point, insisting that critical discourse analysis understands discourse as having a dialectical relationship with social identities, social relationships, and systems of knowledge and belief.[60]

A critical discourse analysis also provides the analytical framework necessary for exploring the relations between discursive practices, which in this case are text, events, and social and cultural processes. This approach allows for the appreciating of the role relations of power and struggles play in constructing text, meaning it helps us understand why different groups of intellectuals are assigning a different set of characteristics to the phenomenon of Wahhabism and why they are using this term in different ways. Critical discourse analysis appreciates the opaque nature of the relations between discourse and society, recognizing these play integral roles in securing positions of influence and achieving hegemony. In describing these relations as opaque, I like Norman Fairclough am suggesting the links between discourse, ideology, and power are often unclear and that our social practices that are bound to these relations are not always apparent.[61]

Like Fairclough I understand 'ideology' to mean those "representations of aspects of the world which contribute to establishing and maintaining relations of power, domination, and exploitation."[62] In this sense we can understand intellectuals' representations of Wahhabism as sites of struggle between movement intellectuals belonging to different intellectual traditions, each of whom are trying to create and recreate the social world in ways that often align and reflect their own interests. Representations of Wahhabism can therefore be understood as a microcosm of a much bigger struggle between intellectuals with competing ideologies.

My interest in how text is used by groups of people to promote particular ideological interests builds on a long tradition of scholarship that includes theorists like Edward Said, Marianne Jørgensen, Louise Phillips,

Ruth Wodak, and Michael Meyer. Said, for example, argues that discursive narratives help create structures of feeling that support, elaborate, and consolidate imperialistic interests. At the same time, he recognizes that discursive narratives can also be used to challenge, resist, and provide alternate structures of feeling.[63] Marianne Jørgensen and Louise Phillips also highlight the ability of critical discourse analysis to be used in the "struggle for radical social change."[64] Wodak agrees:

> For CDA, language is not powerful on its own—it gains power by the use powerful people make of it. This explains why CDA often chooses the perspective of those who suffer, and critically analyzes the language use of those in power, who are responsible for the existence of inequalities and who also have the means and the opportunity to improve conditions. In agreement with its Critical Theory predecessors, CDA emphasizes the need for interdisciplinary work in order to gain a proper understanding of how language functions in constituting and transmitting knowledge, in organizing social institutions or in exercising power.[65]

An important point made by Wodak and Meyer is that we often fail to question or challenge the ideas endorsed by proponents of dominant ideologies.[66] Rather than critiquing and challenging the representations of the social world these intellectuals provide, we often take them to be common sense. I am hoping that this book will at the very minimum help the reader to realize that books and scholarly newspaper and magazine articles about Wahhabism are anything but 'common sense.' In many instances they are carefully constructed portraits designed to achieve very specific political and/or religious aims and goals. A critical discourse analysis emphasizes the importance of not taking ideas at face value, rather it advocates for a thorough critique and challenging of these dominant ideas which have the ability to influence public opinion, policy, and the decision-making processes.

There is no one style of critical discourse analysis approach that is applicable to all kinds of research. Rather it is best understood as a style of critical reading allowing for the use of many different kinds of techniques and approaches. Norman Fairclough maintains that different kinds of approaches are acceptable as long as they satisfy three basic criteria.[67] First, there must be some kind of analysis of language. Second, the researcher must explore the relation between the different ways in which language is used and the author's belief system. Third, the researcher must consider the relation between the author's belief system and reality. My research questions have been purposely designed with these conditions in mind. I will now begin the deconstruction process, first focusing on the major ways in which liberal intellectuals have gone about representing Wahhabism.

4
Spreading the Rule of Reason: Liberal Imaginings of Wahhabism

> . . . total liberty for wolves is death to the lambs . . .
>
> —Isaiah Berlin, *The Pursuit of the Ideal*

Intellectuals writing about Wahhabism in newspapers, magazines, and online are exposing their readers to a particular kind of interpretation or representation. As Bacchi's work illustrates, these intellectuals are representing a problem or a social phenomenon in a particular way.[1] Intellectuals deliberately choose to emphasize, de-emphasize, and completely ignore particular elements. Many of us reading these representations are like novices gazing at paintings by famous French Impressionists—we see the overall picture and the dominant colors but we tend to miss the finer strokes of color. I am certainly not suggesting that an intellectual's representation of Wahhabism is a masterpiece constructed with the same brilliance. What I am saying is that these representations are constructions whose finer elements may not be apparent on first appearances. Just like many of us who rely on the *critique d'art* when visiting art galleries to explain the finer details and complex elements to us, my abstraction and closer analysis of the subtle and complex elements comprising intellectuals' representations of Wahhabism can be of great value to the untrained eye.

In this chapter I take a closer look at some of the dominant representations provided by prominent liberal intellectuals appearing in popular

US-based publications like the *New York Times*, *Wall Street Journal*, *Washington Post*, and *Washington Times*, which are informing current debates particularly in the West about Wahhabism. The first step in our journey is looking at a representation of Wahhabism provided by liberal intellectual, Pulitzer Prize winner, and op-ed columnist for the *New York Times* Maureen Dowd in her article "Loosey Goosey Saudi." Providing a critique of modern Saudi Arabia, in which she understands Wahhabism as the official religion, Dowd expresses concern about the general lack of freedoms in Saudi society: she is concerned by the lack of cultural freedom afforded by the state and the lack of freedom for Saudi women who are forced to live according to Wahhabi religious doctrine. She writes:

> The word progressive, of course, is highly relative when it comes to Saudi Arabia. (Wahhabism, anyone?) But after spending 10 days here, I can confirm that, at their own *galactically glacial pace*, they are *chipping away* at *gender apartheid* and cultural repression.[2] [emphasis added]

I have emphasized the key rhetorical techniques Dowd relies on and indeed which many other liberals rely on when attempting to persuade her readers about the restrictive, oppressive, and discriminatory nature of Wahhabism as practiced in Saudi Arabia. They are the use of neologisms and metaphors.

Dowd uses 'gender apartheid' when referring to a particular political system that relies on different kinds of practices, such as physical and legal practices aimed at relegating women to subordinate positions (relative to men) in society. In addition to first-hand experiences she gathered during her short trip to the kingdom, it is possible that Dowd has been influenced by Western human rights organizations like Amnesty International reporting on the current situation in Saudi Arabia.[3] Dowd has chosen to use the neologism 'gender apartheid' because of its ability to influence readers. It is a much more powerful phrase than 'gender discrimination' or 'sexism.'

Writers use neologisms to encourage readers to view particular situations or events in certain ways. This neologism derives much of its power to influence from its likening of the situation of Saudi women living according to Wahhabism to racial apartheid historically practiced in South Africa. The term 'apartheid' is synonymous with this period of time in South African history, which instituted a system of white supremacy subordinating the nation's majority black population. The implication in Dowd's representation is that gender equality in modern Wahhabi Saudi Arabia is as horrible and worthy of the same widespread condemnation as the institutionalized racism that occurred in South Africa throughout the mid- to late twentieth century.

Dowd's use of metaphorical expressions is the second pertinent rhetorical technique worth deconstructing. Dowd uses the metaphorical expressions "galactically glacial pace" and "chipping away" when representing the progress currently taking place in Saudi Arabia. Both can be understood as Progress is Movement metaphors that are used to represent the slow, incremental, and what she perceives as positive changes taking place in Saudi society. This metaphor considers forward movement to be indicative of social progress and treats backward movement as indicative of societal regression. The metaphorical expression "galactically glacial pace" draws on the extreme slowness with which a glacier moves, while "chipping away" is often used when describing a process where smaller parts are gradually removed from a bigger and usually solid whole, such as a woodchipper using his axe to chip away at a tree trunk. In both instances Dowd represents this slow and incremental change as a positive thing for Saudi society. Dowd is making the point for her audience that Wahhabism is a force that must and will be slowly overcome and that there are positive signs that things are progressing in the right direction. This metaphor also has strong nature elements, which along with the Progress is Movement metaphor I will explore in greater detail later, given its centrality in liberal thinking.

Dowd is making an important point pertinent to the ways in which many liberal intellectuals represent Wahhabism, namely that Wahhabism, which is understood to be the official doctrine of Saudi Arabia, violates the freedoms of its people. While we can understand Dowd as belonging to the liberal tradition, she is also an individual influenced by her own life experiences, interests, and prejudices. Here she chooses to focus on two particular kinds of freedoms important to her: those associated with women and culture. Liberals are united in their belief that Wahhabism violates freedoms. However, they differ with regards to the particular freedoms they value and choose to focus on. This is understandable given the crucial role prejudice plays in influencing the individual sense-making process, which is related to, as Heidegger understands it, 'the time and place into which we are thrown.' Dowd clearly values cultural and women's freedom. However, there are other liberals who have tended to represent Wahhabism as restricting other specific kinds of freedoms.

At this point the reader may well ask, how do I know that Dowd is a liberal and what does it mean to say that someone is a liberal? As I want to indicate, initially there are no easy answers to these questions.

Understanding Liberalism: Many Freedoms?

Jeffrey Lustig famously wrote, "There are many rooms in the liberal mansion."[4] This is an apt metaphor when describing the many themes and approaches constituting the liberal tradition. Liberalism is an umbrella term we use to describe a range of approaches and because it is a fuzzy category it has no clearly definable boundaries. Nonetheless, it is generally acknowledged that it does have a number of core beliefs exerting great influence over the ways in which its intellectuals make sense of the social world. These include a preoccupation with the idea of liberty, which we can trace back to twentieth-century liberal theorist Isaiah Berlin.

Berlin was very interested in our values and how we get along with others holding contrasting values. In his seminal essay *Two Concepts of Liberty*, he argues that we as individuals can hold many values we consider genuine; however, many of these may be incompatible with each other, thereby producing an internal conflict. This conflict can also be external between different groups of people.[5] For Berlin, this conflict is a great tragedy of the human condition that is irremovable: "These collisions of values," writes Berlin, "are of the essence of what they are and what we are."[6] According to Berlin, a world where these conflicts are easily resolved is not one we will ever know or understand. These ideas form a key part of a doctrine we call value pluralism.

Berlin is a prominent figure in the liberal tradition and his ideas provide us with valuable insight into the themes influencing many modern liberal intellectuals writing about Wahhabism. That said, it is also important to point out that the political liberal tradition I am referring to is a particular kind that is at odds with more idealist and rationalist kinds of liberalism. A salient point Berlin is making is that the idea of the perfect whole or an ultimate solution is practically unattainable and conceptually incoherent, which is a position some who promote a more idealist and rationalist kind of liberalism would have trouble accepting. In *The Pursuit of the Ideal* Berlin writes:

> The notion of the perfect whole, the ultimate solution, in which all good things coexist, seems to me to be not merely unattainable—that is a truism—but conceptually incoherent; I do not know what is meant by a harmony of this kind. Some among the Great Goods cannot live together. That is a conceptual truth. We are doomed to choose, and every choice may entail an irreparable loss.[7]

Overcoming these internal and external conflicts between values demands a transformation tantamount to an abandoning of those same values. For Berlin this is not something that will ever happen in this world.

If we are to accept Berlin's proposition like many liberal intellectuals do, our inability to reconcile our internal conflict and the external conflict between holders of different values leaves us with important questions like, which values do we give priority for the purposes of creating a functional society? Unable to completely abandon our own values that we hold so dear, Berlin emphasizes the inescapable need of choosing between different kinds of values. Berlin's value pluralism doctrine holds that in most cases there are no clear right and wrong answers when making this decision.[8] This is why he and many liberal intellectuals inspired by his ideas emphasize the importance of liberty, because this conflict between values implies that different ways of living are unavoidable. It is essential that individuals have the *freedom* to make their own decisions *within reason* about whom they will be and what they choose to do with their limited time on this earth.

The freedom to choose is a core part of the political liberal tradition and plays a major role in influencing how many liberal intellectuals make sense of and represent Wahhabism. This focusing on freedom is certainly a commendable idea that would garner support from many outside of the liberal tradition. Ask the everyday American, Englishman, or Australian, especially the immigrants who have fled war and persecution and found new homes in the West, what they value most, and many would say freedom. However, the fundamental problem in the political liberal tradition that is unavoidable, and which one can only assume modern liberal intellectuals are either ignorant of or deliberately choose to ignore so as to remain content in their delusion, is the paradoxical belief that freedom of choice *must* take place within a specific kind of state.

Liberals believe the modern secular liberal democratic state provides the best framework in which to choose values. However, if we are to truly enjoy and exercise our *a priori* liberty/our freedom to choose, then surely we should be able to choose what kind of state we want to live in? This seemingly obvious internal contradiction that says 'we will choose the kind of state in which we all will live and you can within reason choose how you want to live' has not deterred liberal intellectuals from ardently promoting this ideological belief system.

This internal contradiction has wider implications. Many liberals are left struggling with a variety of other issues pertinent to the governing of any modern secular liberal democratic state. One of the major issues that is relevant to how many modern liberal intellectuals represent Wahhabism in a time of widespread concern about the threat of radical Islam is when totalitarian or fascist movements, groups, or parties use the freedoms of the modern liberal democratic state to impose nondemocratic systems of government. A recent example of this occurred during the Arab Spring with the election of the Muslim Brotherhood in Egypt.

Prior to their rule, Egypt had what is best described as a liberal democratic system of government that afforded its people the right to elect their political representatives. In 2012 the majority of Egyptians elected Muhammad Morsi's Brotherhood in spite of or possibly because of its long and demonstrated commitment to Islamist ideals. In conjunction with other ultraconservative Islamist parties like the Salafist Nour Party, Morsi's government then began implementing nondemocratic reforms.

Changes to the constitution soon followed that gave Morsi far-reaching powers aimed at strengthening and maintaining the government's positions of power.[9] This Islamist political party, with the support of their political allies, who valued a particular interpretation of Islam over key liberal democratic ideals, was able to use the political liberal state against itself.

Another major problem worth mentioning with liberalism is the relation between modern liberal democratic regimes and imperialism. John Gray points out that modern liberal regimes like the United States have invaded sovereign nations under the banner of spreading democracy and freedom.[10] The United States and its coalition of allies maintain that their interventions were aimed at replacing oppressive regimes in sovereign nations like Afghanistan and Iraq with democratic regimes entrusted with the responsibility of safeguarding the liberty of their peoples. The reality is that we now have situations in Iraq and Afghanistan that are arguably worse than before Western intervention. Gray claims the destruction in Iraq has signaled the death of the global liberal project, and as forces belonging to the Islamic State of Iraq and the Levant (ISIS) continue to wreak havoc, it is becoming increasingly difficult to argue that the alleged spreading of freedom and democracy in the region has been a positive experience for the millions of people killed during and since their 'liberation.' Despite liberalism's internal contradictions and the recent experiences in nations like Egypt, Iraq, and Afghanistan, many liberal intellectuals continue to hold an unequivocal faith in their tradition.

I now want to turn my attention to developing an ideal type as a prelude to examining a selection of these intellectuals whose liberal *Weltanschauung* has influenced the way they have made sense of and represented Wahhabism. I make use of the abstraction process that is the Weberian ideal type when constructing my liberalism fuzzy category.

Understanding Liberalism: Toward an Ideal Type

My ideal type consists of four key elements. The first is the assumption that all people are entitled to freedom and liberty. Second, and closely related to the concept of freedom, is the belief in individualism. Third is a belief in secularism as a way of ordering society. Fourth is the liberal belief in progress. It matters that we have a basic understanding of each of these concepts given the major role they play in my deconstruction of liberal intellectual representations of Wahhabism.

Maurice Cranston rightly points out, "by definition a liberal is a man who believes in liberty."[11] That all people are entitled to freedom and liberty and the closely related belief in individualism are core to the liberal *Weltanschauung*. Modern liberals influenced by this idea are drawing on a long and rich tradition of liberal scholarship we can trace back to Isaiah Berlin, John Locke, and John Stuart Mill. Locke writes that humans naturally exist in "a State of perfect Freedom to order their Actions . . . as they think fit . . . without asking leave, or depending on the Will of any other Man."[12] Mill also emphasizes an individual's right to enjoy their freedom, claiming that "the burden of proof is supposed to be with those who are against liberty; who contend for any restriction or prohibition. . . . The *a priori* assumption is in favor of freedom."[13] Locke and Mill are referring to what we commonly call the fundamental liberal principle.

This principle holds liberty to be essential to humankind and assigns the responsibility of justifying the limiting of an individual's freedom to those doing the limiting.[14] For example, those wanting political authority and to legislate laws must offer *reasonable justifications* given their ability to limit the liberty of citizens. This is of tantamount importance when coercive measures have the effect of limiting freedoms.[15] What constitutes *reasonable justification* is highly contentious. This is perhaps best illustrated in the introduction of new counterterror legislation in Western liberal democracies like the United States, the United Kingdom, and Australia that have eroded many of the freedoms those suspected of conspiring or committing acts of terror were previously entitled to.

Closely related to the fundamental liberal principle is the belief in individualism. Mill understood individualism as the key idea underpinning and endorsing freedom.[16] Individualism is the idea that the interests of the individual must take precedence over the interests of the state or any other kind of social group. According to this view, the state or any kind of institution in society, for example, religious bodies like the Wahhabi ulama in Saudi Arabia, should not interfere with the interests of the individual. Locke makes this point when he argues that the rights of the individual exist prepolitically and are therefore beyond the discretion of the state.[17]

This classic liberal view advocated by authors like Locke, which helps inform my thinking about what constitutes a liberal intellectual, views these rights in a more formal or legal way. Rights are understood as negative, in the sense that the state should not interfere or impinge on those rights. This classical view also considers those rights as subject to the no harm principle, which Mill describes as the right for individuals to act however they choose, as long as they are not harming other individuals.[18] An individual's liberty can only be rightfully interfered with when their actions are harming others. Mill distinguishes between 'harm,' which he understands to be physical, and 'offense,' which he understands as actions that may offend the moral sensibilities of others.

Another pertinent aspect of this approach is the relation between the liberal theory of individualism and liberal ideas about our development as human beings. Again, we can refer to the work of Mill for a classical liberal understanding of this relation. Mill writes:

> Individuality is the same thing with development, and . . . it is only the cultivation of individuality which produces, or can produce, well-developed human beings . . . what more can be said of any condition of human affairs, than that it brings human beings themselves nearer to the best thing they can be? or what worse can be said of any obstruction to good, than that it prevents this?[19]

Mill clearly understands individualism as crucial to our development as human beings. Gaus and Courtland point out that this is not just a political theory but also a moral theory about what constitutes 'good.' According to this view we should be committed to promoting development and striving for perfection, and this can only be achieved by a government that secures liberty for its people.[20] The kind of government that is needed is a modern secular liberal democratic regime.

A belief in a secular state forms the third key element of my ideal type for liberal intellectuals. A conventional interpretation of liberal political theory holds that the liberal state must not espouse any specific kind of religion. Rather than aligning itself with any religious belief, the liberal secular state should be committed to tolerating all religions. Paul Starr writes that "the logic of liberalism" is "exemplified" by religious toleration, and should help in the cultivating of many points of view whilst also averting "internecine . . . conflicts."[21] These multitudes of views should not be religious in nature. While I have spoken about this belief, I would like to draw on the contemporary writings of US public intellectual and scholar Stanley Fish to help elucidate the key role secularism plays in the modern liberal intellectual tradition.

Religious views, often the most volatile and divisive of issues, must be kept out of political debate. They are best suited to the private realm. The exception to this rule are those religions that respect the private–public distinction upon which liberalism relies and enforces. Fish describes this process:

> The liberal order does not extinguish religions; it just eviscerates them, unless they are the religions that display the same respect for the public-private distinction that liberalism depends on and enforces. A religion that accepts the partitioning of the secular and the sacred and puts at its center the private transaction between the individual and his God fits the liberal bill perfectly.[22]

Religions that fail to realize this public–private distinction and instead encroach on public life are understood by liberals as extremist, fascist, and authoritarian, or as Fish puts it, "enemies of the public good."[23] While harsh, this judgment is necessary. Liberalism is to be true to itself as long as it opposes any measures or actions that seek to curtail the individualism and liberty of its people.

A belief in secularism has played a major role since the inception of the liberal intellectual tradition and can be traced back to the works of seventeenth-century writer John Milton. In the twentieth century, John Rawls did more than most in helping highlight its key role. Fish draws our attention to the fact that it was Milton who wrote the state should tolerate all religions so long as they do not encroach upon the individual's right to free expression.[24] Later Rawls sought to construct a notion of the political that legitimated reasonable religious doctrines. The major issue is what constitutes 'reasonable,' and modern liberal intellectuals continue to debate this point. The liberal values of pluralism and moderation help provide rough boundaries about what is and what is not considered reasonable within the tradition. Ultimately reasonableness is a subjective notion influenced by individual prejudices. Liberalism like all other categories is fuzzy, meaning it has no clearly definable boundaries but rather what Lotfi Zadeh calls "grades of membership."[25]

The idea of progress is the fourth element making up my ideal type. Liberal proponents of this idea maintain that the human condition is constantly improving.[26] Doctrines of progress in general first appeared in Europe in the eighteenth century. They flourished throughout the continent in the nineteenth century before slightly retreating in the twentieth century in response to the many horrific events like the two world wars, the Holocaust, and the use of nuclear weapons.[27] Ideas influencing modern liberal thinkers making sense of Wahhabism can be traced back to key Enlightenment thinkers like Anne-Robert-Jacques Turgot, the Marquis de Condorcet, and Immanuel Kant and more recently to thinkers like John Rawls and John Stuart Mill.[28]

Modern liberals typically see the modern secular democratic state as the ideal society. Rawls wrote that this kind of society should be well-ordered and guarantee basic political and civil freedoms.[29] Rawls espouses the optimism typically held by modern liberals regarding our ability as humans to create such a society that, once attained, is capable of lasting "in perpetuity."[30] Rawl's ideas are useful when understanding the different steps humans must take and stages societies must pass through in order to create this kind of society. Pertinent here is Rawl's description of how this kind of state deals with religion. Rawls sees religion as having no place in the affairs of the liberal state; however, it does have a place in a liberal society and people must eventually learn to respect and value freedom of religion. This learning process is considered to be progress.

Rawls sees Europe's transition through the early modern period as the quintessential example of this progress. He specifically refers to the conflict between Catholics and Protestants during the sixteenth century: "In this case the acceptance of the principle of toleration would indeed be a mere modus vivendi."[31] This conflict taught Europeans the valuable lesson that freedom of religion is in their self-interest. I have made a point of including Rawls's reference to this situation between Catholics and Protestants because some liberal intellectuals draw the same comparisons when making sense of Wahhabism in the modern Islamic world.

Progress for the modern liberal intellectual also typically involves creating, establishing, and maintaining free institutions. I have already pointed out the major roles that ideas about freedom and individualism play in liberal political theory. Further to this, liberals tend to consider establishing institutions free from political interference as a key part of an ideal society. These institutions serve many important functions in a liberal state, including helping to ensure that no policies, measures, or other forces are impinging upon the liberties of the citizenry and ensuring that an environment is created in which people can work at bettering themselves. This idea of humans working and living in this kind of environment that is conducive to progress is related to liberal ideas about individualism. According to these beliefs the individual's commitment to personal development is an important part of society's overall progression. A standard reading of liberal political theory holds that it is individuals that make society.

Key Enlightenment thinkers like Turgot and the Marquis de Condorcet are among those to emphasize the importance of free institutions to our development as human beings. Making sense of Enlightenment views on progress, which have influenced many in the modern liberal political tradition, Lange points out that both Turgot and Condorcet agreed that scientific discoveries and political freedoms reinforce each other and together help further human wellbeing.[32] Focusing on the relation between science, political freedom, and progress, Turgot believes that free political institutions provide the necessary framework in which scientific genius can flourish, and that it is institutions and not the concentration of genius that are primarily responsible for scientific achievement and consequently human advancement.[33] The key point is that political institutions either help suppress or encourage these processes.

Condorcet claimed that spreading scientific knowledge would help create a more enlightened population free from the shackles of religion and that would ultimately demand greater freedoms.[34] Reiterating the point made by Rawls, this gradual moving away from religion is considered to be progress. Again, there is a specific reason why I have chosen to refer to these particular thinkers. Turgot's and Condorcet's focus on the relation between science, liberty, and progress helps highlight an important aspect of the liberal imagination in general and liberal ideas of progress in particular. Liberal intellectuals tend to see the implementing of their ideas as a scientific process. Also pertinent here are the ideas of Immanuel Kant.

Kant played a formative role in developing the liberal conception of progress. His essay "Idea for a Universal History with a Cosmopolitan Purpose," is based on the *a priori* assumption that all animals have natural faculties that can be developed. He makes the argument that human development in the social world is similar to the development of animals in the natural world. He championed a long-term commitment to the development of human faculties, which act as a yardstick for our overall progress as human beings.[35] Echoing the sentiments of Turgot, Condorcet, and Rawls, Kant maintained that humans need a very particular kind of society in order to fulfill our potential. Kant, in "Toward Perpetual Peace: A Philosophical Sketch," envisioned the ideal society as one in which the rule of law values and guarantees freedom and equality for all its citizens.[36] That is to say, a modern secular liberal democratic state is crucial to providing the framework necessary for our development as individuals.

These four interrelated ideas about progress, individualism, secularism, and freedom comprise my ideal type. Again, it should be reiterated that my ideal type is an abstraction designed with very specific purposes in mind. Liberalism is a large and complex fuzzy category. Providing an exhaustive list of what we understand to be liberal beliefs and then using this list to help guide my deconstruction of liberal intellectual representations of Wahhabism is an unmanageable task that is beyond the scope of this book. My ideal type is combined with a focus on five particular elements apparent in liberal representations of Wahhabism: the intellectuals' use of metaphors, neologisms, similes, analogies, and constructing of violent accounts; this makes my deconstruction process a much more manageable and interesting task. I shall now turn my attention to the deconstruction and analytical processes.

Wahhabism Restricts Freedoms

Individual freedom is key to the liberal imagination, and according to many liberal intellectuals a major problem with the observer-dependent phenomenon they are calling Wahhabism is that it violates the liberties that liberals believe people are *a priori* entitled to. Liberals have tended to represent Wahhabism, especially as implemented and practiced in modern Saudi Arabia, as fundamentally illiberal given the perceived role it plays in restricting thought and behavior. Like many of the other scholars whose works we have focused on, these intellectuals see Saudi Arabia as the home of Wahhabism.

Liberal intellectuals are in general agreement that Wahhabism restricts individual freedoms; however, they differ in their representations with regards to the specific freedoms they focus on. This is understandable given both the fuzzy nature of liberalism and the role prejudice plays in how each individual makes sense of the world. Maurice Cranston points out that a liberal believes in liberty. However, different individual prejudices that are related, as Heidegger puts it, to 'the time and place into which we are thrown,' mean liberals will often differ with regards to the particular kinds of liberties they value. Some, like Thomas Farr, who echoes popular arguments made by key liberal thinkers like Rawls, value religious freedom and have focused their representations on Wahhabism's restriction of this.[37]

Adopting the role of what Eyerman has termed a 'movement intellectual' for the political liberal tradition, Farr blames Wahhabism as practiced and enforced in Saudi Arabia for depriving its people of the ability to choose their own religion and indeed whether or not they even want to be religious. Like many of his liberal colleagues, Farr believes the state should not align itself with a particular religion and that people should be free to practice their own religion, so long as it does not interfere with running the state or harm others. Farr understands Wahhabism as currently practiced and enforced in Saudi Arabia as violating these key liberal principles. Farr even suggests that Wahhabism is responsible for stunting the personal growth of Saudi Arabians and for encouraging people to embrace a radical version of Islam that promotes the harming of others, or as he puts it, Wahhabism encourages "religious-based terrorism." Farr writes:

> The IRF Act [International Religious Freedom Act] was passed unanimously because millions are denied religious liberty . . . 70 percent of the world's population lives in countries where religious freedom is severely restricted. A few recent examples:
> A senior Saudi cleric issued a fatwa mandating the death of anyone arguing that men and women could work together professionally. Such edicts emerge from Wahhabism, a malevolent political theology that *nurtured* Osama bin Laden and continues to be exported worldwide. . . .
> These stories and thousands like them represent more than humanitarian tragedies. They signal a national security threat—and a diplomatic opportunity—for the United States. The absence of religious freedom is highly correlated with unstable democracy, low economic growth, low female literacy rates and religion-based terrorism. Religious liberty could help solve these problems.[38] [emphasis added]

Pertinent here is Farr's use of the metaphorical expression "nurtured" when describing the process of Wahhabism influencing Bin Laden's personal development. Nurture is commonly understood to be the act of caring for and protecting someone or something as they are growing up. A religious belief system like Wahhabism cannot literally be responsible for raising, caring, and protecting a person; in most instances, it is one's parents who are primarily responsible for this task until a certain age is reached. However, this is precisely what Farr is suggesting when using this metaphorical expression. He claims Wahhabism and not any other factors like those ascribed to the domain of nature—the nature versus nurture debate is a common narrative—is responsible for radicalizing Bin Laden and inspiring him to commit acts of terror.

The metaphorical expression "nurtured" is linked to what George Lakoff identifies as the nurturant parent model.[39] Lakoff claims this model is popular among leftists and liberals in the United States, providing them with a conceptual framework for how they make sense of the world. Lakoff writes:

> The principal goal of nurturance is for children to be fulfilled and happy in their lives and to become nurturant themselves. A fulfilling

> life is assumed to be, in significant part, a nurturant life, one committed to family and community responsibility. . . . [W]hat children need to learn most is empathy for others, the capacity for nurturance, cooperation, and the maintenance of social ties. . . . [W]hen children are respected, nurtured, and communicated with from birth, they gradually enter into a lifetime relationship of mutual respect, communication.[40]

Lakoff emphasizes the relation between those who understand morality in terms of nurturance and the use of the conceptual metaphor Community is Family.[41] These individuals tend to view the wider community as having responsibility to help others. When considering the nature versus nurture debate, Lakoff maintains that these individuals generally consider nurturance to be an environmentally determined factor leading them to look at other environmentally determined factors when making sense of the social and political world.[42]

Lakoff's seminal work on metaphors provides valuable insight when making sense of Farr's choice of the metaphorical expression "nurtured" when describing the influence Wahhabism had on Bin Laden. Farr assumes the Saudi community has a responsibility, particularly with regards to instilling important values, in helping raise its people like Bin Laden. According to Farr, this did not happen with Bin Laden and he looks to environmental factors like religious, political, and social forces in an attempt to help explain why Bin Laden became such a violent individual. Farr blames Wahhabism, suggesting it is the community's embrace of this "malevolent political theology" that has failed to encourage the values that liberals believe are necessary to produce good, responsible members of society. The implication is that if Bin Laden and the society in which he lived enjoyed religious freedoms, then it is possible he would not have committed "religious-based terrorism" and he would have avoided becoming another "humanitarian traged[y]." The important point Farr is making is that religious liberty is a fundamental right of humans and that without this liberty humans would likely fail to reach their potential and would therefore be more likely to commit tragic acts like Wahhabi-inspired terrorism.

Like Farr, Doug Bandow is a movement intellectual beholden to the big ideas of the grand liberal narrative. In his article "Befriending Saudi Princes: A High Price for a Dubious Alliance," first published by the libertarian think tank the Cato Institute and then republished by *USA Today*, Bandow accuses Riyadh for its local and global promotion of an "extreme Wahhabi form of Islam" hostile to modernity and the West.[43] Writing soon after the 9/11 attacks in the United States, Bandow adamantly opposes the US-Saudi alliance, which he believes is between a fundamentally liberal regime and an illiberal regime. He sees the United States as valuing secularism and democracy and guaranteeing individualism and religious freedoms, and the Wahhabi Saudi regime as violating the rights of its people. He writes:

> For American administrations that loudly promote democracy, the alliance with Saudi Arabia has been a deep embarrassment. As the Human Rights Watch reported in 2001, "Freedom of expression and association were nonexistent rights, political parties and independent local media were not permitted, and even peaceful anti-government activities remained virtually unthinkable. Infringements on privacy, institutionalized gender discrimination, harsh restrictions on the exercise of religious freedom, and the use of capital and corporal punishment were also major features of the kingdom's human rights record." . . .
>
> *Most ugly*, though, is the religious totalitarianism enforced by Riyadh. Citizens and foreigners alike are prohibited from engaging in non-Muslim worship as well as proselytizing.[44] [emphasis added]

Bandow's article touches on an important and long-lasting point of conjecture within the political liberal tradition. Liberals tend to agree that individualism, secularism, progress, and freedom are crucial values; however, they often hold differing beliefs about foreign policy. Bandow belongs to the school of thought that liberal regimes should not work closely with illiberal regimes like Saudi Arabia. Bandow's ideas resonate with John Rawls's argument that liberals must distinguish between decent and indecent states (i.e., outlaw states), which he sees as having no right in asking liberal regimes for tolerance and support.[45] For Rawls, a key part of being a decent person, and by extension belonging to a decent society, involves not tolerating those who ignore what liberals hold as fundamental human rights.[46] Bandow categorizes Saudi Arabia as one of these outlaw states in part because it imposes Wahhabism at home and accordingly he champions a liberalizing and modernizing project aimed at guaranteeing the freedom of its people. However, he does not see foreign interventionism as a way of achieving this.

In the excerpt above I have highlighted a pertinent rhetorical technique worth deconstructing. Bandow, in using the metaphorical expression "ugly" when describing the religious totalitarian Wahhabi doctrine implemented by the Saudi government, draws on the metaphor (Political) State as a Form of Attraction. As humans we are naturally drawn to and appreciate beautiful things as they arouse positive emotions in us. John Keats famously wrote, "A thing of beauty is a joy forever."[47] Visually displeasing or ugly things tend to arouse negative emotions in us and often leave us feeling disgusted and repulsed. In using this metaphor, Bandow is clearly suggesting that particular kinds of political states, specifically liberal democratic states, can be understood as beautiful, while illiberal regimes can be viewed as ugly. These states are ugly because they do not have the same qualities that make a liberal state beautiful: democratic freedoms, particularly religious freedom. Beautiful things are expressions of humankind's greatest talents and Immanuel Kant would argue that developing ourselves, which best occurs within a liberal state guaranteeing our individualism and freedom, would greatly increase our ability to create and produce beautiful things. Echoing Kant's sentiments, liberals like Bandow believe the modern liberal democratic state is one of humanity's greatest creations as it provides the framework necessary for an individual to realize their full potential. The implication is that oppressive regimes like Wahhabi Saudi Arabia are stunting the development of their peoples.

Believing in freedom is integral to the liberal imagination. However, each individual is influenced by their personal preferences and prejudices, meaning they may focus on the kinds of freedoms that are most important to them. The relation between Wahhabism and the lack of religious freedoms is of major importance to Bandow and Farr. Liberals like Maureen Dowd, Fareed Zakaria, and Azeem Ibrahim have chosen to represent a relation between Wahhabism and a lack of freedom for women. Earlier I described how Dowd used the neologism "gender apartheid" and the metaphorical expressions "galactically glacial pace" and "chipping away" when describing the situation for women forced to live according to Wahhabi religious doctrine in Saudi Arabia.[48] Zakaria and Ibrahim share these concerns; however, they use different rhetorical techniques when representing this situation to their readers.

Fareed Zakaria is one of the more prominent liberal intellectuals to have written about Wahhabism. Zakaria has hosted his own television show "Fareed Zakaria GPS" on CNN since 2008, has been editor of publications like *TIME* magazine, *Newsweek International*, and *Foreign Affairs* and was named by *Forbes* as one of the top twenty-five most influential liberals in American media. The *New York Times* reported that he and Thomas Friedman (whose representations of Wahhabism I also analyze) had been "sounded out" by US President Barack Obama about the situation in the Middle East: "He is searching for a way to pull back and weave a larger picture," Zakaria is quoted as saying when asked about his dealings with the president.[49]

In his article "The Saudi Trap" for *Newsweek*, Zakaria writes:

> Every noxious version of Wahhabism has had free rein in Saudi Arabia, and yet all liberal ideas and debates have always been closed down. . . . The tragedy is that Saudi Arabia has one of the largest groups of reform-minded liberals in the Middle East. It's an odd combination: the most conservative society and a vast swath of modernists. . . . [Saudi Arabia's students] want to see change. . . . They hope that Saudi Arabia will soon become a member of the World Trade Organization and that this will unleash even more economic reforms, . . . that educational reform will flourish, that women will be moved *out of the shadows* of everyday life. . . . Saudi Arabia will probably weather this storm and beat back the terrorists. . . . But without wrenching change, Saudi Arabia will not achieve the promise of genuine modernization that its liberals and reformers hope for.[50] [emphasis added]

Pertinent is Zakaria's use of the metaphorical expression "out of the shadows" when describing the situation for Saudi women forced to live according to "noxious" Wahhabism. A shadow is the point between lightness and darkness and the general understanding is that it owes more to the latter than the former. Zakaria is suggesting there are many men living their lives in full view/in lightness, while there are many women forced to live in places where they are largely unseen/in the shadows. This metaphorical expression can be interpreted in a number of ways.

For example, Western readers will often associate light with good entities like God and angels. Conversely, popular myths in the West typically associate evil entities like monsters and vampires as living in darkness. According to this interpretation, Wahhabism legitimizes Saudi men's treatment of women as evil entities. The implication is the liberalization or modernization of Saudi Arabian society would create the necessary conditions that would allow Saudi women to emerge from the shadows and be treated like human beings.

Ibrahim also represents Wahhabism as practiced and enforced in Saudi Arabia as responsible for denying women their freedoms.[51] Ibrahim is an academic by trade who has served as a national security and defense policy advisor to the then leader of the British Labour Party, Ed Miliband, and as a strategic policy advisor to the former chairman of Pakistan's PTI Party, Imran Kahn. The European Social Think Tank named him as a Top 100 Global Thinker in 2010. Like Thomas Farr, Ibrahim believes that denying freedoms is partly responsible for inspiring Islamic radicalism. However, while Farr links the lack of religious freedom to religious-based terrorism, Ibrahim draws a longer bow by also associating denying women their freedoms with Islamic radicalism. Ibrahim writes:

> The U.S. has always been aware of Saudi Arabia's role in funding and spreading Wahhabism—an extremist ideology which provides the ideological foundation for groups like Al Qaeda. . . . [T]he conservative cult of Wahhabism advocates anti-Semitism, *misogyny* and inter-action with non-Muslims only in cases of necessity. It therefore provides the ideological justification for animosity and hatred of wider society, thus

> providing the perfect foundation for radical preachers to then advocate violence as a *religious duty*.[52] [emphasis added]

Here I want to abstract two elements for closer analysis. The first concerns Ibrahim's use of the term "misogyny" and its relation to Wahhabism and radicalism. This is what Karen Cerulo describes as the assigning of gender characteristics to the victim. Emphasizing the victim's female gender is likely to result in the reader understanding and categorizing the violent act as deviant, illegitimate, and unjustifiable. In contrast, focusing on the male gender of the victim is more likely to result in the reader understanding the violent act to be normal.[53] Ibrahim's choice to use the term "misogyny" clearly identifies females rather than males as the subject of concern. The term comes from the Greek term *misogynes* meaning 'woman-hater' and is today typically used when referring to the 'dislike of, contempt for, or ingrained prejudice against women.' Ibrahim's key point is that Wahhabism promotes discrimination against women and that this is in part responsible for promoting radicalism.

Also pertinent is Ibrahim's use of the phrase "religious duty," involving what Cerulo calls the assigning of instrumental aims to the perpetrators of violence, which in this instance are the Wahhabi "radical preachers."[54] Ibrahim represents the preachers as promoting acts of violence with clear religious aims (they are said to have a "religious duty"). Using the phrase "religious duty" implies there are religious rewards for the perpetrators of the violence. Cerulo maintains that readers are more likely to condemn violent acts if they believe the perpetrator will receive some kind of reward.[55] In using this technique Ibrahim is taking advantage of a common political narrative dominating modern Western discourse, particularly among right-wing and conservative commentators, political groups, and sometimes by Islamic militants, which states that Muslims committing violence as a way of defending their faith will be rewarded in the afterlife. These kinds of representations are just a small part of a wider liberal effort condemning Wahhabism and Saudi Arabia and championing the global liberal agenda.

Since the 9/11 terrorist attacks the representation of Wahhabism as restricting freedoms in general is one of the clearest messages emanating from modern liberal intellectuals. As I have shown, liberals have gone about communicating this message in a variety of ways. Some like Dowd have made use of rather simple rhetorical techniques like the using of the neologism "gender apartheid" when attempting to persuade audiences of the oppressive nature of Wahhabism as practiced in Saudi Arabia, others like Ẓakaria have deployed metaphorical expressions like "out of the shadows" that draw on well-known myths about good and evil, while liberals like Ibrahim have made use of more subtle rhetorical techniques focusing on the cognitive structuring of violent accounts. These representations are part of a multipronged attack against Wahhabism that also encompasses representing it as backward and an obstacle to progress.

Wahhabism as Backward and an Obstacle to Progress

Earlier I referred to Dowd's description of the glacially slow progress of Saudi society. This idea that the human condition has and must continue to progress is integral to liberalism and has a major influence on how many modern liberal intellectuals represent Wahhabism. Influenced by these ideas, there is a strong tendency among modern liberal intellectuals to represent the existence of Wahhabism as indicative of a society that is backward, antimodern, and regressive. Liberals often claim that these backward societies need to free themselves from the shackles of Wahhabism in order to progress. Progress here is typically understood as adopting measures that lead to the creation of a modern liberal secular democratic state. Friedman, Dowd, and Zakaria are among the key liberal intellectuals representing Wahhabism in these ways, and their views have appeared in popular US newspapers like the *New York Times*, *Washington Post*, and *USA Today*. I will now take a look at how each of these intellectuals has represented Wahhabism, focusing on some of the specific rhetorical techniques employed by each in an attempt to persuade their audiences.

Thomas Friedman is a three-time Pulitzer Prize winner, *New York Times* columnist, and self-described liberal who championed the war in Iraq, calling for the left to support the US invasion:

> Believe me, being a liberal on every issue other than this war, I have great sympathy for where the left is coming from. . . . But here's why

> the left needs to get beyond its opposition to the war and start pitching in with its own ideas and moral support to try to make lemons into lemonade in Baghdad: First, even though the Bush team came to this theme late in the day, this war is the most important liberal, revolutionary U.S. democracy-building project since the Marshall Plan. The primary focus of U.S. forces in Iraq today is erecting a decent, legitimate, tolerant, pluralistic representative government from the ground up. . . . For my money, the right liberal approach to Iraq is to say: We can do it better. . . . "Thanks, Mr. Bush. We'll take it from here."[56]

As I mentioned before, Friedman like Zakaria has been 'sounded out' by US President Barack Obama about the situation in the Middle East. Friedman has also written about Wahhabism. In his *New York Times* article "An Islamic Reformation," he laments the prevalence of the phenomenon, apportioning it some of the blame for the poor relationship between the Western and Islamic worlds post–9/11.[57] Extremely critical of Saudi Arabian clerics promoting Wahhabism, Friedman claims the existence of this version of Islam is evidence of the backwardness of the Islamic world. He tells his readers that Islam in general must experience an Islamic reformation and that he sees the beginnings of this transformation in the grassroots movements in Iran. Friedman writes:

> What's going on in Iran today is . . . the most promising trend in the Muslim world. It is a combination of Martin Luther and Tiananmen Square—a drive for an Islamic *reformation*. . . . This movement faces a formidable opponent in Iran's conservative clerical leadership. It can't provide a quick fix to what ails relations between Islam and the West today. . . .
>
> But . . . it reflects a deepening understanding by many Iranian Muslims that to thrive in the *modern era* they, and other Muslims, need an Islam different from the lifeless, *anti-modern*, anti-Western fundamentalism being imposed in Iran and propagated by the Saudi Wahhabi clerics.[58] [emphasis added]

Pertinent here are the terms "modern era" and "anti-modern," which with a little digging helps reveal a lot of about Friedman's thinking. The modern period in Western history that Friedman is referring to is roughly between the years AD 1500 and 1815 and is important to many in the liberal intellectual tradition because it is when both the Protestant Reformation and French Revolution occurred. Both events saw people challenging the dominant role religion played in governing the state. In the Reformation it was the authority of the Catholic Church that was the target. The French Revolution saw the end of medieval Christianity and the welcoming of a new secular phase in mankind's development.

The implication in Friedman's work is that the Islamic world that Wahhabism pervades is stuck about four to five centuries behind the Western world in terms of development. Wahhabism is partly to blame for this backwardness because its proponents oppose secularism, instead championing a society ruled according to an interpretation of religious doctrine. In this sense Friedman wants his readers to understand Wahhabism as an obstacle to both progress in the region and cordial relations between the two worlds. Calling for an Islamic reformation, which is an argument commonly employed by right-wing political groups and conservative commentators in the West, can be understood as an ethnocentric point of view given that it relies on the historical development of the West as a yardstick for progress.

Friedman's article was written in 2002 when many in the world, particularly Americans, were still dealing with the immediate effects of the 9/11 terrorist attacks. However, over a decade later liberal thinkers are still making similar comparisons when making sense of Wahhabism and the situation in the Middle East. Zakaria, for example, has claimed, "The Middle East is in the midst of a sectarian struggle, like those between Catholics and Protestants in Europe in the age of the Reformation."[59] This analogy suggests that the entire Middle East, including Wahhabi Saudi Arabia, is backward and less developed when contrasted with the liberal democratic West. Again the implication is that the West has evolved from an age of religiously inspired violence into a world comprised of modern liberal secular democratic regimes. The Middle East is still far away from reaching this ideal society.

Bandow is another liberal thinker who likens the situation in Wahhabi-affected nations like Saudi Arabia to a particular historical period in Western history that nations have since progressed beyond. Employing analogy as a key rhetorical technique, Bandow writes:

> **Repression** and **corruption**. Saudi Arabia is an absolute monarchy, an almost *medieval theocracy*. . . . Political opposition and even criticism are forbidden. . . . [T]here are few procedural protections for anyone arrested or charged by the government. . . . The government may invade homes and violate privacy whenever it chooses, and travel is limited. Women are covered, cloistered, and confined, much as they were in Afghanistan under the Taliban. . . .[60] [italics added]

Bandow is making the point that Wahhabi Saudi Arabia shares many similar characteristics with medieval theocracies specifically with regard to the lack of freedoms. Bandow wants to convince his readers that modern states like Saudi Arabia ruled according to Wahhabism are just like medieval forms of government that appeared in Western history centuries ago.

Bandow, like Zakaria and Friedman, is a movement intellectual for the political liberal tradition, influenced by the idea that we can rank different kinds of governments on a linear scale, from least developed–regressive–backward to most developed–progressive–modern. Bandow situates Saudi Arabia, because of its adherence to Wahhabism, near the beginning of this spectrum, akin to the medieval period in Western human history. The standard political liberal understanding is that the medieval period in Western human history was characterized by an irrational belief in religion that needed to be overcome in order for society to progress. Again, the implication is that societies in which Wahhabism plays a crucial role, like Saudi Arabia, must go through this same process in order to progress and catch up with the West.

Friedman provides another interesting example of how some liberal intellectuals represent the backwardness of Wahhabism when using the term "evolution" to describe the current situation in the Gulf states, including Saudi Arabia. Friedman claims Wahhabi-ruled Saudi Arabia, like the other Gulf nations, needs an "evolution" and not a "revolution," which is what he understands as currently occurring in other Middle Eastern nations (these are a part of what Friedman calls the "Arab Awakening"; the use of this term suggests that the Arab nations have 'been asleep' and are only now becoming consciously aware of what is happening in their countries). Making sense of the recent turmoil in the Arab and Muslim world for his readers, Friedman writes:

> There are the radical *revolutions* you've read about in Tunisia, Egypt, Syria, Yemen and Libya, none of which yet have built stable, inclusive democracies. But then there are the radical *evolutions* that you've not read about, playing out in Saudi Arabia and other Arab Gulf monarchies.[61]

Friedman also writes:

> I heard many of these stories during group conversations with young Saudis and Emiratis, who I found to be as impressive, connected and high-aspiring to reform their countries as any of their revolutionary cohorts in Egypt. But they want *evolution* not *revolution*. They've seen the footage from Cairo and Damascus. You can feel their energy—from the grass-roots movement to let women drive to the young Saudi who whispers that he's so fed up with the puritanical Islam that dominates his country he's become an atheist, and he is not alone. Saudi atheists? Who knew?[62] [emphasis added]

Friedman's choosing to use the term "evolution" says a lot about how he sees the world. 'Evolution' comes from the Latin *evolutio* meaning the 'unrolling' (of a scroll). During the seventeenth century the term 'evolution' was then commonly used by scholars working in the fields of medicine, mathematics, and literature to refer to the 'growth to maturing and development of an individual thing.' It was Scottish geologist Charles Lyell who gave the term a sense of progress when using it to describe changes in nature.[63] These connotations have stuck with the term and when writers like Friedman use it when describing the current political situation in places like Saudi Arabia, we can see an underlying belief in the natural progression or maturing of a society.

The implication is that societies like Saudi Arabia are currently immature, infantile, or underdeveloped because of the influence religious interpretations like Wahhabism continue to have on them. Clearly influenced by the communitarian approach within the liberal tradition, as well as ideas about human perfection promoted by key liberal writers like J.S. Mill, Friedman sees the Gulf nations as still in the early stages of the maturing process. Friedman understands states and societies as groups of people working toward an end goal of human perfection, and the term "evolution" helps to describe this journey.

Liberal movement intellectuals Maureen Dowd and Thomas Farr represent the backwardness of Wahhabism in slightly different ways. In describing the situation in Wahhabi Saudi Arabia for readers of the *New York Times*, Dowd writes:

> The attempts at more tolerance are belated baby steps to the outside world but in this veiled, curtained and obscured fortress, they are *'60s-style cataclysmic social changes*. Last week, Sheik Abdul Rahman al-Barrak, a pugnacious cleric, shocked Saudis by issuing a fatwa against those who facilitate the mixing of men and women. Given that such a fatwa clearly would include the king, Prince Saud dismissed it.
>
> "I think the trend for reform is set, and there is *no looking back*," he told me. "Clerics who every now and then come with statements in the *opposite direction* are releasing frustration rather than believing that they can stop the trend and *turn back the clock*."[64] [emphasis added]

Here we see the use of a variety of metaphorical expressions: "no looking back," "opposite direction," and "turn back the clock," that all draw on the Progress is Movement metaphor. This metaphor considers forward movement to be indicative of societal progress and backward movement as indicative of societal regression. Like many liberal intellectuals, Dowd considers the modern liberal democratic state to be the ideal form of government and she uses instances of democratic freedoms as a yardstick against which this progress is measured. Dowd represents democratic reform in Wahhabi Saudi Arabia as a natural, incremental, progressive, and positive process that cannot be undone, reversed, or stopped: there is no turning back the clock.

I have also highlighted Dowd's use of the phrase "60s-style cataclysmic social changes." Again we see a liberal intellectual using the West as a yardstick against which progress can be measured. In this instance the ideal kind of society to which Dowd refers is the United States, and the state that fails to measure up to this progress is Wahhabi Saudi Arabia. We know she is referring to the United States because it was experiencing "cataclysmic social changes" during the 1960s.[65] The implication is that the liberal democratic West typified by the US state is far more advanced than a nation like Saudi Arabia, which is held back by Wahhabism and therefore still has a lot of catching up to do.

Like Dowd, Farr also draws on the metaphor Progress is Movement when representing Wahhabism as an obstacle to the development of a society for readers of the *Washington Post*. Farr joins Dowd in critiquing the role Wahhabism plays in Saudi Arabia; however, for Farr this is a part of a wider critique of the role Islam plays in the modern Muslim world. He writes:

> A senior Saudi cleric issued a fatwa mandating the death of anyone arguing that men and women could work together professionally. Such edicts emerge from Wahhabism, a malevolent political theology that nurtured Osama bin Laden and continues to be exported worldwide. . . .
>
> Among other things, Muslims need religious liberty to undermine Islamist extremism and to *advance* women's rights. . . .[66] [emphasis added]

We can abstract the metaphorical term "advance" for closer analysis, which Farr uses when describing the relation between religious liberty and women's rights in Saudi Arabia. In drawing on the Progress is Movement metaphor and using this particular metaphorical term, Farr is suggesting that Saudi Arabian society does not currently provide women the liberty to which they are entitled and which forms a key part of a modern society.

Farr's use of the term "advance" also provides valuable insight into the ways some liberals think about history. The liberal intellectual tradition typically promotes a linear understanding of human history, where the purpose of mankind is to progress and advance in creating a liberal democratic utopia. A woman's ability to enjoy her liberty is an integral part of this ideal society. According to Farr this is the opposite of what is currently happening in Saudi Arabia, where women are forced to live according to Wahhabism. Farr represents Wahhabism, with its restrictions of religious and women's freedoms, as an obstacle that needs to be overcome.

Wahhabism Is a Threat to the Ideal Secular Society

What Farr is getting at, and what many liberals have intimated, is the crucial role they believe secularism plays in ordering modern liberal democratic society. The third prominent representation of Wahhabism provided by liberal intellectuals since 9/11 that I now want to focus on is the supposed threat this religious phenomenon poses to achieving a secular society.

Many liberal intellectuals resent the modern Saudi state because it violates many of the principles they hold dear. Liberal intellectuals typically believe an ideal society is secular, meaning the state does not espouse or promote any particular kind of religion. They believe that a state should be committed to tolerating all religions, so as long as they do not impinge upon the daily operations of the state or individual freedoms, or harm individuals. For many liberals, the problem with a state like Saudi Arabia, which they understand as organized according to Wahhabi religious doctrine, is that it violates these principles. Liberal intellectuals do not tend to see Wahhabism as a religion that accepts the partitioning of the secular and sacred.

Fareed Zakaria is also among those liberal intellectuals whose belief in secularism plays a major role in influencing his representation of Wahhabism. Zakaria provides an assessment of the current religious and political situation in the Middle East for readers of the *New York Times*, claiming the region has become more violent than usual. He blames Wahhabism for inspiring and motivating this violence that he interestingly terms a "*rising tide* of Islamic fundamentalism"[67] (emphasis added).

According to Zakaria, "Its causes are various—the rise of Saudi Arabia and its export of puritanical Wahhabi . . . and the discrediting of Westernization as the secular republics in the region morphed into military dictatorships."[68] Apparent in this representation is the belief that secularization is an effective tool in countering modern Islamic extremism. The implication is that secular republics, which for liberals are the ideal forms of government for the Middle East, provide people with what they deserve, need, and are *a priori* entitled to—liberty. Without liberty, people in the region are likely to become frustrated with oppressive forms of government and embrace Islamic fundamentalism as an outlet for their anger.

Pertinent is Zakaria's use of the metaphorical expression "rising tide" when describing the increasing popularity of Islamic fundamentalism in the region. The phrase's literal meaning is the occurrence of incoming water between a low tide and following high tide. Rising tides are the result of gravitational forces exerted by the moon and the sun on the rotating Earth. Rising tides, especially when accompanied by strong winds, often result in severe flooding. Zakaria uses this metaphorical expression to help represent Islamic fundamentalism as a natural relation of nonsecular governments that are denying people their liberty and of Saudi Arabia's global promotion of Wahhabism. His key point is that where there is Wahhabism and military dictatorships, there will also be Islamic fundamentalism.

Dan Bilefsky's article, which also appeared in the *New York Times*, is another example worthy of analysis.[69] While most liberal intellectuals have tended to focus on the prevalence of Wahhabism in the Middle East, Bilefsky looks at the spread of Wahhabism in Europe, specifically how he believes it has influenced the social, religious, and political situation in Bosnia. Influenced by a strong belief in secularism, Bilefsky claims Wahhabism is a threat to the emerging modern and secular Bosnian nation that values separation of "mosque and state" and an individual's right to practice religion privately.[70] Secularism and not Wahhabism is represented as the will of the Bosnian people: "A recently conducted detailed survey of 600 Bosnian Muslims, said 60 percent favored keeping religion a private matter."[71] Like many other intellectuals belonging to different intellectual traditions, Bilefsky blames Wahhabism/Salafism (he uses the terms interchangeably) for motivating and inspiring violence in Bosnia.[72]

Of major concern to Bilefsky is the influence that Islam in general and Wahhabism in particular are having on the Bosnian secular education system, especially in public kindergartens. Bilefsky communicates this concern to his readers by giving voice to the opinions of locals and "a prominent liberal Muslim intellectual" who is critical of Islam's encroachment on civic life. Bilefsky writes:

> Mustafa Effendi Spahic, a prominent liberal Muslim intellectual and professor at the Gazri Husrev-beg Madrasa in Sarajevo, went further, calling the introduction of religious education in kindergarten "a crime against children."
>
> "The Prophet says to teach children to kneel as Muslims, only after the age of 7," said Professor Spahic, who was imprisoned under Communism for Islamic activism. "No one has any right to do that before then because it is an affront to freedom, the imagination and fun of the child's world."[73]

This excerpt helps illustrate many of the beliefs that liberal intellectuals value, like individualism and the relation between freedom and the development of the self, evident in Bilefsky implying that religious education for children hinders their "imagination." Early modern liberal thinkers like Turgot and Condorcet treated imagination as a key part of individual genius and therefore key to the progress and development of society.

Also pertinent is Bilefsky's use of analogy when likening the current situation in Bosnia, which is experiencing a rise in popularity of Wahhabism, to the situation in Iran. He writes:

> Muharem Bazdulj, deputy editor of the daily Oslobodjenje, the voice of liberal, secular Bosnia, said he feared the growth of Wahhabism, the conservative Sunni movement originating in Saudi Arabia that aims to strip away foreign and corrupting influences.
>
> Analysts say Saudi-financed organizations have invested about $700 million in Bosnia since the war, often in mosques.

> Wahhabism arrived via hundreds of warriors from the Arab world during the war and with Arab humanitarian and charity workers since, though sociologists here stress that most Bosnian Muslims still believe that Islam has no place in public life. . . .
>
> Milorad Dodik, prime minister of Bosnia's Serb Republic, has referred to Sarajevo as the *new Tehran*, and talks of a "political Islam and a fight against people *who don't share the same vision*."[74] [emphasis added]

Understanding the context in which these remarks are made is crucial. Bilefsky's article was published in December 2008 and appeared during a period of time when Iran was understood by many as an Islamic superpower keen on spreading its version of Islam and hence its influence throughout the world. In more recent times the supposed threat of Iran has taken a back seat to the perceived threat posed by ISIS, which has tended to dominate Western media commentary.

Bilefsky uses this analogy to help make the point that Saudi Arabia spreading Wahhabism in Bosnia is similar to Iran. Like the Islamic regime in Tehran, Saudi Arabia wants to encourage the implementation of a version of Islam as a way of ordering civic society. Both nations adhere to different versions of Islam (Iran officially subscribes to a Shi'a interpretation of Islam); however, Bilefsky wants the reader to think of the two as both belonging to "political Islam." As an intellectual influenced by key liberal ideas, Bilefsky understands political Islam as a threat to key liberal values like the separation of religion and state.

Like Bilefsky, Friedman is a liberal intellectual promoting the triumph of secular liberal democratic regimes throughout the world. Friedman, in his article "Caution, Curves Ahead," published in the *New York Times* in 2013, focuses his attention on the Middle East, particularly Syria, which is in the midst of a civil war now involving international forces.[75] Friedman provides his readers with an assessment of the aims and goals of the major players in the conflict and picks the groups he believes Western nations should support.

Friedman sees both Qatar and Saudi Arabia as key players in the Syrian conflict. He describes both as "Wahhabi fundamentalist monarchies" and as "the two main funders and arms suppliers of the Syrian uprising."

He blames their adherence to Wahhabism for their nations' failure to embrace democracy and for the sectarian violence each are currently experiencing. According to Friedman, their adherence to Wahhabism at home reveals their true intentions motivating their interference in Syria:

> Are we to believe that these two archrival Wahhabi fundamentalist monarchies, the two main funders and arms suppliers of the Syrian uprising, are really both interested in creating a multisectarian, multiparty democracy in Syria, which they would not tolerate in their own countries?[76]

This flies in the face of what liberals and Western liberal democratic regimes want for Syria. As we can see, Friedman is also suggesting that there is a relation between Qatar's and Saudi Arabia's non-democratic Wahhabi beliefs and their support for violence.

Friedman identifies three "rebel groups" in Syria engaged in the conflict that could potentially emerge as rulers of a new post-Assad Syria:

> . . . those democrats who want to be free to be citizens in a country where everyone has the same rights; those who want to be free to be more Islamic; and those who want to be free to be more sectarian—to see Syria's Sunni majority oust the ruling Alawite minority.[77]

He claims the West should support the group that is more likely to get Syrians "to think and act like *citizens* than *sects* or *tribes*"[78] (emphasis added). Friedman understands the term 'citizen' in liberal terms, meaning someone who values things like a democratic secular government. Here we see a clear ranking of different kinds of people and societies. At the top are citizens and below them are those who belong to "sects or tribes." The implication is that Wahhabism is incompatible with the liberal belief in a secular state because it encourages people to act in ways contrary to what liberalism values. Western readers tend to associate the term 'tribe' with an earlier period in human history where society was organized according to a common ancestry. It is also a biological term used to describe a taxonomic category placed between a subfamily and a genus or between a suborder and a family. These understandings support the claim that Friedman is categorizing adherents of Wahhabism as behind or below the non-Wahhabi and nonreligious people living in advanced liberal secular democratic states.

This helps us to understand why Friedman believes the "secular-nationalist rebels" who are "those democrats who want to be free to be citizens in a country where everyone has the same rights" are the only potentially viable group the West can support. The West must not support the Sunni groups who are themselves supported and armed by a "Wahhabi fundamentalist monarchy," because if they emerge victorious, then it is likely they will create a state that rejects democracy, secularism, and stability in favor of a monarchy ruled according to Wahhabi religious doctrine. They will likely create a state that encourages treating its people as "sects or tribes" rather than as "citizens" who respect the freedom of others, including religious freedom. Friedman writes:

> I'm dubious that just arming "nice" rebels will produce the Syria we want; it could, though, drag us in in ways we might not want. But if someone can make the case that arming the secular-nationalist rebels increases the chances of forcing Assad and the Russians into a settlement, and defeating the Islamists rebels after Assad falls, I'm ready to listen.[79]

The liberal intellectuals whose works I analyze in this chapter are clear in their message: Wahhabism is an affront to the values they hold dear. Liberals value freedom, a modern secular liberal democratic government, and an environment providing its people with the best chance to develop to their full potential. These intellectuals see Wahhabism as denying individual freedoms, particularly religious and gender freedoms, failing to appreciate the divide between the secular and the sacred, and creating an environment that hinders the development of its people. As we have seen, these liberal intellectuals deploy a number of different rhetorical techniques when representing Wahhabism in this way. Having conducted this preliminary analysis, I now want to take a look at some of the themata and generative metaphors influencing how liberals are making sense of the social world in general and the phenomenon they are calling Wahhabism in particular. However, before doing this it matters that we know what themata and generative metaphors are and how they work.

5

Themata, Generative Metaphors, and Making Sense of Liberal Intellectuals' Representations of Wahhabism

Most of the evil in this world is done
by people with good intentions.—T.S. Eliot

I have argued to date that liberal intellectuals representing Wahhabism rely on particular notions of history, human nature, the relationship between individuals and their society, and the ideal ordering of a community. I showed how these beliefs characterize and define how liberals make sense of the world, understand the aims and goals of human existence, and shape their representations of Wahhabism, hence their characterization of societies in which Wahhabism is prevalent as relatively backward, unevolved, antimodern, and regressive when contrasted with states in the West. We also saw many liberals championing the introduction of measures aimed at creating a modern secular liberal democratic state guaranteeing and valuing the liberties of its people. Yet it seems there is still more to be understood about the 'why' of these representations.

Here we confront the allure of various kinds of interpretative or explanatory approaches. As I have noted there is certainly a rich tradition of the sociology of knowledge that offers a structural and determinist account of ideas couched in terms of class and gender. Other thinkers like Hannah Arendt in her book *Rahel Varnhagen: The Life of a Jewess* have offered a rich historical and phenomenological account of how personal preferences and prejudice intersect with historical circumstance to play a major role in how individuals make sense of the world.[1] For reasons already spelled out and without seeking to controvert the findings generated by these traditions, I have determined on using a more formal analysis couched in terms of significant metaphoric and discursive features. Here I show that if we dig deeper we can establish several important elements playing a major role in constituting these kinds of representations. These elements are what Gerald Holton calls "themata" and what Kurt Danziger calls "generative metaphors."[2]

My ability to make sense of liberal and neoconservative representations of Wahhabism relies in part on my ability to abstract and describe the roles both of these processes play in how these intellectuals make sense of the world and the representing process. I dedicate the first part of this chapter to describing precisely what themata and generative concepts are and how they work. I dedicate the second part of the chapter to identifying and describing some of the key themata and generative metaphors influencing the thinking of liberal intellectuals and describing the implications these have for the ways in which they represent Wahhabism.

It should be noted from the outset that Holton and Danziger are historians seeking to make sense of the history of European physics from Kepler to Einstein and the rise of modern psychology, respectively. They have set out to demonstrate the key role played by two kinds of discursive and generative factors at work in these rich and complex intellectual projects. On the premise that the proof of the pudding is in its eating, I propose to establish the value of drawing on these two discursive devices by applying them to situations in the social world, as when looking at the different ways intellectuals represent Wahhabism. In adapting and using these theories in this way I am building on a tradition of scholarship in social science that includes important work like that undertaken by Robert Nisbet.[3]

Themata

Gerald Holton's account of the origins of scientific thought established the value of studying what he called themata.[4] Holton defined themata as those presuppositions often existing for long periods of history and which are not derivable "from either observation or analytic ratiocination."[5] As such, these presuppositions "required a term of their own, and thus the author called them themata (singular, *thema*, from the Greek θέμα: that which is laid down; proposition; primary word)."[6] Holton sees themata as "often-hidden mechanisms[s]" that have and continue to play powerful and motivating roles in advancing science, and claims they have been so influential that they have "repeatedly fashioned the foundations of sciences."[7] They are "motivating aids," inspiring and motivating researchers that also "tend to be suppressed or disappear from view."[8] Other authors have used alternative terms when referring to these same assumptions or presuppositions people tend to take for granted when making sense of the world and which are often taken as literal truth. A popular term is "master themes," which is used by Robert Nisbet in his study of the parallels between sociology and art.[9]

Holton's account of the thematic origins of scientific thought lead him to argue that there were a number of presuppositions, each with their own discreet set of thematic elements pervading and silently shaping the work of modern scientists. These included themata like evolution–steadystate–devolution and mechanistic–materialistic–mathematical models, which have proven to be fundamental frameworks shaping the development of scientific thought, especially in terms of the process Popper insisted was critical in testing and refuting established theories.[10] Holton's studies concentrating on themata have influenced researchers in the physical sciences. However, as he notes, the same findings are applicable to the other sciences.[11] Holton's indexing of themata in the physical sciences helps highlight an important point that is pertinent to considering the themata used by liberal and neoconservative intellectuals. Namely, different groups of people tend to use different themata and these absolutely fundamental beliefs tend to influence the ways in which these different groups of people make sense of the world. Holton finds that:

> All these [themata] become visible most strikingly during a conflict between individuals or groups that are committed to opposing themata, or within the developing work of a scientist holding on to a thematic concept before the data have given sufficient confidence in its value.[12]

Because they are not usually acknowledged or explicitly taught, the influential role themata play is often ignored by historians of science who want to understand things like what motivates and inspires scientists in their research, why they select particular conceptual tools, and why researchers treat data in particular ways.[13] Holton observes how some scientists, consciously or otherwise

> use highly motivating and very general presuppositions or hypotheses that are not directly derivable from the phenomena and are not provable or falsifiable. . . . [T]hese motivating aids—which the author has termed thematic presuppositions or thematic hypotheses—tend to be suppressed, and disappear from view.[14]

Holton is very critical of those adopting what he calls a "two-dimensional approach" that fails to appreciate the integral and influential role themata play in how researchers make sense of the world, highlighting four major problems with this kind of approach. One is that by consciously or unconsciously ignoring or overlooking these themata, researchers also tend to overlook the "positive, motivating and emancipatory potential of certain presuppositions, as well as the negative and enslaving role that sometimes has led promising scientists into disastrous error."[15] Two, failing to recognize the influential role played by themata "does nothing to explain why at any given time the choice of problems or the reception of theories may be strikingly different among individuals or like-minded groups who face the same corpus of data."[16] Three,

> this limited view does not explain what a historian, looking at laboratory notebooks or drafts of a distinguished scientist, often sees with stark clarity: the willingness, particularly at the early stages, privately to cling, firmly, and sometimes at great risk, to what can only be called a suspension of disbelief about the possible falsification of their hypotheses, emerging from the data before them.[17]

And four, this kind of two-dimensional definition treats 'science' "as if it were a cold and lifeless imposition of an authoritarian, dogmatic excess of rationalism . . . [leaving] no room for creative play of the intuition or personal preferences."[18] This last point is especially pertinent to this study and speaks to the point raised by others like Gadamer and Arendt about the effect of personal preferences on how individuals make sense of the world. Recognizing the major role themata play and undertaking a thematic analysis aimed at drawing some of these out for closer analysis are crucial to understanding what motivates and inspires researchers in their creative processes. This becomes especially important when we consider that many of these themata can persist for very long periods of time.

While Holton is concerned with research undertaken in the physical sciences, this approach can be applied to the social sciences: "the role of . . . themata is not so different from the guiding presuppositions and framing worldviews expressed in other creative activities, from the arts to politics."[19] In many instances "some themata in a particular science are exemplifications of the same fundamental themata in other sciences, or even in cultural productions far from that of the sciences."[20] Robert Nisbet is among those authors who have heeded Holton's advice, using his ideas to study the parallels between sociology and art.

As has been the case with Western science, Nisbet finds that researchers working in the sociology and art fields have tended to draw on and interpret a set of what he calls "master themes" when undertaking research. One of the dominant master themes identified by Nisbet and which is pertinent to how liberals make sense of the world is individualism. Nisbet writes:

> The rise of the modern conception of the *individual*, free and secular, liberated, as it were, from the religious community, is of course a hallmark of the painting of the Italian Renaissance. Individuality in its own right thus becomes a theme. . . . In more recent times, roughly since the 1950s, the individual self, consciousness, reflexive awareness, have given a certain priority to subjectivism in literature and art. And no one acquainted with the history of sociology during the last decade or two will be unaware of the dominance of precisely these same styles and themes in this area.[21]

Some of the representations provided by liberal intellectuals in this study suggest that this search for the self is best traced back to the Protestant Reformation rather than the Renaissance. Irrespective of this, individualism continues to be a key thematic element that has become a central imperative of contemporary thought, including contemporary political liberal thought. Freedom, secularism, and progress are also key thematic elements central to contemporary liberal thinking.

Nisbet points out that researchers in modern social science have also been preoccupied with and pursued other common themata, including ideas dealing with community, authority, status, the sacred, and alienation. Nisbet finds that these themata have helped form a "thematic palette" that has been used by the founders of sociology when creating portraits of the "European social landscape."[22] We can also say that some of these same themata have helped form a thematic palette used by Western intellectuals when creating portraits of the Middle Eastern and Islamic landscapes for Western audiences in recent times. Nisbet also suggests there are three dominant metaphorical systems, namely growth, genealogy, and mechanism that have influenced and motivated scholars using these themata. While these specific metaphors described by Nisbet are of varying relevance to this book, what is important is the relation between a researcher's use of themata and the metaphors helping constitute, generate, and support this kind of thinking.

Generative Metaphors

We can refer to the seminal work of Kurt Danziger for a deeper understanding of the generative role or theory-constitutive function metaphors play in this process.[23]

Danziger's analysis of metaphor takes us beyond the literal surface of discourse and into the realm of assumptions and preoccupations, an important point when we start to consider the ways in which liberal and neoconservatives make sense of the world. Danziger argues that individuals and groups of individuals who have contributed to the evolution of psychology tend to draw on similar metaphorical descriptions that have been used over long periods of time and which have come to be thought of "as expressing some kind of literal truth."[24] This makes the role played by metaphors historically significant as it allow us to "improve our understanding of patterns of . . . thought . . . characteristic of a period, or a culture, or a particular intellectual community."[25] The study of generative metaphors can therefore be understood as pertinent to our making sense of the liberal and neoconservative intellectual representations of Wahhabism in the post–9/11 period in which there is a heightened anxiety about the threat posed by Islamic radicalism.

Danziger provides an illuminating example of the ways in which psychologists Bain and McDougall used metaphors when writing about psychology. This account is illuminating in the sense that it can help us to understand the ways in which intellectuals in this study use metaphors and the theory-constitutive function role metaphors can play. Danziger writes that Bain describes the learning process in terms of "tracks" and "turning off steam" and that McDougall describes an organism without instincts as a "steam engine whose fires had been drawn."[26] Both Bain and McDougall were very deliberate in the language they choose to use, and their use of particular metaphors helped create particular images that fitted their psychological theories in fundamental ways. Danziger points out that Bain and McDougall's use of metaphorical language has a theory-constitutive function and that our studying of these can provide us with valuable insight into the underlying assumptions and concerns expressed in their psychological theories.[27]

Danziger finds that both authors employ a similar image of the Mind as an Energy System, yet they emphasize different aspects of this image. This illuminates an important characteristic of fundamental psychological metaphors and metaphors in general, including those used by intellectuals belonging to the same tradition providing representations of Wahhabism. Danziger writes:

> They [basic metaphors] provide a basic common framework within which communication is possible, while at the same time providing scope for differences of emphasis. Basic metaphors, like that of psychological energy, provide a kind of rough schema that, when held in common, can constitute one of the minimal conditions for effective human communication. But because metaphors link two domains

> (such as mind and energy) in rather undefined ways, these schemata leave open the issue of precisely which assumptions and questions are to be transferred from the one domain to the other. So metaphorical schemata not only provide a framework for shared discourse, but encourage differences of emphasis and therefore provide conditions favourable for theoretical development.[28]

Similarly, Nisbet finds that authors influenced by the master theme individualism are influenced by a number of common and basic metaphors, namely those relating to growth, genealogy, and mechanism. Nisbet, for example, emphasizes the key role 'growth' has played in the way Western intellectuals have made sense of the world:

> Growth is change, yes, but when we declare some change a manifestation of growth in the social sphere we are speaking metaphorically. We are endowing an institution or social structure with a process drawn from the organic world. Few perspectives, few themes, have been more vital in Western thought than that of growth or development, which is a conceptual product of metaphor.[29]

The key point is there are common metaphorical systems that provide a framework for a shared discourse for intellectuals belonging to a particular tradition. As Danziger puts it, "underlying metaphorical systems have *generative* properties that give a certain cast to surface discourse" and "the identification of such schemata is therefore important from the point of view of understanding the cognitive factors that provide some of the conditions of both coherence and novelty in the historical development of . . . discourse."[30] Identifying these metaphorical systems in addition to identifying the key thematic elements is therefore integral to making sense of liberal and neoconservative intellectuals' representations of Wahhabism.

It is also important to point out that metaphors are more than just cognitive constructions; they also have what Danziger calls a "programmatic aspect." Reiterating the important point made by Donald Schön, Danziger writes, "When we define a certain part of the world metaphorically, this is not just an invitation to *think* about it in a certain way, it is also an invitation to *act* in terms of certain implied assumptions."[31] Using metaphors to define an object in a particular way encourages certain expectations, focuses our attention on particular features, and highlights priorities for practical action. Now we have a basic understanding of what themata and generative metaphors are and how they work, I want to turn our attention to those specifically influencing liberal intellectuals in their representations of Wahhabism.

Individualism, Progress: The Key Themata and Generative Metaphors Influencing Liberal Thinking

We have seen that the idea of individualism is a key idea influencing liberal thinking. This themata has long existed in American political culture in general and has been taken for granted by many American intellectuals, at least since the founding of the American republic in 1783. Zhenghuan Zhou is among the authors to write about the prominent role this themata has played in the American political experience:

> While the republic was founded upon the values and beliefs that go to the heart of modern individualism, the absence of a historical tradition, the vastness of uncultivated and rich land, and ultimately a divinely ordained sense of mission, combined to foster a strong and unique form of individualist culture that is unparalleled in any other nation in the world . . . to read American history—from the Puritan settlers in pursuit of religious liberty to the revolutionary war that led to political independence, from the lonesome frontierman chasing his "manifest destiny" to the economically self-made capitalist—is to watch individualism grow. To observe the ordinary lives of ordinary men and women in America is to see individualism in action."[32]

Zhou is expressing an opinion commonly held by many sociologists studying the American political experience, that the United States is the embodiment of individualism *par excellence*. Nearly all the liberal intellectuals analyzed in this book are Americans writing in popular US publications like the *New York Times* for primarily American audiences. Of course, the fact that these newspapers publish their articles online means they also have a global audience—the *New York Times* in particular is widely understood to be one of the most reputable and leading newspapers in the Western world and has a large global following. Because these authors are Americans first, it is therefore unsurprising that such an influential American themata like individualism that has dominated the modern American experience should play such an influential role in the American intellectual tradition in general.

What is key for American liberal intellectuals is that this presupposition resonates with similar ideas about individualism that have also played such an integral role in modern political liberal thought. Furthermore, individualism has acted as a motivating aid for many modern liberals making sense of and representing Wahhabism.

In my analysis in Chapter 4 we saw that there were some liberal intellectuals referring to a very specific period of time in Western history, namely the Protestant Reformation, when representing Wahhabism. Thomas Friedman describes the modern Islamic world in which Wahhabism is pervasive as currently undergoing a much-needed "Islamic reformation" to help push it into the "modern era."[33] Fareed Zakaria likens the current sectarian struggle in the Middle East involving Wahhabi forces as similar to the past struggles "between Catholics and Protestants in Europe in the age of the Reformation."[34] The use of the term 'reformation' and the analogizing of this period in time when making sense of the current situation in the Middle East is very telling.

Holton points out that themata often exist for long periods of time and this is certainly the case when we consider the prominent and long-term role individualism has played in the liberal intellectual tradition. This idea at the very least dates back to a time that intellectuals like Zakaria and Friedman are referring to, that is, the Protestant Reformation that took place during the eighteenth century. Neither Zakaria nor Friedman or any other liberal intellectual explicitly refer to the importance or lessons of this period. However, as Holton describes, this lack of explicit acknowledgement is a key aspect of themata. Despite not acknowledging the importance of this era, we can see that some of the key ideas associated with this period, namely the concept of individualism, are clearly acting as motivating aids for some liberal intellectuals when making sense of Wahhabism in the modern political environment.

A cursory review of the liberal tradition tells us that the Reformation played a prominent role in laying the foundation for the emergence of the master theme individualism and the ideas typically associated with it: freedom of religion and secularism. This themata has been so prominent that liberal intellectuals have since taken it as expressing a kind of literal truth about the modern existence of humankind. What authors like Zakaria and Friedman do not explicitly acknowledge is that the Reformation marked an important transition in the Western world, namely a moving away from the idea that the church and state (which were interlinked) controlled the individual, and embracing the idea of an individual's freedom to their own decision, free from coercion and interference from state and faith-based institutions.

In the religious age immediately prior to the Reformation it was generally accepted that it was the key function of the (religious) state in the West to define and articulate a specific (religious) conception of the good for its citizens. The events taking place during the Reformation helped usher in a new understanding of the function of the state. Influenced by the writings of key Protestant intellectuals like Martin Luther and John Calvin, and by key liberal thinkers like John Locke, John Stuart Mill, and Immanuel Kant, a conception of individualism emerged that continues to pervade liberal thinking. In the new postreligious and secular age, people began to value an individual freedom that allowed them to think and act as they pleased, so as long as they did not harm or impinge on the freedom of others within a state that valued and guaranteed people's liberty. That is to say, people were free to develop and pursue their own conception of the good.

Closely related with this way of thinking, and which has also influenced the ways in which liberals represent Wahhabism, is the themata regarding 'progress.' We saw how many liberal intellectuals describe Wahhabism and societies in which this faith was enforced or practiced as backward and antimodern. Doug Bandow uses the phrase "medieval theocracy" to describe a state like Saudi Arabia that is ruled according to Wahhabi doctrine and therefore does not value or grant their people individual freedoms to make their own choices.[35] Thomas Friedman describes Wahhabism as "anti-modern," suggesting that changes must be made in Middle Eastern nations in order for them to "thrive in the modern era."[36]

What these authors are getting at, but are often not explicitly stating, is that they are motivated and inspired by the idea that people and the societies they comprise have the ability to achieve progress, or put another way to realize their full potential as human beings. The implications associated with this kind of thinking is that we can measure progress or the lack thereof of individuals and societies on some kind of continuum, and that there exist better and worse ways of living. This themata has a long tradition in Western scientific thinking in general and in liberal political theory in particular and can at the very least be traced back to the works of Jean-Baptiste Lamarck, Herbert Spencer, and John Stuart Mill.

It was Lamarck who provided the first modern attempt to account for the diversity of life on the planet without relying on the ideas of divine creation. Inspired by Lamarck's work, Spencer then used materials from the biological sciences to construct a framework aimed at describing the development of the human race. Spencer promoted the idea that the human race like the animal kingdom is constantly evolving and that these processes were elements of a universe in a constant state of evolution and progression. Spencer's evolutionary theory holds that human development can be categorized into a hierarchy, and we can rank humans according to race, ethnicity, and mental ability. Progress can be understood as "an advance from homogeneity of structure to heterogeneity of structure."[37]

These ideas resonate with modern European literature about progress, in which authors typically proclaim the superiority of European science, culture, and institutions. As Margaret Lange puts it, "the paradigmatic progress narrative shows Europeans setting the standards and then the rest of the world catching up until everyone is a full participant in an enlightened order."[38] Lange makes the point that this introduction of scientific theories about biological evolution into writings about the progress of humankind helped to create a new kind of Eurocentrism based on biologically racist ideas. Inspired by this evolutionary theory, Spencer argued that different races of human beings exist and form a clear hierarchy: "The civilized man departs more widely from the general type of the placental mammalia than do the lower human races."[39]

This kind of thinking inspired many prominent liberal theorists like Mill, who combined it with other key ideas like those associated with individualism. Mill argued that the development of the individual could be best achieved within a liberal democracy given the individual freedoms it values and guarantees. According to Mill, it was liberal secular regimes that provide the necessary conditions for a conflict between ideologies, which he saw as a powerful driver of ideological development.[40] This would mean that Mill would have major problems with modern nations that do not allow for a conflict of ideas within a liberal democratic state, which is necessary for the development of society. For many modern liberal intellectuals, Saudi Arabia is one of these states. It is also important to note that unlike many Marxists, who consider human and societal progress to be an inevitable process, Mill believed progress was possible and desirable but not necessarily assured.

Many of the modern liberal intellectuals are influenced by a similar themata about progress and this shows in their representations of Wahhabism. Friedman shows signs of subscribing to the same racist beliefs associated with progress that are espoused by thinkers like Spencer when arguing that "young Saudis" forced to live according to Wahhabi doctrine in Saudi Arabia want "evolution" and not "revolution."[41] Friedman also ranks the different societies in the Middle East, categorizing non-Wahhabi societies like Tunisia, Egypt, Syria, Yemen, and Libya as above or more enlightened than societies like Saudi Arabia and other Gulf states. He writes:

> There are the radical *revolutions* you've read about in Tunisia, Egypt, Syria, Yemen and Libya, none of which yet have built stable, inclusive democracies. But then there are the radical *evolutions* that you've not read about, playing out in Saudi Arabia and other Arab Gulf monarchies.[42]

It is people and not animals that tend to experience 'revolutions,' while we tend to use the term 'evolution' generally when we are talking about biological theories dealing with animals. The implication is that Wahhabism does not provide the same individualism or freedom as the modern liberal democratic state and which is needed for humans and societies to progress.

There are also important generative metaphors helping constitute this master theme. Danziger points out that metaphors commonly used by authors belonging to particular traditions often take them "as expressing some kind of literal truth" and that we must identify and analyze these metaphors if we are serious about "improv[ing] our understanding of patterns of . . . thought characteristic of a period, or a culture, or a particular intellectual community."[43] Abstracting the "underlying metaphorical systems" that "have generative properties" and "that give a certain cast to a surface discourse" is therefore of major importance when making sense of liberal representations of Wahhabism.[44]

An important metaphorical system I identify in my deconstructing of liberal intellectuals' representations of Wahhabism, and which fits perfectly with the liberal themata about progress, is the metaphor Progress is Movement. In one example Maureen Dowd describes Wahhabi Saudi Arabia as making "*galactically glacial*" progress with regards to gender and cultural freedoms.[45] In another example she maintains there is "*no looking back*," that Wahhabi clerics are "looking in the *opposite direction*," and "that they [the Wahhabi clerics] can[not] stop the trend and *turn back the clock*" (emphasis added).[46] The "trend" she is talking about is the granting of new freedoms to Saudi Arabians forced to live according to Wahhabi doctrine. Thomas Farr draws on the same metaphorical system when representing Wahhabism as an obstacle to the development of a society. He describes the need to "*advance* women's rights" so as to create a modern liberal secular democratic state (emphasis added).[47]

As we can see, these liberals literally believe that there is a purpose, endpoint, or a highest state of evolution for humankind and that we as individuals and a society must always be working to move forward until we reach this goal. For many liberal intellectuals it is taken for granted that this end goal is a world full of modern liberal democratic states that value and guarantee citizens' freedom. However, the obvious point is that not all people think in this way. Not everyone subscribes to a linear conception of human progress and believes that we can rank or order people and societies. There are some people, for example, who have a cyclical understanding of the universe and human nature, while others believe life is chaotic and is without rhyme or reason. This was pointed out by David Hume in 1757 and more recently by Terry Eagleton. Hume writes:

> We are placed in this world, as in a great theatre, where the true springs and causes of every event, are entirely unknown to us; nor have we either sufficient wisdom to foresee, or power to prevent those ills, with which we are continually threatened. We hang in perpetual suspense betwixt life and death, health and sickness, plenty and want; which are distributed amongst the human species by secret and unknown causes, whose operation is oft unexpected, and always accountable.[48]

And Eagleton writes:

> The cosmos is something of the whorling, spiraling, self-involved quality of traditional Celtic art. Like such art, it exists purely for its own self delight, not to accomplish some mighty goal. . . . Like [James] Joyce's fiction, the world is not designed to get anywhere in particular. For [John Scotus] Eriugena, as for modern physics, Nature is a dynamic process which varies according to the observer's shifting vantage point. It is an infinity of partial perspectives, an endless sport of multiple viewpoints.[49]

In this sense the linear thinking held by many liberals can be understood as a coping mechanism designed to impose a sense of order and purpose on a world and universe that for many lacks both. The inability of many liberal intellectuals to accept the whirling nature of the universe, and their desire to believe that we as a society are heading toward an end goal, can be understood as a refusal to accept the seemingly inherent meaninglessness and emptiness of our own existence. In this sense, developing and subscribing to a particular linear conception of history that places themselves and the societies to which they belong ahead of other people and societies, including those living according to Wahhabi religious doctrine, can be understood as an egoistic attempt to instill meaning in their lives by showing they are somehow better, more advanced, or more evolved than the (Wahhabi Muslim) Other.

Scottish philosopher Alasdair McIntyre is among those to highlight the important role teleology plays in intellectual traditions.[50] The term 'teleology' comes from the Greek *telos* meaning 'end' and *logos* meaning 'reason.' McIntyre understands teleology as any kind of philosophical account holding that final causes exist in nature, meaning nature inherently tends toward definite ends. Without a religious belief in God and an eternal afterlife filled with rewards, the liberal teleology helps to provide a standard by which to judge the quality of one's life. Put another way, it helps provide meaning where perhaps there is none. The liberal intellectuals' representation of Wahhabism can therefore be understood as an exercise designed to imbue their life with meaning and purpose, as they are able to point to it and say, '*we* are better than *them* and *we* can show *them* how to create a heaven on earth.'

In the next chapter I continue the analytic and interpretive process, this time focusing our attention on what can be described as the neoconservative assault on Wahhabism, Saudi Arabia, and the Palestinian struggle for self-determination. In the proceeding chapter I combine my making sense of neoconservative intellectuals' representations of Wahhabism with my deconstruction of the dominant representations appearing in the public sphere.

6

Those Evil and Violent Savages: The Neoconservative Assault on Wahhabism, Saudi Arabia, and the Palestinian Struggle for Self-Determination

Both read the Bible day and night,
But thou read'st black where I read white.
—William Blake, *The Everlasting Gospel*

On September 20, 2001, President George W. Bush stood before the US Congress and declared:

> The enemy of America is not our many Muslim friends; it is not our many Arab friends. Our enemy is a radical network of terrorists, and every government that supports them. . . . Every nation, every region, now has a decision to make. Either you are with us, or you are with the terrorists.[1]

For many outside observers this was the precise moment in time in which the Bush administration drew clear boundaries dividing the nations of the world into one of two groups: either they support the United States in its global war on terror and are treated as friends and allies, or they oppose or remain silent, thereby siding with the terrorists.

Bush's speech has since proven to be pertinent for a number of reasons. It highlighted the administration's simplistic and stark binary foreign policy view that was central to what became known as the Bush Doctrine. It also revealed a number of key beliefs that have come to characterize what is commonly referred to as a neoconservative worldview. It was President Bush who delivered this speech to rapturous applause from a Congress that appeared as eager as the president to exact revenge on those responsible for the 9/11 terrorist attacks. The speech itself has proven testimony to the influence wielded by a group of neoconservative intellectuals in shaping US foreign policy in the first decade of the twenty-first century.[2] Together the Bush Administration and its neoconservative allies constructed a coherent worldview that attempted to account for why the 9/11 terrorist attacks on the United States occurred and the policies that needed to be adopted to prevent these kinds of attacks from happening again. What they devised was pretty simple: 'they hate us because we're free' and 'we must go on the offensive to spread democracy in the Middle East.'[3]

In this chapter I begin as I did in my treatment of the liberal tradition, by outlining a Weberian ideal type to help with deconstructing neoconservative intellectuals' representations of Wahhabism. Second, I characterize some of the ways neoconservatives represent Wahhabism. Third, drawing on Holton and Danziger's ideas about themata and generative metaphors, I go about making sense of these representations. This involves paying close attention to the central role religious themata, specifically those concerning the Jewish state of Israel and the coming of the savior, play in neoconservative thinking. Closely related to this is the important role played by the good versus evil themata. The two generative metaphors I identify as playing key roles in neoconservative representations are the Wahhabi Other as an animal and savage. But first a little more about the neoconservative movement and the kind of influence it has had on the US political process.

Introducing the Neoconservatives

The neoconservative intellectuals who wielded significant if not hegemonic influence on the making of US foreign policy by the Bush administration from 2001–08 belong to a movement in the United States originating in the 1960s. Its first-generation sponsors include prominent intellectuals like Samuel Huntington, Daniel Patrick Moynihan, Jeane Kirkpatrick, and Irving Kristol.[4] There has been a tendency among commentators and scholars to mistakenly pick out the controversial figure

Leo Strauss as the source of the neoconservative movement because many of the intellectuals believed to be involved were either students of Strauss, or claimed to be influenced by him.[5] While its roots are often traced back to the works of intellectuals in the 1960s, the term 'neo-conservative' itself was popularized early in the 1970s when Michael Harrington used it to describe the group of American intellectuals that included Kristol, who had moved away from the anti-Stalinist socialist left and embraced American conservatism.[6] The term then came to be used as a self-identifying label by Kristol, the godfather of the movement, in 1979, who described neoconservatism as a 'persuasion' and a particular way of thinking about the world and politics.[7] Expressing his distaste for the American liberal tradition, which he and many neoconservatives held responsible for what they perceived to be a cultural and moral breakdown in US society, Kristol famously declared a neoconservative to be a "liberal mugged by reality."[8]

The term neoconservatism again became extremely popular during the presidency of George W. Bush, with commentators often using it when referring to a group of intellectuals who were influential in the Bush administration, especially with regards to US foreign policy.[9] The Bush Doctrine, a term coined by prominent neoconservative intellectual Charles Krauthammer and which was the approach to foreign policy that promoted unilateral regime change and the spreading of democracy in the Middle East, is widely understood to be the quintessential expression of a neoconservative foreign policy.[10]

While the neoconservatives exerted major influence over US foreign policy during President Bush's time in the White House, the election of the Obama administration in 2008 and its governing until 2016 has seen a marked decrease in the movement's ability to influence US foreign policy. This is because for the most part neoconservatives do not enjoy as close a relationship with members of the Democratic Party as they do with the Republican Party. When the Democrats took office in 2008, many of the neoconservatives momentarily retreated to the vast and well-resourced network of right-wing think tanks primarily located in Washington, DC, where they have continued to work tirelessly while patiently awaiting the next election of the Republican Party.

The ability of think tanks to influence the policy- and decision-making processes, especially the network of neoconservative think tanks operating in and around Washington, DC, is perhaps best described by Muhammad Idrees in his book *The Road to Iraq: The Making of a Neoconservative War*.[11] Idrees explains how think tanks focus a lot of their efforts on members of the US Congress and their staffers, including scrutinizing their policy proposals, monitoring congressional proceedings, and inviting the members to seminars hosted by the organizations. They can even get their ideas across by placing staffers and interns in their offices. During elections think tanks will compete to provide advisors to candidates who if elected would be responsible for filling thousands of bureaucratic positions. The plethora of neoconservative think tanks, many of which are located near Capitol Hill and include the Washington Institute for Near East Policy, the Council on Foreign Relations (CFR), the American Enterprise Institute (AEI), the Heritage Foundation, and the Foundation for Defense of Democracies (FDD), tend to focus their efforts on the Departments of Defense, State, and Homeland Security. These organizations are well funded by some of the richest individuals in the United States and they allocate millions of dollars each year to public relations campaigns and to producing studies and reports that aim to influence US policy.[12]

Neoconservative think tanks have been very successful in getting their messages into the media with the AEI, Heritage, and the CFR making up three of the top five most-cited think tanks.[13] The Brookings Institute was recently ranked as the most-cited think tank, and while it is not a bona fide neoconservative organization, it has become more hospitable to the neoconservative persuasion since 9/11.[14] Many of its right-wing intellectuals have collaborated with neoconservatives and it has recently employed some prominent neoconservative intellectuals like Robert Kagan. What this means is that the US media (major US newspapers, television, and radio) have sought the 'expert' opinions of neoconservative intellectuals rather than seeking those of more centrist or leftist intellectuals.

In recent times the neoconservatives were extremely active in campaigning for the Republican members they believe would best represent their interests. Many in the movement sought to influence the outcome of the 2016 Republican Party's presidential primaries, where they strongly supported Texan senator Ted Cruz. The flagship neoconservative publication *The Weekly Standard* published articles describing Cruz as a "dynamic," "strong," and "extremely clever candidate," celebrating his victories in Republican state primary elections, and endorsing him as the next commander-in-chief. [15] At the same time it published articles describing his chief opponent, Donald Trump, as a "conspiracy theorist," "a serial nutter," and "unfit to lead," imploring Republican voters not to support a "buffoon and opportunist" prone to making "idiotic and racist comments."[16]

Well-known neoconservatives involved in the Cruz campaign included former director of the CIA James Woolsey, Elliot Abrams, who is a senior fellow at the Council on Foreign Relations and former advisor on Middle Eastern foreign policy to the Bush administration, and Frank Gaffney, who is the director of the Center for Security Policy. Neoconservatives mostly concern themselves with US foreign policy and it is therefore unsurprising that Woolsey, Abrams, and Gaffney were all part of Cruz's foreign policy team. Unfortunately for the neoconservatives, Trump won the Republican nomination and ultimately the US election and the neoconservatives appear not to have assumed the positions of influence they so eagerly sought. While they may not have direct access to US foreign policymaking at this point, they will continue to champion a policy that remains steadfast in its support for Israel, promotes a black and white view of the world, clearly categorizing groups and nations as either friends or enemies, and promotes spreading democracy abroad, particularly in the Middle East. These three beliefs have formed key components of the neoconservative worldview since 9/11. They also comprise my ideal type.

Toward an Ideal Type

I want to first look at the neoconservative belief in the global promotion of democracy. Inspiring and motivating this approach to foreign policy initiatives is the idea that a safe world is one comprised of democratic states.[17] According to neoconservative logic, a world with fewer autocracies means less anti-Americanism, which in turn means a reduced threat to US national security and US interests abroad.[18] Democracy promotion abroad is seen both as a normative prerogative and a pragmatic way of strengthening US security and advancing its geopolitical preeminence.[19] Neoconservatives tend to equate democracy with freedom, believing a democratic state to be the freest kind of state. To quote George W. Bush, "every step toward freedom in the world makes our country safer."[20] In his 2006 State of the Union address, Bush argued that ending global tyranny and replacing it with democracy was one of America's defining moral commitments.[21] Not only was this "the right thing to do" according to Bush, but it was also in the nation's best interests: "Democracies replace resentment with hope, respect the rights of their citizens and their neighbors, and join the fight against terror."[22]

Closely related to this is the idea that nation-states are either friends or enemies, invoking what John Mearshimer has described as a black hats–white hats view of the world.[23] President Bush famously expressed this idea when declaring, "Either you are with us, or you are with the terrorists."[24] Neoconservatives typically consider democratic nations as holders of benign motives and as having a natural inclination to act peacefully toward other states, especially the United States. The popular idea among neoconservatives is that democratic states only act aggressively when provoked by the black hats.[25] This belief can be understood as an expression of democratic peace theory, which holds that democratic states rarely engage in conflict with other democratic states. This is why neoconservatives promote the global spread of democracy, because they believe it helps transform enemies into friends or black hats into white hats. One-time prominent neoconservative intellectual Francis Fukuyama describes this global democratizing project of turning black hats into white hats as the end of history.[26] A motivating idea that we will explore in greater detail is that of good eventually emerging triumphant over evil.

As I will soon show, neoconservatives are unequivocal in their understanding and representation of Saudi Arabia, the home of Wahhabism, as a black hat that must embrace democratic freedoms in order to become a white hat. They understand Wahhabism as a religion responsible for inspiring and motivating modern Islamic terrorism and violence and the Saudi kingdom as its chief sponsor. If we are to believe the rhetoric emanating from the neoconservative movement since 9/11 then any future influence they have on US foreign policy will no doubt result in the United States adopting a much harsher stance toward the Saudi kingdom.

An unwavering support for Israel is the third key feature of my ideal type, which plays a major role in influencing how neoconservative intellectuals represent Wahhabism, Saudi Arabia, and the ongoing conflict between Israel and Palestine. So strong is their support for Israel that outside observers have described the neoconservative movement as a uniquely Jewish phenomenon. Neoconservative critic Jacob Heilbrunn writes, “Indeed, as much as they may deny it, neoconservatism is in a decisive respect a Jewish phenomenon, reflecting a subset of Jewish concerns.”[27] In attempting to account for this pro-Israeli posture, many of those studying the movement have highlighted the integral role pro-Israeli Jewish-American intellectuals have played in shaping the movement. Many of these Jewish-American neoconservatives have been influenced by their experiences of persistent anti-Jewish discrimination and extremely traumatizing events like the Holocaust.[28]

This steadfast commitment to the state of Israel has often involved promoting a US foreign policy prioritizing the aims and goals of the Jewish state ahead of those of the United States. These policies have also tended to align with those promoted by right-wing and Zionist Israeli political parties and commentators whose ideas rest on claims to Biblical authority.[29] So strong is the neoconservative support for Israel that there has also been a tendency to defend what many understand as the indefensible. For example, while many criticize Israel’s ongoing occupation of Gaza and the West Bank, which has resulted in humanitarian crises in these areas, neoconservatives like Gaffney have supported Israel’s actions, arguing that withdrawing its forces would result in the creation of a terrorist state he terms “Palestan.”[30] It should however be noted that not all neoconservatives are Jewish and identifying as Jewish does not necessarily entail unconditional support for policies adopted by the state of Israel.

Many neoconservatives have for a long time been riled by what they understand to be a constant spewing of anti-Israel and anti-Jewish propaganda coming from within Saudi Arabia. They perceive the state-sanctioned Wahhabism to be fundamentally hostile to Judaism and have felt especially aggrieved in recent times by what they perceive as anti-Jewish and anti-Israeli views promoted in Saudi school texts. Often claiming they are worried by the intergenerational views held by Saudi Arabians, neoconservative intellectuals and neoconservative publications and organizations have published and circulated documents blaming the Saudi school system for not recognizing the state of Israel, and for describing Jews as "apes" and "wicked."[31] Some have taken aim at Saudi-sponsored schools in the United States, which they claim are key parts of the Wahhabi Saudi plan of "destroying the US from within."[32] They have also dismissed claims that Saudi Arabia has since 9/11 taken steps to remove intolerant views from its curriculum.[33]

Neoconservatives have also resented Saudi Arabia's vocal support for Palestinians in the context of Israeli-Arab disputes and its efforts at brokering peace deals between Israel and Palestine. Saudi authorities lambasted "Israeli inhuman aggression" during its summer 2014 Gaza war with Hamas, pledging their support "to the Palestinian brothers in the West Bank and Gaza Strip to alleviate the difficult conditions in which they live because of the Israeli aggression and terrorism."[34] The kingdom's ongoing efforts to help broker peace in the region include the peace initiative put forward under the auspices of the Arab League in 2002, calling for the normalization of Arab relations with Israel if it were to withdraw fully from the territories it occupied in 1967, for the establishment of a Palestinian state with a capital in East Jerusalem, and for the achievement of a just solution to the Palestinian refugee problem in accordance with the UN General Assembly Resolution 194.[35] Neoconservatives claim this kind of peace deal would surely endanger the Jewish state.[36]

Despite some recent commentary suggesting the Saudi kingdom is better placed than the United States to broker a peace deal, given its relatively friendly relations with both Hamas and the Palestinian Authority (which along with Israel are the three political factions that must commit to ending hostilities in order for a peace deal to be somewhat effective), the neoconservatives remain adamantly opposed to any Saudi Arabian involvement.[37] Neoconservatives oppose any kind of peace deal that formally recognizes a Palestinian state as they believe Israel has a divine right to the land in question because God had promised it to the Jews. These are key religious themata I explore in greater detail later in the chapter.

Now that we have a basic understanding of the movement and the ideal type I am drawing on, I want to focus on some of the popular representations of Wahhabism provided by neoconservative intellectuals in the post–9/11 period characterized by a heightened anxiety about radical Islam and take a closer look at some of the different rhetorical techniques they have deployed when attempting to persuade their audiences. As we will see, the ways in which neoconservatives have represented Wahhabism have greatly contributed to this anxiety felt by many people, particularly those living in the West, toward the Muslim Other.

The Wahhabi Is a Savage

There has been an orchestrated effort by neoconservative intellectuals to represent adherents of Wahhabism as less-evolved, inferior human beings or, put another way, as savages. Neoconservatives representing adherents of Wahhabism in this way typically hold the Judeo-Christian Westerner to be the ideal kind of human living in the ideal society. Often neoconservatives will combine these representations of the Wahhabi Other with representations of groups and states that they perceive as adhering to Wahhabism as enemies of the United States, Israel, and the Western democratic world. They are drawing Imagined communities to which Israel, the United States, and the West belong and the Wahhabi Other does not. They are also creating Imagined geographies in which Islamic states adhering to Wahhabism are represented as backward, antimodern, violent, and brutish. The examples I want to abstract for closer analysis are provided by prominent neoconservative intellectuals Bret Stephens, David Pryce-Jones, and Reuel Marc Gerecht. These representations appear in the neoconservative publication *The Weekly Standard* and in the popular US mainstream newspaper the *Wall Street Journal*.

Stephens, like Dore Gold, is keen to represent Wahhabism as a global threat.[38] Also like Gold, he is keen to represent Saudi Arabia as the chief promoter of this radical version of Islam and therefore as the source of modern Islamic terrorism. Providing an interpretation of the political situation in Indonesia, Stephens claims that Saudi-sponsored Wahhabism has influenced the radical Islamist group Front for the Defense of Islam.

Stephens represents this group as threatening US interests, specifically its stated aim of promoting democracy abroad. Stephens makes use of a number of rhetorical techniques when dehumanizing the Wahhabi Other. He uses analogies aimed at representing members of this group as less-evolved humans and savages, metaphorical expressions representing Saudi-sponsored Wahhabism as a disease, and describes brutish acts of violence one typically associates with the savage and which Cerulo claims evoke condemnation on the part of the reader. Stephens writes:

> The headquarters of the *Front for the Defense of Islam* is reached by a narrow alley just off a one-lane street in a residential neighbourhood near downtown Jakarta. But step inside the carpeted reception area, decorated by a mural of a *desert mosque* and partially open to the sky, and it's as if you've arrived in a *Bedouin kingdom*.
>
> Your host is Habib Mohammad Rizieq Shihab, 41. He is dressed entirely in white, a religious conceit far from typical of most Indonesian ulama, or experts in Islamic theology. To the question, "Where are you from?" Mr. Rizieq is quick to explain that he is descended from the Quraishi *tribe*, from what is now Yemen. Just how he knows this isn't clear, but it's the symbolism that counts: The Prophet Mohammad was a Quraishi, and the *tribe* is entrusted with the responsibility for protecting God's House, the Qe'eba, in Mecca. Mr. Rizieq, in fact, is a native of Jakarta. . . .
>
> The source of Mr. Rizieq's views—and of the Islamic radicalism that increasingly *infects* this country—becomes a little clearer as he tells his life story. A poor but talented student, he won a full scholarship to study at King Saud University in Riyadh. He says he was "not influenced by Wahhabism," which he found excessively literal in its readings of the Qur'an and Islamic law. As evidence of his moderation, he observes that in his future Shariah state, authorities would not "*cut off people's hands for stealing right away. First, you have to raise people up*."
>
> Still, Saudi attitudes plainly rubbed off on Mr. Rizieq.[39] [emphasis added]

Pertinent are the phrases "Bedouin kingdom" and "tribe," both of which evoke the idea of the noble savage. Stephens repeatedly uses the word "tribe," which when viewed historically or developmentally is typically understood as a social group existing prior to the development of or existing outside of the modern nation-state. The nation-state is a nineteenth-century European creation that accompanied a change in views with regards to our understanding of indigenous peoples.[40] Tribes are therefore generally understood as reflecting a particular way of life predating the modern era.

In addition to having links with colonialism, the term also has racial implications, often used to favor one ethnic group based on racial superiority. The implication is the 'tribe' to which Stephens refers exists outside the modern world inhabited by the democratic West. The suggestion is that the version of radical Islam the leader of this group subscribes to, which has been influenced by his experience in Saudi Arabia living according to Wahhabism, is a religion for the backward and the regressive. Furthermore, the areas in which this religion flourishes are in need of democratic advancements in order to help the inhabitants become more enlightened human beings living in more enlightened societies.

These ideas align with Stephens's reference to a "Bedouin kingdom" when describing the residence of the Front for the Defense of Islam. The term 'Bedouin' comes from the Arabic term *badw* (singular) or *badawiyyun/badawiyyin* (plural) and is typically used when referring to a desert-dwelling Arabian ethnic group divided into 'tribes.' The Bedouin are originally from a region in the Arabian Peninsula incorporating modern Saudi Arabia. It is here we begin to see Stephens's link between the Wahhabism of Saudi Arabia and the radical Islam he believes has "infected" Indonesia like a disease does a host. Stephens identifies Saudi Arabia as an enemy of the United States, blaming it for its global propagation of Wahhabism, which has now spread around the world. Stephens wants his audience to understand Saudi Arabia as the source of the modern radical Islamist threat. Considering the impact this would have on US foreign policy, any antiterror or prodemocratic efforts and policies must focus on Saudi Arabia: we have to treat the source of the disease to stop the infection.

Also worth abstracting for closer analysis is Stephens's claim that in Mr. Rizieq's future sharia state, authorities would not "cut off people's hands for stealing right away. First, you have to raise people up." Karen Cerulo, in *Deciphering Violence: The Cognitive Structure of Right and Wrong*, makes important points worth considering. First, regarding the nature of the violent act, Cerulo states that its specific characteristics have the ability to influence audience perception. Physical violence as opposed to nonphysical violence is far more likely to be perceived as deviant.[41] Additionally, audience perception is greatly influenced by the magnitude of force, with excessive force seen as the "hallmark of deviant violence."[42] Second, Cerulo notes the importance regarding the consequences of the violent act. Violence resulting in serious consequences is likely to be judged by audiences as deviant, whereas violence leaving no visible injury tends to be seen as more normal.[43]

Stephens here is writing about a man who is the leader of the radical Islamist Indonesian group and who has been influenced by his time in Saudi Arabia, where he was exposed to Wahhabism. While in Saudi Arabia they 'cut off people's hands,' this man wants to go a step further and have people 'raised up' before this forced amputation process. This is physical violence using excessive force that leaves visible injury, considering that theft is typically viewed as a misdemeanor by Western audiences. Stephens wants his audience to understand this man as a savage with a brutish appetite for violence and Wahhabism as a practice promoted by Saudi Arabia as a kind of gateway drug: spreading Saudi attitudes and practices to people around the world will inspire more violent acts. Gustav Jahoda's historical catalogue highlights the tendency in Western thought to think of these racial, ethnic, and religious Others as barbarians lacking in culture, self-restraint, moral sensibility, and cognitive capacity.[44] These cultural, moral, and cognitive deficiencies are usually accompanied by excessive violence, and the savage has often been represented as having a brutish appetite for violence.[45] This brutish appetite for violence Jahoda identifies in historical Western imperial and colonial representations resonates with Stephens's description of this radical Islamist leader influenced by "Saudi attitudes."

Gerecht is another neoconservative keen to represent the Wahhabi Other as a savage with a brutish appetite for violence. Gerecht writes:

> There's not a soul in Washington or New York or London who would defend the sybaritic Saudi royals and their *head-and-hand-chopping* Wahhabi clergy were it not for the cash. Without oil, Saudis would have the same appeal as the Afghan Taliban.[46] [emphasis added]

Gerecht's use of the phrase "head-and-hand-chopping" when describing the actions of the "Wahhabi clergy" highlights the physical and brutal nature of a society ordered according to Wahhabi religious doctrine. Again, Western audiences would associate such brutal acts of violence with earlier periods in Western civilization, implying that the West, unlike Saudi Arabia, has progressed beyond this uncivilized behavior. According to Gerecht, Wahhabism as practiced by the "Wahhabi clergy" is responsible for inspiring and motivating these unjustified and deviant violent acts. Gerecht's representation also invites his readers to ask questions like, "if the Wahhabi clergy is able to act in this way against its own people, what are they willing to do to non-believers?"

These acts of physical violence for crimes resonate with some of the reports issued by Western human rights organizations.[47] What is of interest however is the way neoconservatives stress the motivating role Wahhabism plays in enforcing this Saudi law. Neoconservatives assume, and they want their readers to do the same, that this punishment is a product of Wahhabism and not a cultural practice or a tactic employed by a ruling class to maintain its position of authority. Neoconservatives do not pose these kinds of questions because they do not resonate with their political aims and goals. This is similar to the representations of the Israeli–Palestinian conflict provided by Dore Gold that we explored earlier: as an ardent supporter of Israel who believes in its divine right to the land in question, Gold does not even consider the possibility that pro-Palestinian groups are motivated by political goals such as self-determination. Instead he represents the conflict as religiously motivated. These representations become particularly important when considering the implication they have for the policy and the decision-making processes. If these issues are framed and viewed as religious and not cultural or political in nature, then what kinds of opinions are likely going to be formed about these situations?

Lastly, I want to take a closer look at the article "The Saudi Revolution," written by David Pryce-Jones for the *Wall Street Journal*. Written a couple years after the 9/11 terrorist attacks, Pryce-Jones is keen to advance the Bush administration's stated goal of global democracy promotion. He represents Saudi Arabia as a black hat and a major obstacle: "The Arab world is having to come to terms with the U.S. campaign in Iraq, and President Bush's insistence on democracy and freedom for everyone. Everyone, Mr. Bush made clear, includes Saudi Arabia."[48] Pryce-Jones blames Saudi Arabia's adherence to Wahhabism for its failure to accept democratic changes and for making the Saudi regime not only "a danger to itself" but also to "the rest of the world."[49] A key part of his representing Wahhabi Saudi Arabia as an enemy of the United States involves representing its people as savages and Wahhabism as a religion for backward people.

> There [Saudi Arabia], 5,000 or more princes control all power and resources, sharing out ministries and governorships and oil revenues as they see fit. Their idea of democracy is to appoint an advisory council and religious leaders carefully vetted to provide a facade of legitimacy.
>
> *Immemorial tribal custom* and the local Wahhabi brand of Islam are defended and perpetuated to create the impression that this is *the natural order of things*. The Shiite minority forms about 20% of the population, but on the grounds that they are not Wahhabis they are arrested without trial, tortured and often disappear. Rights and the rule of law are only what the ruling family says they are. The Saudi family of course has a large and privileged security and police apparatus at its service. No blueprint exists in any of the textbooks for successfully *modernizing* a society like this one.[50] [emphasis added]

Pertinent is Pryce-Jones's use of the phrase "immemorial tribal custom" when coupling it with the "local Wahhabi brand of Islam" to describe the situation in Saudi society. The word 'immemorial' means 'originating in the distant past or very old,' and it comes from the French term *immémorial* meaning 'old beyond memory.' By associating this with Wahhabism

Jones wants his readers to see Saudi society as backward, regressive, and antimodern.

Pryce-Jones reinforces this idea by likening the current internal instability in Wahhabi Saudi Arabia to the situation in eighteenth-century France. Jones goes on to say:

> "Is it a revolt?" Louis XVI asked in 1789. "No, sire, it is a revolution," answered one of his courtiers. In Saudi Arabia the ruling family has long been presiding over a denial of reality to match that of the Bourbon monarchy. The bombing this weekend in Riyadh, which killed 17 people and wounded over 100, suggests that the thousands of princes who control the wealth of that country have trouble in store.[51]

Here Pryce-Jones is drawing parallels between the current political situation in Saudi Arabia and the Bourbon monarchy in eighteenth-century France. The abolition of the French monarchy during the French revolution ushered in the modern Western era defined by reason and science. The implication is that Wahhabi Saudi Arabia is centuries behind the West in terms of progress and it is assumed that it will eventually succumb to progress, experience its Enlightenment, and shun Wahhabism in favor of valuing science and reason. Pryce-Jones is a well-known neoconservative and his likening of the situation in Wahhabi Saudi Arabia to that of pre-Enlightenment France is a technique also used by liberal intellectuals. While there are core distinguishable beliefs defining the two intellectual traditions, they can at times deploy similar rhetorical devices. I now want to take a closer look at another dominant representation of Wahhabism provided by neoconservative intellectuals post–9/11.

An Unwavering Support for Israel: Wahhabism and Saudi Arabia as Enemies of the Jewish State

Neoconservatives are steadfast and unconditional in their support for the state of Israel. This belief motivates and inspires many neoconservatives to criticize any individual, group, movement, or state they perceive as providing some kind of threat to Israeli interests. This extreme sensitivity, as

Susan George points out in her book *Hijacking America: How the Religious and Secular Right Changed What Americans Think*, often leads neoconservatives to label critics of Israel's actions, including Palestinians or anyone questioning American support for Israel, as "anti-Semites" and "self-hating Jews," if they happen to be Jewish.[52] George makes the point that the neoconservative response combined with that of the larger pro-Israeli lobby in the United States has made it nearly impossible for US politicians to have a rational discussion about Middle Eastern policy and the Israeli–Palestinian conflict. George claims "such extreme reactions" by neoconservatives are linked to their perception that Israel is the only democratic outpost in the Middle East.[53] This is certainly an important belief worth considering and we must be careful of offering deterministic explanations reducing the neoconservative *Weltanschauung* to only a theological dogma.

However, what George and many other scholars have failed to see and which my analysis helps reveal is the key role religious themata play in neoconservative thinking, particularly when it comes to their unwavering support for Israel. Wahhabism has certainly received a bad rap in the United States post–9/11 and neoconservatives have used representations of this phenomenon as responsible for inspiring and motivating modern Islamic terrorism in their ongoing public relations campaign against pro-Palestinian groups and organizations. More specifically, many neoconservatives use representations of Wahhabism to help heighten the threat posed by these different groups, thereby helping to contribute to the moral panic currently gripping much of the (Western) world. Underscoring these representations is the desire to further the aims and goals of the modern Israeli state, including helping to legitimize Israel's action in the Occupied Territories.

The first example which I want to take a closer look at involves prominent neoconservative intellectuals using representations of Wahhabism to help discredit the two-state peace initiatives proposed and endorsed by Saudi leaders. Frank Gaffney is among those making this link, using his position as a writer for the *Washington Times* to argue that an independent Palestinian state free from Israeli control should not be created on the grounds that it would pose a security threat to Israel.[54] He criticizes

Saudi Arabia's interference and proposed peace initiatives, representing the kingdom as a black hat that supports Islamic terrorism:

> [T]hanks to Saudi Arabia, the latest effort to kill Americans with sophisticated bombs failed. Thanks to Saudi Arabia, we are certain to be subjected to more such attacks in the future. . . . [It is a] double game we confront from a kingdom that, on the one hand, is routinely characterized by American officials as a reliable US ally. . . . On the other hand, it is also the wellspring of Shariah, the supremacist totalitarian doctrine. . . .[55]

Citing another report as supporting evidence, Gaffney goes on to say:

> "The puritanical strain of Islam fostered by the state, sometimes called Wahhabism, was breeding extremists who were willing to kill even Muslims for their cause. Now . . . Saudi Arabia's problem . . . has become the world's problem."[56]

Gaffney also states, "Their contribution to instability in the Middle East is discounted, and their "peace plan" for ending the Israeli–Palestinian conflict on terms that assuredly would endanger the Jewish state is enthusiastically embraced."[57] Gaffney makes a similar argument in his article "Undesirable Influence," also published in the *Washington Times* and circulated by the neoconservative think tank Center for Security Policy where he is president.[58] Unable to fathom why President Bush would consider proposing a peace plan for the Israeli–Palestinian conflict, Gaffney concludes that he must have been manipulated by what he calls the Wahhabi lobby operating in Washington.[59] The creating of a Palestinian state, Gaffney argues, is in the best interests of this powerful and radical lobby and certainly not in the best interests of US and Israel. Gaffney writes:

> The question occurs: Could the President's recent decision to pursue a "road map" for Mideast peace that is, in important respects (notably with respect to the need for a new Palestinian leadership "untainted

> by terror," the dismantling of Palestinian terrorist infrastructure and an end to Palestinian incitement as preconditions to U.S. recognition of a state of Palestine) at odds with the "vision" he enunciated last June also be a product of the undesirable influence of the *Wahhabi Lobby*? The far-reaching changes were reportedly the subject of major internal fights between top administration officials.[60] [emphasis added]

Gaffney wants to discredit the peace process by linking this Wahhabi lobby to pro-Palestinian enemy terrorist organizations like Hamas, Hezbollah, and Islamic Jihad. Again it is important to be aware of Gaffney's political prejudice: like Dore Gold, Gonzalez-Perez, and all neoconservatives and in contrast to authors like Khaled Hroub and Zaki Chehab, Gaffney categorizes these groups as terrorists and not as primarily anticolonial and anti-imperialist groups. Gaffney writes:

> Even as President Bush stresses his opposition to such terrorist organizations as Hamas, Hezbollah and Islamic Jihad, their advocates and/or apologists in this country with ties to Saudi Arabia's radical Wahhabi sect (dubbed the "*Wahhabi Lobby*") are routinely turned to when the administration seeks to reach out to Muslims. Worse yet, such "outreach" usually excludes those representing the majority of Muslims who are not Islamist sympathizers. That is undesirable influence.[61] [emphasis added]

Pertinent is Gaffney's repeated use of the neologism "Wahhabi lobby," which aims at convincing readers that there is a Wahhabi movement in the United States and that it is coordinated, influential, and taking its cues from Saudi Arabia. Motivated and inspired by his unwavering support for Israel, Gaffney's use of this neologism can be understood as a technique aimed at deflecting attention from the well-known pro-Israeli lobby currently exerting huge influence in the United States and which has at times been a focus of criticism.[62] In categorizing and linking pro-Palestinian groups Hamas, Hezbollah, and Islamic Jihad to the Wahhabi lobby, neoconservatives like Gaffney are representing the Israeli–Palestinian conflict as a part of the wider global war on terror. This challenges the competing narrative that says Palestinians are primarily engaged in a struggle for self-determination against an Israeli colonizing force.

A third article worth considering, also written by Frank Gaffney, is titled "Seeing the threat for what it is," published by the *Washington Times*.[63] It should now become clear that Gaffney has certainly been at the forefront of this neoconservative campaign linking representations of Wahhabism with the Israeli–Palestinian conflict, and that this, on Gaffney's part in particular, has been a sustained effort. The three articles I have abstracted for closer analysis were published in 2003, 2006, and 2010. In this article, Gaffney identifies "Islamofascism" as the black hat posing a global threat to the United States and Israel. This umbrella term includes Osama Bin Laden's ideology and Saudi Arabia's Wahhabism, and Gaffney represents a contest among the two for new believers:

> [T]he Saudis—the world's most aggressive and generous champions of Islamofascism—are trying to ensure their young men adhere to the Wahhabi strain of this ideology, rather than bin Laden's. The only perceptible difference between the two is that the former holds that it is Allah's will to kill non-Islamist Muslims and non-Muslims outside the Kingdom; the latter includes among his target list Saudi royals who have adopted Western ways and mores.[64]

Gaffney goes on to criticize then Israeli Prime Minister Ehud Olmert's proposed withdrawal of Israeli forces from the West Bank as a "retreat," arguing that Israel's withdrawal in Gaza has allowed "Islamofascist entities" to move in, and any future withdrawal of Israeli forces from the West Bank would result in the creating of a terrorist state—"call it Palestan."[65] For Gaffney the world is clearly divided between the black hat Islamofascists, which includes those who are a part of the Saudi-funded Wahhabi movement, pro-Palestinian organizations, and Bin Laden's followers, and the white hat 'free world,' which includes the United States and Israel. Gaffney cannot however understand why others cannot see the world in this binary:

> So why do ostensibly friendly governments not recognize the threat posed by *Islamofascism* for what it is: a viral ideology that threatens

> non-Islamist Muslims as much as the rest of us, one that cannot be appeased and must be rooted out and destroyed?[66] [emphasis added]

What I am interested in is Gaffney's repeated use of the neologisms "Islamofascism" and "Islamofascist" when describing the threats to the free world. These terms work by analogizing the ideological characteristics of radical Islamist groups with a range of twentieth-century European fascist movements. In using these terms, Gaffney wants his audience to think of adherents of Wahhabism, followers of Bin Laden, and pro-Palestinian groups as terrorists that are very similar in their beliefs and actions to popular past European fascist movements, which are just as hostile to modernity, nostalgic for past empires, obsessed with humiliating their enemies, and vehemently anti-Jewish.[67] Many nations in the West joined forces to help defeat the threat posed by fascist regimes in the twentieth century and Gaffney now wants the same thing to happen with regards to the threat posed by these radical Islamists. Gaffney is creating both an Imagined community to which Israel and the United States belong, called the free world, and an Imagined geography in the Palestinian Territories that is lawless, crime-ridden, and needing Western intervention. Gaffney's representation again helps to feed into the wider neoconservative narrative that the Israeli–Palestinian conflict is a microcosm of the wider global war on terror and not, as many have argued, a struggle between colonizers and the colonized.

Gaffney is not the only neoconservative whose representations of Wahhabism are in part motivated and inspired by a strong support for Israel. Two more articles I want to abstract for closer analysis are written by Clifford May and Michael Ledeen and have appeared online, in popular US newspapers, and have been circulated by neoconservative think tanks. I have chosen these articles to help demonstrate some of the other popular rhetorical techniques neoconservatives make use of when persuading their audiences of the threat posed by Wahhabism.

May's professional positions include working for the Foundation for Defense of Democracies (FDD), the foreign policy interest group the Committee on the Present Danger, and as a panelist for Christians United for Israel. May was also a former board member of the Republican

Jewish Coalition. Michael Ledeen has worked for the neoconservative think tank the American Enterprise Institute and now also works for the FDD. A former consultant to the US National Security Council, the US Department of State, and the US Department of Defense, it was also revealed in e-mails dumped online by Wikileaks that Ledeen was described by Hillary Clinton's aid Sidney Blumenthal as "a channel for Israeli Intel[ligence]."[68]

In his article, "No Peace While World War Rages," which appears in *Moment Magazine*, May uses representations of Wahhabism as responsible for inspiring and motivating Islamic terrorism to help frame the Palestinians as the aggressors in their conflict with Israel.[69] May claims the United States, Israel, and the West/the white hats are fighting a world war against the black hat radical Islamists, which includes terrorists inspired by Wahhabism and pro-Palestinian groups Hamas and Hezbollah. May frames the Palestinian-Israel conflict as a microcosm of this world war initiated by the black hats, who are inspired by radical Islamist ideologies like Wahhabism:

> Israel's American supporters spend a lot of energy trying to convince people that Israelis want peace, are working for peace and are prepared to sacrifice for peace. All that's true but it misses this point: Militant jihadis are waging a war against the "*infidel*" West. They see Israel as a frontline state. There is no way they will permit a separate peace for Israel. . . .
>
> Today, we confront ideologies that are similarly violent and supremacist—e.g. Khomeinism, bin Ladenism, Wahhabism—and no less intent on the conquest and destruction of free nations. Too many Americans do not grasp this and are not prepared for the tough measures necessary to limit, contain and eventually defeat these enemies. . . .
>
> The beliefs and goals of Al Qaeda, the Taliban, Iran's mullahs, Hezbollah, Hamas and a long list of other Islamist groups are not identical, but much more unites them than divides them. All embrace a militant understanding of Islam. All justify their aggression and their terrorism *theologically*. All believe that a final, decisive and *divinely ordained jihad-holy war* is now under way.[70] [emphasis added]

Key are the rhetorical techniques May uses when representing the religious factors motivating the black hats' desire to destroy the free world, US, and Israel. First, May uses the term "infidel," which is commonly used in Islam when describing those with no religious beliefs or who reject the central tenets of one's own religion. Second, he claims the enemy, including pro-Palestinian groups Hamas and Hezbollah, justify their violence "theologically" and believe they are currently taking part in a "divinely ordained jihad-holy war."

What May is doing here is assigning these perpetrators of violence a particular psychological profile in which their intentions become especially salient. Cerulo's framework for analysis would deem this violence motivated by 'instrumental goals' and a 'clear presence of intention.' The instrumental goals are obvious as the enemies are motivated by clear religious aims. Cerulo notes that violence motivated by instrumental goals is generally perceived by the audience as deviant in kind.[71] This is not violence for the greater good; this is violence perpetrated by the Other in the name of a religion most Western readers do not personally identify with. Furthermore, the 'clear presence of intention' is the enemies' desire to win this religious war for which they will receive religious rewards. Again readers are likely to condemn these acts of violence given they do not identify with the religious cause.

May uses the same technique later in the article when providing a more detailed description of the religious beliefs motivating and inspiring the radical Islamist enemy.

> On one side is the dar al-Islam, literally the "realm of submission," the parts of the world governed by Sharia, Islamic law as they [the Militant Jihadis] interpret it. On the other side is the dar al-Harb, literally "the realm of war," those countries ruled by Christians, Jews, Hindus and moderate Muslims who oppose them and therefore are "enemies of God."[72]

Again we have a neoconservative intellectual keen to tell readers who is in the free world and who are its enemies. These enemies, which include followers of Wahhabism as well as pro-Palestinian groups, want to destroy

Israel, the United States, and the wider Western world because it is their religious duty.

We see the same division of the world into black and white hats in Ledeen's article, "The Wider War," published in the *Wall Street Journal* and by the neoconservative think tank the American Enterprise Institute.[73] Ledeen advocates for a US-led war on multiple fronts, claiming fighting one at a time "isn't good enough, because it gives our enemies the luxury of attacking us where, when and how they choose."[74] He identifies four states as the primary enemies given their support for terrorists: "Iraq, Iran, Syria and Saudi Arabia," blaming the Saudi Kingdom for "provid[ing] money for terrorist groups and support[ing] a global network of radical Wahhabi mosques and schools that indoctrinate young Muslims in the ways of jihad."[75] Stopping Saudi Arabia would in turn help quell the threat facing Israel. Ledeen writes:

> [T]he many Palestinian terrorist organizations that keep their offices in Damascus would find it very difficult to relocate and maintain their effectiveness. All would be weakened by the loss of Saudi funding, and moderate Muslims everywhere, including in the U.S., would breathe a sigh of relief if the Wahhabi mosques were closed.
>
> It [this counter-terrorism approach] doesn't require more boots on the ground or bombing raids. It requires a traditional American policy: support for democratic revolution against our tyrannical enemies.[76]

Ledeen goes on to say:

> A free Iran would deliver a devastating global blow to the terrorists, and would no doubt change the calculus—and perhaps the regime—of Syria. Under those happy circumstances, we might muster the will to insist that the Saudis shut down the Wahhabi schools and mosques, which constitute an *assembly line* of fanatics all over the world.[77] [emphasis added]

Pertinent is Ledeen's use of the metaphorical expression "assembly line of fanatics" when describing the relation between "Wahhabi schools and mosques" and modern Islamic terrorism. This is an interesting way of characterizing the Wahhabi Other. It dehumanizes the enemy in a mechanical rather than animalistic way. Neoconservatives have traditionally relied upon animalistic metaphors when representing the Wahhabi Other as inhuman. An 'assembly line' is a series of workers and machines in a factory dedicated to making items that are generally identical in nature. In using this metaphorical expression, Ledeen encourages his audience to think of "Wahhabi schools and mosques" as factories dedicated to producing a very specific product, the "Wahhabi fanatic." In addition to helping dehumanize the Wahhabi enemy, this also persuades the reader to ignore the possibility there may be other factors, such as Israel's ongoing occupation of Palestine, which may be responsible for radicalizing the Islamist enemy.

Coupled with the animalistic metaphors used by other neoconservative intellectuals, we can understand Ledeen's representation as a part of the wider effort by neoconservatives to dehumanize the Wahhabi enemy. This has the potential effect of making any deaths taking place in the context of military or security operations more palatable, as it is less distressing to kill animals or destroy machines than it is to harm people. Now that we have an understanding of how some neoconservatives strategically use representations of Wahhabism when representing the threat posed to Israel and the wider free world, I want to extend my analysis by turning to the role played by certain themata and generative metaphors.

Key Themata: The Holy Land and Welcoming the Savior

Neoconservative intellectuals are unwavering in their support for Israel. What has received scant attention to date is the integral role key religious themata have played in underpinning, inspiring, and motivating neoconservatives' representations of Wahhabism. We get a glimpse of this when abstracting and deconstructing Gerecht's use of the metaphorical expression, "There is scant evidence to suggest that the Wahhabi establishment has changed its spots," when arguing that this Saudi institution continues to promote radical Islam.[78] On first appearances, many readers may think this comes from the common saying, 'a leopard cannot change its spots.' However, if we dig a little a deeper we find that this phrase actually comes from the Book of Jeremiah in the Hebrew and Christian Bibles. We begin to see that perhaps there is a religious link to how Gerecht is making sense of the social world in general and Wahhabism in particular. The important point is that there are certain religious themata that are acting at a conscious or subconscious level as motivating aids for neoconservatives and which have tended to be "suppressed or disappear from view," as Holton points out; this is the hallmark of themata.[79]

There are two key themata that are sustaining the ways in which neoconservatives make sense of the Israeli–Palestinian conflict and the role played by Wahhabism. One is Israel's 'theological right,' understood as a God-given covenant conferring on the Jewish people certain territory, conventionally referred to as the Holy Land. The second is that the state of Israel must have control of this land so as to welcome the coming of the savior.

The themata of the covenant has its roots in the Bible, particularly the Book of Genesis. There we find texts supporting the idea that God entered into a covenant to give certain lands to the people of Abraham. The relevant text says:

> And I will establish My covenant between Me and you and your descendants after you throughout their generations for an everlasting covenant, to be God to you and to your descendants after you. And I will give to you and to your descendants after you, the land of your sojourning, all the land of Canaan, for an everlasting possession; and I will be their God. (Genesis 17:7)

Biblical text also records a specific agreement between Abraham and God:

> Then God said, "Yes, but your wife Sarah will bear you a son, and you will call him Isaac. I will establish my covenant with him as an everlasting covenant for his descendants after him." (Genesis 17:9)

The book of Genesis is the first Book of the Pentateuch of the Christian Old Testament. A basic and typical understanding of the narrative in Genesis is that God first created the world and made the first man (Adam) his regent. That man disobeyed God and was ejected from the Garden of Eden. Later, God expressed his displeasure at the way his people were behaving and punished them by flooding the world, saving only Noah and his family. The new human order created in the wake of the flood proved equally corrupt. This time God decided not to destroy the world but instead gave one man the responsibility of securing a righteous order. That man was Abraham, and it is his story and relationship with God, centering especially on the covenant, that has had major implications for many believers in the world, including many intellectuals who are part of the neoconservative movement.

The conventional interpretation of this religious text, which is taken as expressing a literal truth by many Jews and Christians, is that God promised the land that is now modern Israel, including what is now the Palestinian territories, to the offspring of Abraham's son, Isaac. Isaac was born to Abraham's first wife Sarah and it is through them that Jews trace their lineage. Jews typically refer to Abraham as *Avraham Avinu*, which roughly translates to 'our father Abraham.' Understanding the history and future of humankind in this way has major implications for the modern conflict between Israel and Palestine. For example, according to this biblical interpretation, the land acquired by Israel in the 1967 war, which biblically is referred to as Judea and Samaria, is not seen as Palestinian land but rather Israel's birthright as authorized by God. This is why many neoconservatives will use these biblical terms when referring to this land.[80] This themata helps us to understand why many neoconservatives, including those whose works are deconstructed in this book, oppose Israel's withdrawal from these areas. To them this is land God gave to his people.

A closely related religious themata influencing neoconservatives in their thinking involves a standard Judaic interpretation of the end of times. This holds that Israel must be in possession of the Promised Land, especially Jerusalem, which contains Judaism's holiest site, the Temple Mount, so as to successfully welcome the messiah, thereby fulfilling Biblical prophecy. Jeremiah 46:27–28 in the Hebrew Bible is often understood by believers as God promising Israel to the Jews and protecting and ensuring their safe return to the land:

27 "But fear not, O Jacob my servant,
nor be dismayed, O Israel,
for behold, I will save you from far away,
and your offspring from the land of their captivity.
Jacob shall return and have quiet and ease,
and none shall make him afraid.
28 Fear not, O Jacob my servant,
declares the Lord,
for I am with you.
I will make a full end of all the nations
to which I have driven you,
but of you I will not make a full end.
I will discipline you in just measure,
and I will by no means leave you unpunished."

Isaiah 11:1–12.6 is typically understood as prophesizing the restoration of Jewish Israel in future messianic times:

12 He will raise a signal for the nations
and will assemble the banished of Israel,
and gather the dispersed of Judah
from the four corners of the earth.

These are just a few examples of some of the core tenets of Jewish eschatology that are elaborated in the Books of Isaiah, Jeremiah, and Ezekiel detailing the end of the world, God's redemption of Israel, God returning the Jewish people to Israel, God's restoring the temple in Jerusalem and the House of David, and people's recognition of the God of Israel as the only God. Appreciating the influence these themata have had on the way neoconservative intellectuals make sense of the world also helps us to understand their use of generative metaphors sustaining the idea that Israel and the United States are engaged in a religious war with the radical Wahhabi Islamists, and why neoconservatives like May, Ledeen, and Gaffney are so vocal in opposing Israel's withdrawal from the areas God has given to *His* people.

Here it is worth drawing on Donald Schön's illuminating description of the different ways of understanding slum housing.[81] Schön claims that if the underlying metaphor frames slum housing as a blight or a disease then we are encouraged to think about medical remedies to help cure or remove the blight. Alternatively, if the underlying metaphor describes the slum as a natural community then we are encouraged to adopt measures that help enhance the life of that community. These two generative metaphors promote very different perceptions and approaches and have different implications when it comes to dealing with issues associated with slum housing. The key point is that the problem does not exist in any simple or real way but is generated or constituted in the use of metaphor.

This is relevant when considering the typical approach adopted by neoconservatives when representing the Israeli–Palestinian conflict. These intellectuals are generating or constituting the conflict as a religious war fought between the radical Islamists, which includes, on one side, Saudi- and Wahhabi-inspired and -influenced pro-Palestinian terrorist groups, and Israel, the United States, and the free world on the other. As we have seen, this conflict is often represented as theological in nature. In representing the conflict in this way, these neoconservative intellectuals are de-emphasizing or ignoring the possibility that there are alternative interpretations, like the idea that Palestinians simply want self-determination and a Palestinian state.

Danziger writes that generating or constituting the world in particular ways not only invites readers to think about it in certain ways but also to act in terms of certain implied assumptions.[82] Not only are these neoconservatives wanting their audience to think of the Palestinian struggle as primarily religious in nature, but they also want policy- and decision-makers to think in the same way and for their readers to support foreign policy and counterterror measures aimed at securing the safety of the state of Israel. According to intellectuals like Gaffney, this includes Israel having an ongoing presence in the Palestinian territories so as to prevent the establishment of a terrorist state.[83]

Good versus Evil

A closely related religious themata neoconservatives have drawn on is the presumption that the world God created is fated to an endless conflict between good and evil. This master theme holds conflict between good and evil as a condition of the natural, God-created order and neoconservatives presume that good will eventually emerge triumphant over evil. Naturally the neoconservatives also assume that they are the good guys dedicated to conquering the evil posed by the radical Islamist bad guys. Neoconservatives are not alone in thinking about the world in this way. Walter Wink identifies the pervasiveness of this motivating aid in Western thinking, which he calls the myth of redemptive violence.[84]

Wink's myth of redemptive violence holds that "violence saves, war brings peace, that might makes right."[85] Violence appears to be the natural order of things and is therefore understood to be inevitable in conflict rather than a more measured approach like talking through differences without violence. Violence has a religious character because it demands absolute obedience from its devotees. Wink traces this themata back to the creation myth of Babylon around 1250 BC, which holds humankind's creation to be an act of violence. According to Wink, the Babylonian myth is diametrically opposed to the creation myth recounted in the Book of Genesis, which can perhaps help us to distinguish the neoconservative worldview from more general Western ways of thinking—remembering that the Book of Genesis is the first book of the Hebrew Bible and many neoconservatives are influenced by Judaism.

The biblical myth originally created in direct rebuttal to the Babylonian myth represents a good God existing before evil. Evil and violence are not part of creation, but come later as a result of Adam's and Eve's sin and the serpent's connivance. Wink notes this is the first evidence of a problem emerging that demands a solution. This is telling when we consider that this part of the Hebrew Bible also provides the narrative about God's creating of the world, his covenant with Abraham, and his promise regarding the land of Israel. All of these ideas inform Jewish religious thought in general, and neoconservative thinking in particular, especially with regards to the Jewish people's claim to what many others understand as Palestinian land. A God-created world that is fated to endless conflict between good and evil is a key part of both the Babylonian and Biblical creation myths. The major point of difference between the two is what comes first: are we creatures born of violent creation or are we, as the Bible says, born good?

The evil versus good themata has certainly been prevalent since the neoconservative movement's inception in the twentieth century. The movement was founded by a group of intellectuals united by a fervent anticommunism and angered by what they saw as a failure on the part of liberal intellectuals to fully appreciate the evil nature of global communism. The neoconservative movement was founded by former socialists/Trotskyists like Kristol, Lipset, Lasky, Burnham, and Himmelfarb, and together they "blazed a wide political trail leading from left to right."[86]

This evil versus good themata continues to inform modern neoconservative thinking, with many intellectuals understanding radical Islam as the modern manifestation of the evil once posed by communism. It was good that triumphed over evil during the Cold War, and now many neoconservatives are motivated by the idea that the forces of good must confront and defeat the latest reincarnation of this evil. This idea is motivating prominent neoconservative intellectuals like David Frum and Richard Perle when they write:

> Like communism, this [militant Islamic] ideology perverts the language of justice and equality to justify oppression and murder. Like Nazism, it exploits the injured pride of once-mighty nations. Like both communism and Nazism, militant Islam is opportunistic—it works willingly with all manner of unlikely allies, as the communists and Nazis worked with each other against the democratic West.[87]

This analogy is basic to neoconservative thinking and highlights the movement's two key threats since its inception: communism and radical Islam. Frum and Perle are proposing a war of broad similarity, given what they see as the commonality of the enemy in both eras.[88] They also go on to say, "the war against extremist Islam is as much an ideological war as the cold war ever was."[89]

Neoconservatives typically consider Wahhabism as promoted by the Saudi kingdom and which influences and inspires pro-Palestinian terrorist organizations as key parts of this evil. We can therefore understand their representations as motivated and inspired by the religious idea that they are engaging in a religious or cosmic struggle in which they represent good and have God on their side. Violence forms a key part of this struggle, which neoconservatives willingly promote. However, one of the problems they do face is that the Wahhabi-inspired Other, whether that is a Palestinian fighting for Hamas, a radicalized leader of an Indonesian terrorist organization, or a Saudi citizen, is human. And people by large do not support the killing of other humans. Neoconservatives attempt to deal with this quandary by representing the Other as inhuman, knowing their audiences are more inclined to support violent acts and a more hostile foreign policy if it is aimed at killing savages and animals. This leads to the last part of this interpretive exercise, which looks at animal generative metaphors and the concept of the noble savage.

Animal Metaphors and the Noble Savage

The Human as Animal metaphor is one of the key generative metaphors motivating many neoconservative intellectuals. It serves to both dehumanize and encourage readers to think of the Wahhabi Other as inferior when compared to those living in the modern Judeo-Christian democratic Western world. Earlier we saw Ledeen use a metaphorical expression representing the Wahhabi Other as a machine. Ledeen is unique in his use of this kind of dehumanizing metaphor, as neoconservatives typically employ animalistic rather than mechanistic metaphors. Of course both help in denying the humanity of the Other and both have the potential effect of making any deaths occurring in the context of military or security operations more palatable, given that it is generally less confronting killing animals or destroying machines than it is killing people.

This carrying over of frames or perspectives from one domain to another, as Schön argues, is characteristic of generative metaphors. The carrying over of animalistic frames into the domain of the human, which denies the humanity of others and encourages cruelty and suffering, has its roots in Western imperialist thinking. In his seminal work *Images of Savages: Ancient Roots of Modern Prejudice*, Gustav Jahoda offers a comprehensive analysis of the many different ways the ethnic and racial Other has been represented in Western popular culture and scholarship.[90] He finds the Human as Animal metaphor to be a particularly popular rhetorical technique used by writers when likening Africans to apes and groups of Others to dogs, parasites, insects, and rats. These kinds of representations have formed an integral part of Western colonial projects as they help justify and legitimize the oppression and subjugation of native people. Dehumanization has also proven to be a popular technique in genocidal conflicts. Animal metaphors, particularly those likening the victims to vermin, have been commonly used by writers championing the killing of Jews in the Holocaust, Tutsis in Rwanda, and Bosnians in the Balkan wars.[91] In these instances the Other was dehumanized, helping justify and legitimize violence against them.

The orchestrated effort by neoconservatives in denying the humanity of the Wahhabi Other adds to this large body of racist Western scholarship that is generally aimed at supporting or justifying violence. Ledeen's mechanistic metaphor can be understood as an outlier in the wider neoconservative effort that typically makes use of animal framing. Many neoconservatives have employed this technique with the aim of persuading their audience to think of the Wahhabi Other as an inferior being, particularly when compared with the Judeo-Christian living in the modern democratic Western world. The dehumanizing of the Wahhabi Other works by encouraging readers to think of followers of Wahhabism as animals and to treat them in this way. There are a plethora of examples of neoconservatives describing Wahhabism and its followers in this way. While the use of this generative metaphor is common, there are notable differences in terms of the kind of language employed and the particular animal serving as the reference point.

Again, the work of prominent neoconservative Frank Gaffney provides a wealth of examples. Infuriated by the United States's treatment of Saudi Arabia as a white hat, Gaffney blames the kingdom for promoting Wahhabism, which he believes "animates and enables Jihadists worldwide."[92] He calls the Wahhabism practiced and promoted by Saudi Arabia a "supremacist totalitarian doctrine" responsible for "*breeding* extremists who were willing to kill even Muslims for their cause" (emphasis added).[93] One ordinarily uses the term breeding when describing the reproductive process of animals. Rats and rabbits breed, while we typically understand humans as giving birth to their offspring. There are many implications associated with this term worth considering. When breeding gets out of control (in the case of wild animals like rabbits), it can create problems for humans who typically respond by trapping, killing, or culling these pests. Describing adherents of Wahhabism in this way can encourage the adoption of foreign policies by the United States aimed at limiting, preventing, and killing the perceived threat.

Neoconservative intellectual Bret Stephens, who is a former Pulitzer Prize winner, former editor of the neoconservative flagship magazine *Commentary*, Fox News regular, and columnist for the *Wall Street Journal*, provides another representation of Wahhabism worthy of closer analysis.[94] He argues that Saudi Arabia is responsible for providing the "ideological inspiration and financial support" for Islamic radicals in Indonesia.[95] He claims Saudi Arabia has "infected" Indonesia with its Wahhabi doctrine, and, making use of an animal metaphor, he provides a quote describing the Islamic radicals as "all drinking from the same breast."[96]

There are many different kinds of animals like dogs, pigs, cats, and cows where the mothers breastfeed their young. Humans also breastfeed; however, Stephens's description of many people "drinking from the same breast" suggests he is referring to animals and not humans because of the former's propensity to have numerous babies at the same time. In choosing to use this metaphorical expression, Stephens wants his audience to think of Wahhabi Saudi Arabia as the mother providing her Islamic radicals, who are the baby animals, with the nutrients or sustenance they need to survive. When it comes to making foreign policy, the implication is that if the United States wants to combat modern Islamic terrorism, specifically the threat it poses to the United States and its interests abroad, then it needs to deal with Saudi Arabia. Supporting representations provided by authors like Gaffney, Stephens is clear in his message that Saudi Arabia is the source of the problem and should therefore be treated as a black hat.

Another example worth taking a closer look at, particularly for its religious overtones, is provided by Reuel Marc Gerecht. He dismisses claims that the Wahhabi establishment in Saudi Arabia has made progress in introducing democratic reform. Gerecht writes:

> There is scant evidence to suggest that the Wahhabi establishment has *changed its spots* (philosophically it can't). The Wahhabis should have to compete for their *flock*. Inside the country and out, the United States should be relentlessly pushing for democracy. As in Egypt, we should increasingly tie government-to-government relations and joint programs directly to Saudi progress with real national elections.[97] [emphasis added]

This excerpt is very interesting because of its ability to reveal a number of beliefs influencing how a neoconservative intellectual makes sense of the world and Wahhabism. We can see Gerecht's use of animal metaphors in his using of the terms "changed its spots" and "flock." The former metaphorical expression has its roots in the well-known phrase 'a leopard cannot change its spots,' which implies that things have an innate nature that cannot be altered. The phrase has Biblical origins, which is telling when we consider the prominent role Judaism plays in the neoconservative movement. The phrase appears in the Book of Jeremiah, which is the second of the Latter Prophets in the Hebrew Bible. Jeremiah 13:23 reads, "Can the Ethiopian change his skin, or the leopard his spots? Then may ye also do good, that are accustomed to do evil." In addition to highlighting the role religion plays in Gerecht's thinking, the use of this metaphorical expression also helps dehumanize the Wahhabi Other. The suggestion is the "Wahhabi establishment" are animals that are inherently evil and because they cannot become good, they must be treated as enemies.

Sticking with this dehumanizing of the Wahhabi Other, Gerecht also writes that "the Wahhabis should have to compete for their flock."[98] When used as a noun, the term 'flock' describes a group of animals, typically birds or sheep, that often group or are herded together. Gerecht is suggesting that Wahhabi adherents are unthinking animals following the directions of their herders/leaders. The term 'flock' can also refer to sheep and to 'follow like a sheep' is to uncritically accept or follow the instructions of a leader. This helps to deny the faculties humans possess that enable them to think deeply about a given situation and make their own choices. Gerecht's use of the term "compete" also resonates with the typical neoconservative ontological view of the world as an anarchic place where states and groups must compete against each other to satisfy their aims and goals. Also apparent is the foreign policy belief in the global promotion of democracy.

While I have chosen to explicate these examples to help illustrate how some neoconservative intellectuals go about representing Wahhabism to their audiences, there are many more instances of neoconservatives using animal metaphors to dehumanize adherents of Wahhabism. For example, Michael W. Schwartz describes followers of the global "Saudi Wahhabist enterprise" as "creatures."[99] Clifford May describes Wahhabis in Saudi Arabia as a "strong horse" ridden by the House of Sa'ud "at full gallop," and likens the Saudi ruling family's use of the Wahhabi establishment to the 'riding of a tiger.'[100] Michael Ledeen calls Saudi-funded Wahhabi mosques and schools "breeding grounds for future terrorists."[101] Furthermore, editors of neoconservative flagship publications like *FrontPageMag* and *The Weekly Standard* have given voice to anti-Saudi and anti-Wahhabi intellectuals like Stephen Schwartz, who describes Wahhabis as a "breed" and has claimed that Saudi-sponsoring of this "totalitarian ideology," which is a "radical system of social control . . . has now come home to roost."[102]

Describing followers, proponents, and sponsors of Wahhabism in terms usually reserved for animals is a popular technique employed by neoconservative intellectuals; however, it is not the only dehumanizing technique they make use of. Many neoconservatives have also likened them to savages and suggested that the religion is fit for the less-evolved. These kinds of representations of the Wahhabi Other resonate with how Western popular culture and scholarship have represented the ethnic, racial, and religious Other.

There has been a tendency in Western thought to think of racial, ethnic, and religious Others as barbarians lacking in culture, self-restraint, moral sensibility, and cognitive capacity.[103] These deficiencies are typically accompanied by excesses: the racial, ethnic, or religious Other is a savage with a brutish appetite for violence, prone to criminality, who can tolerate excessive amounts of pain.[104] The brutish appetite for violence in particular is a favorite rhetorical technique of Reuel Marc Gerecht who, in wanting his audience to think of Wahhabis as savages, talks about the "head-and-hand-chopping" practices adopted by the "Wahhabi-clergy," the "Wahhabi-Saudi thirst for power and pillage," and the likelihood of Saudi Arabia becoming a "Wahhabi police state" that "tortures" its own people.[105]

There are many neoconservatives who like to represent adherents of Wahhabism as less-evolved beings. For example, Daniel Pipes tweeted to his tens of thousands of followers that the Wahhabi Saudi Arabian ruling regime are "barbarians" for recent structural developments they have undertaken in the city of Mecca; Bret Stephens uses the terms "tribe" and "Bedouin kingdom" when describing an Islamic group in Indonesia influenced by Wahhabism to readers of the *Wall Street Journal*; David Pryce-Jones says that in Saudi Arabia "immemorial tribal custom and the local Wahhabi brand of Islam are defended and perpetuated to create the impression that this is the natural order of things."[106] Gerecht also suggests the Wahhabis from Najd in Saudi Arabia are antimodern:

> We would be wise not to assume that the Saudi royal family is more "modern" than the people of the country. It may well be more "modern" than the average Wahhabi in the Najd region, the heartland of Wahhabi power. But Saudi Arabia is much larger than the Najd.[107]

He also argues that Wahhabi Saudi Arabia must experience some internal violence in order to "evolve" into a democracy.[108]

There are a plethora of examples of neoconservative intellectuals using specific rhetorical techniques to represent followers of Wahhabism as less evolved and the societies and groups that practice it as antimodern, backward, and barbaric. There are a variety of reasons why I have chosen to draw attention to these representations. First, Daniel Pipes's tweet is indicative of the neoconservative movement's embracing social media as a tool for getting their message out into the public sphere. The typical neoconservative intellectual is older, white, religious, and male and on first appearances one might assume that this could equate to a failure to embrace new social media. This is certainly not the case with the well-funded and well-orchestrated movement, which has a number of intellectuals and neoconservative organizations using Twitter (#Wahhabi is a popular hashtag) to provide concise representations of Wahhabism, criticize contrasting viewpoints, and provide links to articles they have written in mainstream newspapers and online.

Second, the ways in which Stephens, Pryce-Jones, and Gerecht use language when representing Wahhabism tells us a lot about how they make sense of the world, particularly with regard to the different kinds of themata and generative metaphors influencing their thinking. Their representations tell us a lot about how they view Saudi Arabia and help us to understand both why they have long criticized the United States for treating the kingdom as a white hat instead of championing a more aggressive and hostile foreign policy that is worthy of a black hat.

Phrases like 'Bedouin kingdom' and 'tribe' evoke the idea of the noble savage. Ter Ellingson, in *The Myth of the Noble Savage*, notes that it was British anthropologists who created the noble savage myth for propaganda purposes, wanting to encourage and legitimize the enslavement and genocide of indigenous peoples.[109] Many have credited eighteenth-century philosopher Jean-Jacques Rousseau with creating the myth; however, Ellingson says this is incorrect: "Rousseau did not promote the idea of the Noble Savage nor did he ever mention it. The idea he did is one of the most widespread misbeliefs of all time."[110] This misbelief is the product of a nineteenth-century racist's claim, who cited Rousseau to help support his notion of inferior races. The myth was a vital tool in enabling the British to promote the centrality of race as a scientific ideology while also advocating violently racist modes of ordering society.[111]

Order is an important idea to many neoconservatives. Neoconservatives work from the ontological assumption that people are naturally evil, violent, and conflictual and therefore need order to prevent themselves from giving in to their natural inclinations.[112] This sense of order is often seen as lacking in indigenous or savage societies, which is why, according to neoconservative logic, they often give in to their violent tendencies. We also know that the global promotion of democracy is a key part of neoconservative foreign policy. Thinking and representing the Wahhabi Other as a savage can therefore encourage and justify policies and actions aimed at recreating or ordering these societies in ways that align with neoconservative beliefs about the world.

Inspired by democratic peace theory, most neoconservatives want all the world's nations outside of the United States, particularly Middle Eastern regimes, to be democracies. Using Wahhabism to represent these societies and the people belonging to them as savages encourages and justifies the adopting of policies and actions aimed at democratizing and 'civilizing' these people. We have seen this in Iraq and Afghanistan, and according to these representations there are many neoconservatives who would also like the United States to promote democracy in Wahhabi Saudi Arabia.

The messages coming from the neoconservative movement are clear: Wahhabism is responsible for inspiring and motivating Islamic terrorism and the Saudi kingdom is its chief propagator. Saudi Arabia is not to be viewed as a white hat; rather, it is a black hat that through their global promotion of Wahhabism poses a security threat to the United States, Israel, and the rest of the free world. The Saudi influence has stretched as far as places like Indonesia but, more importantly, it has helped to corrupt pro-Palestinian organizations whose desire to destroy the modern state of Israel is represented as primarily theological in nature. Neoconservatives want us to understand that Israel's conflict with the Palestinians is a microcosm of the wider global war on terror; they do not under any circumstances want readers entertaining the idea that this could be a struggle between an occupier and the occupied.

Conclusion

From the end spring new beginnings.
—Pliny the Elder

I began research for this book with clear aims and goals in mind. I wanted to show readers how scholars were representing Wahhabism and I wanted to identify some of the major problems with these representations. I wanted to address certain kinds of problems evident in the sociology of intellectuals tradition and how and why intellectuals belonging to two of the most prominent Western intellectual traditions, liberalism and neoconservatism, have chosen to represent Wahhabism in particular ways. My initial interest in doing all these things was provoked by those conversations I had with my Palestinian friend in suburban Stockholm during lunch breaks and after Swedish language classes.

It is hoped that this work serves as a valuable contribution to a tradition of scholarship that has to date treated Wahhabism as a historical phenomenon or a monolithic theological ideology, and as having a normative definition provided by authors with ideological axes to grind and geopolitical interests to promote. The originality of this work is found in its treating the phenomenon Wahhabism as a discursive construct crafted and popularized by a Western intellectual elite. Originality is also found in how this work looks at the different ways in which intellectuals belonging to two specific traditions, liberalism and neoconservatism, have rhetorically and socially constructed Wahhabism, and in its consideration of the implications these representations have for policy- and decision-making processes, particularly in regards to the global war on terror.

Situated within the sociology of intellectuals tradition, it is hoped that this scholarly monograph encourages readers to think about the larger role intellectuals are currently playing in helping shape and drive intellectual discourse and contemporary geopolitics. It is also hoped that this work inspires readers to think about what kinds of roles intellectuals *should* be adopting. We are living in a moment in time where many are suffering from a heightened anxiety brought about by the perceived threat posed by radical Islam. Is this a time for promoting partisan political and religious interests, or should those who enjoy privileged positions as the producers and mediators of knowledge in the modern world be more concerned with speaking truth to power and helping shine a light on injustice? This question becomes especially important when considering the ongoing Israeli–Palestinian conflict, which is only becoming increasingly brutal.

This work, like all others, has its limitations, which I prefer to see as opportunities for further investigation. I have only focused on five elements of discourse when deconstructing liberal and neoconservative representations of Wahhabism. While these play crucial roles in the myth-making process, there are other elements that can also be analyzed, which in turn could help reveal other kinds of themata and generative metaphors influencing liberal and neoconservative thinking. Opportunities also exist for future study into how intellectuals belonging to different traditions have represented Wahhabism. I hope this work helps open these doors.

Notes

Introduction

1 Ferdinand de Saussure, "Signs and language," 56.
2 Gustav Bergmann, *Logic and Reality*.
3 Aristotle, "Poetics IV," cited in "Representation," by W.J.T. Mitchell, paragraph 1.
4 Cassirer's works on the philosophy of symbolic forms appeared as studies and lectures of the Warburg Library from 1922 to 1925 and the three-volume *Philosophy of Symbolic Forms* appeared in 1923, 1925, and 1929. See Ernst Cassirer, *Philosophie der symbolischen Formen. Erster Teil: Die Sprache*. Translated as *The Philosophy of Symbolic Forms. Volume One: Language*. *Philosophie der symbolischen Formen. Zweiter Teil: Das mythische Denken*. Translated as *The Philosophy of Symbolic Forms. Volume Two: Mythical Thought*. *Philosophie der symbolischen Formen. Dritter Teil: Phänomenologie der Erkenntnis*. Translated as *The Philosophy of Symbolic Forms. Volume Three: The Phenomenology of Knowledge*.
5 Mitchell, "Representation," paragraph 2.
6 Edmund Burke, *Philosophical Enquiry*.
7 Aristotle, "Poetics IV," in "Representation," Mitchell, paragraph 7.
8 Mitchell, "Representation," paragraph 8.
9 Ludwig Wittgenstein, *Philosophical Investigations*. Throughout the *Philosophical Investigations* Wittgenstein constantly returns to the concept of language-games to make clear his lines of thought about language. See, for example, §2, §23, §65, and §66.
10 Ian Hacking, *The Social Construction of What?*
11 Ian Hacking, *Mad Travelers: Reflections on the Reality of Transient Mental Illnesses*.

12 Cited in Mitchell, "Representation," paragraph 9.
13 Ibid.
14 Some of the better studies include Alexander Knysh, "A Clear and Present Danger: 'Wahhabism' as a Rhetorical Foil"; Muriel Atkin, "The Rhetoric of Islamophobia"; Quintan Wiktorowicz, "Anatomy of the Salafi Movement."
15 Joseph Nevo, "Religion and National Identity in Saudi Arabia," 36–50; Joseph A. Kechichian, "The Role of the Ulama in the Politics of an Islamic State: The Case of Saudi Arabia," 56–59; William Wager Cooper and Piyu Yue, *Challenges of the Muslim World: Present, Future and Past*, 271–72; Stephen E. Atkins, "Wahhabism (Saudi Arabia)."
16 David Commins, *The Wahhabi Mission and Saudi Arabia*, 104–29; Jon Armajani, "Saudi Arabia," 122–33; Madawi al-Rasheed, *A History of Saudi Arabia*, 15–17; Khalid S. al-Dakhil, "Social Origins of the Wahhabi Movement," 1–19; Natana DeLong-Bas, *Wahhabi Islam: From Revival and Reform to Global Jihad*, see chapters "Muhammad Ibn Abd al-Wahhab and the Origin of Wahhabism: The Eighteenth-Century Context," 7–40, and "The Theology and Worldview of Muhammad Ibn Abd al-Wahhab," 41–92; Charles Allen, *God's Terrorists: The Wahhabi Cult and The Hidden Roots of Modern Jihad*, 20.
17 Michael Cook, "On the Origins of Wahhabism," 191.
18 W.F. Smalley, "The Wahhabis and Ibn Sa'ud," 230.
19 Ibid.
20 Ibid., 231.
21 Robert Lacy, *Inside the Kingdom: Kings, Clerics, Modernists, Terrorists, and the Struggle for Saudi Arabia*, 10–11; Allen, *God's Terrorists*, 21; Smalley, "The Wahhabis and Ibn Sa'ud," 232; Abdulaziz H. al-Fahad, "The Imama vs. the 'Iqal: Hadari-Bedouin Conflict and the Formation of the Saudi State," 12.
22 Christopher M. Blanchard, *CRS Report for Congress: The Islamic Traditions of Wahhabism and Salafiyya*, 3.
23 Khaled Abou El Fadl, "Islam and the Theology of Power," 32.
24 Sebastiano Andreotti, "The Ikhwan Movement and Its Role in Saudi Arabia's State-Building," 88.
25 Joseph Kostiner, "On Instruments and Their Designers: The Ikhwan of the Najd and the Emergence of the Saudi State," 298.
26 Matt Stefon, *Islamic Beliefs and Practices*, 173; Marko Rakic and Dragisa Jurisic, "Wahhabism as a Militant Form of Islam on Europe's Doorstep," 650; Yahya Hakim, "The Hashemite-Umayyad Divide and its Impact on the Future of Islam," 95.
27 Rakic and Jurisic, "Wahhabism as a Militant Form of Islam on Europe's Doorstep," 650.
28 DeLong-Bas, *Wahhabi Islam*, 18; Nevo, "Religion and National Identity in Saudi Arabia," 37.

29 DeLong-Bas, *Wahhabi Islam.*
30 Ibid.
31 Ibid., 25.
32 Febe Armanios, *CRS Report for Congress: The Islamic Traditions of Wahhabism and Salafiyya*, 2.
33 Ibid; Nabil Mouline, *Les clercs de l'Islam: autorité religieuse et pouvoir politique en Arabie Saoudite, XVIIIe–XXIe siècle*; Muhammad Al-Atawneh, *Wahhabi Islam Facing the Challenges of Modernity: Dar Al-Ifta in the Modern Saudi State: Studies in Islamic Law and Society*; Nevo, "Religion and National Identity in Saudi Arabia," 36–37.
34 Abdulaziz H. Al-Fahad, "From Exclusivism to Accommodation: Doctrinal and Legal Evolution of Wahhabism," 488.
35 Cameron Zargar, "The Hanbali and Wahhabi Schools of Thought: As Observed Through the Case of *Ziyarah*," 85–86.
36 Uriya Shavit, "Raising *Salafi* Children in the West," 2; Innes Bowen, *Medina in Birmingham, Najaf in Brent: Inside British Islam*, 58; Commins, *The Wahhabi Mission and Saudi Arabia*, ix; Al-Fahad, "From Exclusivism to Accommodation," 487–88; Hamid Algar, *Wahhabism: A Critical Essay*, 1.
37 Armanios, *CRS Report for Congress*, 2.
38 Ibid.
39 Claude Moniquet, *The involvement of Salafism/Wahhabism in the support and supply of arms to rebel groups around the world.*
40 Barry M. Rubin, ed. *Guide to Islamist Movements*, 308.
41 Armanios, *CRS Report for Congress*, 2.
42 Wikipedia, "Wahhabi Movement."
43 Blanchard, *CRS Report for Congress.*
44 Moniquet, *The involvement of Salafism/Wahhabism in the support and supply of arms to rebel groups around the world.*
45 Wael Mahdi, "There is no such thing as Wahabism, Saudi prince says"; Mohammed bin Nawaf Al Saud, "Saudi Arabia does not support Islamic State terrorists—or any others."
46 Trevor Stanley, "Understanding the Origins of Wahhabism and Salafism," paragraph 1.
47 Khaled Abou El Fadl, *The Great Theft: Wrestling Islam from the Extremists*; Stephen Schwartz, *The Two Faces of Islam: The House of Sa'ud from Tradition to Terror.*
48 Benedict Anderson, *Imagined Communities: Reflections on the Origins and Spread of Nationalism.*
49 Charles Kurzman and Lynn Owens, "The Sociology of Intellectuals"; Karl Mannheim, "The Sociology of Intellectuals"; Patrick Baert and Joel Isaac, "Intellectuals and Society: Sociological and Historical Perspectives."
50 Thomas Osborne, "On Mediators: Intellectuals and the Ideas Trade in the Knowledge Society"; Hisham M. Nazer, *Power of a Third Kind: The Western*

Attempt to Colonize the Global Village, 13–24; James Q. Wilson, ""Policy Intellectuals" and public policy"; Edward Said, "The Public Role of Writers and Intellectuals."

51 Rob Watts, "Truth and Politics: Thinking About Evidence-Based Policy in the Age of Spin," 35–36.

52 Ibid., 36.

53 "Iraq's Weapons of Mass Destruction: The Assessment of the British Government," also known as the "September Dossier," was published by the British government on September 24, 2002. It alleged that Iraq possessed weapons of mass destruction, including chemical weapons and biological weapons. It also alleged that Iraq had reconstituted its nuclear weapons program. All of the allegations have since been proved false. The US Senate Intelligence Committee found many of the administration's prewar statements about Iraqi WMD like Bush's claim, "The people of the United States and our friends and allies will not live at the mercy of an outlaw regime that threatens the peace with weapons of mass murder," were not supported by the intelligence. See "Press Release of Intelligence Committee Senate Intelligence Committee Unveils Final Phase II Reports on Prewar Iraq Intelligence—Two Bipartisan Reports Detail Administration Misstatements on Prewar Iraq Intelligence, and Inappropriate Intelligence Activities by Pentagon Policy Office."

54 Hannah Arendt, "Truth and Politics," 257.

55 See Karl Mannheim, "The Sociological Problem of the 'Intelligentsia,'" "The Sociology of Intellectuals," and "The Problem of the Intelligentsia."

56 Antonio Gramsci, *Selections from the Prison Notebooks*; Jürgen Habermas, "Heinrich Heine und die Rolle des Intellektuellen in Deutschland"; Jean-Paul Sartre, *Anti-Semite and Jew*; Raymond Aron, *The Opium of the Intellectuals*; Edward Shils, *The Intellectuals and the Powers and Other Essays*; J.P. Nettl, "Ideas, Intellectuals, and Structures of Dissent"; Peter Berger, *Invitation to Sociology: A Humanistic Perspective*; Michel Foucault and Gilles Deleuze, "The Intellectuals and Power: A Discussion Between Gilles Deleuze and Michel Foucault"; Noam Chomsky, "The Responsibility of Intellectuals"; Judith Butler and Gayatri Chakravorty Spivak, *Who Sings the Nation State? Language, Politics, Belonging*; Michael Walzer, *The Company of Critics*; Edward Said, *Representations of the Intellectual: The 1993 Reith Lectures*. For a critique of the sociology of intellectual tradition in general, and of works by Theodor W. Adorno and Jürgen Habermas in particular, see Stefan Müller-Doohm, "Two Ways of Being a Public Intellectual: Sociological Observations Concerning the Transformation of a Social Figure of Modernity."

57 Foucault and Deleuze, "The Intellectuals and Power," 103–109; Said, *Representations of the Intellectual*, see chapter "Speaking Truth to Power," 85–102.

58 Habermas, "Heinrich Heine," 274–76.
59 Gramsci writes, "Every social group, coming into existence on the original terrain of an essential function in the world of economic production, creates together with itself, organically, one or more strata of intellectuals which give it homogeneity and an awareness of its own function not only in the economic but also in the social and political fields." See Antonio Gramsci, "The Intellectuals," 5.
60 See Jürgen Habermas, *The Structural Transformation of the Public Sphere: An Inquiry into a Category of Bourgeois Society*.
61 Ari Adut, "A Theory of the Public Sphere."
62 Peter Dahlgren is a prominent author studying the key role the Internet plays in the public sphere. See, for example, Peter Dahlgren, "The Internet, public spheres, and political communication: Dispersion and deliberation."
63 See chapter "Intellectual Exile: Expatriates and Marginals" in Said, *Representations of the Intellectual*, 47–64; Foucault and Deleuze, "The Intellectuals and Power."
64 Anderson, *Imagined Communities*; Edward Said, *Orientalism*.
65 Eric Hobsbawm, *Nations and Nationalism Since 1780: Programme, Myth, Reality*; Anthony Smith, *Theories of Nationalism*; Ronald G. Suny and Michael D. Kennedy, eds., *Intellectuals and the Articulation of the Nation*.
66 Carl Schmitt, *The Concept of the Political*; Max Weber, "The Profession and Vocation of Politics."
67 Bernard Crick, *In Defence of Politics*; Simon Critchley, *Infinitely Demanding: Ethics of Commitment, Politics of Resistance*.
68 The concept of the Other is key to Edward Said's work on Orientalism. See Edward Said, *Orientalism*.
69 Carol Bacchi, *What's the Problem Represented to Be?*
70 Arendt, "Truth and Politics," 252.
71 Stephen Toulmin, *Human Understanding: The Evolution of Concepts*; John Caputo, *Truth*.
72 Hannah Arendt, *Was Ist Politik?*, 19.
73 Jim George, "Leo Strauss, Neoconservatism and US Foreign Policy: Esoteric Nihilism and the Bush Doctrine"; Scott Kline, "The Culture War Gone Global: 'Family Values' and the Shape of US Foreign Policy"; David Grondin, "Mistaking Hegemony for Empire: Neoconservatives, the Bush doctrine, and the Democratic empire."
74 John Gray, *Black Mass: Apocalyptic Religion and the Death of Utopia*; Eric A. Heinze, "The New Utopianism: Liberalism, American Foreign Policy, and the War in Iraq"; Nick Bisley, *Great Powers in the Changing International Order*; James Mayall and Ricardo Soares de Oliveira, eds., *The New Protectorates: International Tutelage and the Making of Liberal States*; Georg Sorensen, *A Liberal Order in Crisis: Choosing between Imposition and Restraint*.
75 Justin Vaïsse, *Neoconservatism: The Biography of a Movement*; Brandon High,

"The Recent Historiography of American Neoconservatism."

76 In March 2013 the Alliance for Audited Media reported that the *Wall Street Journal* (the most circulated newspaper in the United States), the *New York Times* (second most circulated), *USA Today* (third), and the *Washington Post* (seventh) were among the ten most circulated newspapers, including print and digital subscriptions in the United States. In June 2014, Cision Research reported that *USA Today*, the *Wall Street Journal*, and the *New York Times* respectively were the top three most circulated daily newspapers in the United States, while the *Washington Post* was ranked tenth. For precise circulation numbers see *Huffington Post*, "Top 10 Newspapers By Circulation: Wall Street Journal Leads Weekly Circulation," and *Cision*, "Top 10 Daily Newspapers."

77 Bertell Ollman and Tony Smith, "Dialectics: The New Frontier"; Bertell Ollman, *Dance of the Dialectic: Steps in Marx's Method*; Bertell Ollman, *Alienation: Marx's Conception of Man in Capitalist Society*, 52–70.

78 Ollman and Smith, "Dialectics," 333–34.

79 Gerald Holton, "The Role of Themata in Science"; Kurt Danziger, "Generative metaphor and the history of psychological discourse."

80 Holton, "The Role of Themata in Science," 456.

81 Danziger, "Generative metaphor and the history of psychological discourse," 332.

82 Norman Fairclough and Clive Holes, *Critical Discourse Analysis: The Critical Study of Language*; Ruth Wodak, "What CDA is About—A Summary of its History, Important Concepts and Its Development."

83 George Lakoff, "The Conceptual Metaphor: The Contemporary Theory of Metaphor"; George Lakoff, *Moral Politics: How Liberals and Conservatives Think*; George Lakoff and Mark Johnson, *Metaphors We Live By*; George Lakoff and Mark Turner, *More than Cool Reason: A Field Guide to Poetic Metaphor*; Douglas Hofstadter and Emmanuel Sander, *Surfaces and Essences: Analogy as the Fuel and Fire of Thinking*.

84 Mary Midgley, *The Myths We Live By*, 1–20.

85 Frank Gaffney Jr., "Seeing the threat for what it is."

86 Karen Cerulo, *Deciphering Violence: The Cognitive Structure of Right and Wrong*.

1. Wahhabism as a Contested Category

1 Nevo, "Religion and National Identity in Saudi Arabia," 36–50; Kechichian, "The Role of the Ulama," 56–59; Cooper and Yue, *Challenges of the Muslim World*, 271–72; Atkins, "Wahhabism (Saudi Arabia)."

2 Bernard Lewis, "Freedom and Justice in Islam"; Commins, *The Wahhabi Mission and Saudi Arabia*; Dore Gold, *Hatred's Kingdom: How Saudi Arabia Supports the New Global Terrorism*; Anderson, *Imagined Communities*; Said, *Orientalism*. I draw on Anderson's and Said's work but discuss this fully in chapter two.

3 Ron Eyerman, *Between Culture and Politics: Intellectuals in Modern Society*, 198.

4 Anderson, *Imagined Communities*, 6.

5 Said, *Orientalism*.

6 Dore Gold, *Hatred's Kingdom*. Gold joins a number of Israeli scholars and other writers who suggest the Israeli occupation of Palestine is fabricated and that Palestinians are incorrect in believing they have some kind of historical claim to the land. See, for example, Alex Joffe, "Fabricating Palestinian History: The Rhetoric of Nonsense"; Brian Wimborne, "The Tactical Myth of Palestinian Identity."

7 The full report is titled "Terrorism Financing: Origination, Organization, and Prevention: Hearing before the Committee On Governmental Affairs United States Senate: One Hundred Eight Congress First Session." Refer to pp. 25–31 for Dore Gold's testimony.

8 Gold, *Hatred's Kingdom*, 5–6.

9 Commins, *The Wahhabi Mission*.

10 Margaret Gonzalez-Perez, "The False Islamization of Female Suicide Bombers." For a basic understanding of the feminist tradition see Genevieve Lloyd, ed., *Feminism and History of Philosophy*, and Charlotte Witt and Lisa Shapiro, "Feminist History of Philosophy."

11 Khaled Hroub, *Hamas: A Beginner's Guide*.

12 Zaki Chehab, *Inside Hamas: The Untold Story of Militants, Martyrs and Spies*.

13 Gonzalez-Perez, "The False Islamization of Female Suicide Bombers," 62.

14 Ibid., 51–52.

15 Eleanor Abdella Doumato, "Manning the Barricades: Islam According to Saudi Arabia's School Texts"; Michaela Prokop, "Saudi Arabia: The Politics of Education."

16 United States Congress Senate, "Terrorism financing," 31.

17 Ibid., 31–32.

18 See, for example, Middle East Media Research Institute, "Special Dispatch No. 4345, Saudi Textbook: The Enmity between the Muslims and the Jews is Everlasting"; "Special Dispatch No. 2571, Liberal Saudi Columnist: With Wahhabism as State Religion, There's No Chance of Reform for Saudi Schools."

19 Ibid.

20 Middle East Media Research Institute TV, "#5059, Saudi Education Ministry Textbooks Used in Remote Burkina Faso Village."

21 For an in-depth analysis of MEMRI, see Right Web, "Middle East Media Research."

22 Louis Althusser, "Ideology and Ideological State Apparatuses"; Gramsci, *Selections from the Prison Notebooks*.

23 Doumato, "Manning the Barricades," 242.

24 Prokop, "Saudi Arabia: The Politics of Education," 80.

25 Ibid.

26 Martin Müller, "What's in a Word? Problematizing Translation between

Languages," 207.

27 Caputo, *Truth*.

28 Müller, "What's in a Word?," 207.

29 Ibid.

30 Ibid., 207–209; H.P. Phillips, "Problems of Translation and Menacing in Fieldwork," 291; Pamela Shurmer-Smith, "The Trouble with Theory," 11–18; Gustavo Esteva and Madhu Suri Prakash, *Grassroots Post-Modernism: Remaking the Soil of Cultures*, 118–19; Bogusia Temple and Alys Young, "Qualitative research and translation dilemmas," 165–71.

31 Phillips, "Problems of Translation and Menacing in Fieldwork," 291.

32 Müller, "What's in a Word?," 207.

33 Doumato, "Manning the Barricades," 242.

34 Ibid., 243.

35 Prokop, *Saudi Arabia: The Politics of Education*, 82.

36 Juan Cole, *Engaging the Muslim World.*

37 Ibid., 97–98.

38 Ibid., 2.

39 Ibid., 97.

40 Chomsky, "The Responsibility of Intellectuals," paragraph 4.

41 Muhammad Al-Atawneh, "Wahhabi Self-Examination Post-9/11: Rethinking the 'Other', 'Otherness' and Tolerance," 255–71.

42 See, for example, Schmitt, *The Concept of the Political.*

43 Crick, *In Defence of Politics*; Critchley, *Infinitely Demanding*.

44 Al-Atawneh, "Wahhabi Self-Examination Post-9/11," 259.

45 Chomsky, "The Responsibility of Intellectuals," paragraph 2.

46 DeLong-Bas, *Wahhabi Islam.*

47 Ibid., 281.

48 Ibid.

49 Schwartz, *The Two Faces of Islam*; *Real Clear Politics*, "Natana DeLong-Bas: American Professor, Wahhabi Apologist."

50 See Caroline B. Glick, "Brandeis' Jewish Problem." At the time of writing Glick was a deputy managing editor of the *Jerusalem Post*. Her opinion piece was originally published in the *Jewish Press* and was also published in the well-known online neoconservative publication *FrontPageMag*.

51 Haneef James Oliver, *The Wahhabi Myth: Dispelling Prevalent Fallacies and the Fictitious Link with Bin Laden*.

52 Oliver, *The Wahhabi Myth*; Schwartz, *The Two Faces of Islam*; El Fadl, *The Great Theft*.

53 Oliver, *The Wahhabi Myth*, 1.

54 Haneef James Oliver joins Khaled Abou El Fadl and Stephen Schwartz as intellectuals who represent the 'Wahhabi' community as existing outside of the mainstream Islamic community. Oliver, El Fadl, and Schwartz all have particular ideas about what 'true' Islam is and is not and all reject

Wahhabism. While united in their representing Wahhabism as a corrupted version of Islam, they each differ in their understanding of what constitutes 'real Islam,' or rather what is a 'truthful' and 'objective' interpretation of Islam. Schwartz's representing of Wahhabism is influenced by his desire to promote a particular interpretation of Sufi Islam. Contra Schwartz, El Fadl is influenced by his desire to promote what he considers to be a moderate and progressive interpretation of Islam. See Schwartz, *The Two Faces of Islam*; El Fadl, *The Great Theft*.

55 Wiktorowicz, "Anatomy of the Salafi Movement."

56 Ibid., 216.

57 Hans-Georg Gadamer, "The Problem of Historical Consciousness"; Hannah Arendt, "Truth and Politics."

58 Gadamer, "The Problem of Historical Consciousness."

2. On Intellectuals, Prejudice, and Understanding the Social World

1 Gregory Vlastos, *Studies in Greek Philosophy*.

2 Plato, *Apology*, 41.

3 This is not to ignore his foundational status in setting off the sociology of knowledge. See Volker Meja and Nico Stehr, eds., *Knowledge and Politics: The Sociology of Knowledge Dispute*.

4 David Kettler and Volka Meja, *Karl Mannheim and the Crisis of Liberalism*, 11.

5 Karl Mannheim, *Ideology and Utopia: An Introduction to the Sociology of Knowledge*.

6 Mannheim says the following about ideology: "The concept "ideology" reflects the one discovery which emerged from political conflict, namely, that ruling groups can in their thinking become so intensively interest-bound to a situation that they are simply no longer able to see certain facts which would undermine their sense of domination. There is implicit in the word 'ideology' the insight that in certain situations the collective unconscious of certain groups obscures the real condition of society both to itself and to others and thereby stabilises it." Ibid., 36.

7 Ibid., 268.

8 Karl Mannheim, *Freedom, Power, and Democratic Planning*, xvii.

9 Alfred Schutz, "The Problem of Transcendental Intersubjectivity in Husserl"; Charles Taylor, "The Politics of Recognition."

10 Ludwig Wittgenstein. *On Certainty*; Rudolf Carnap, "Empiricism, Semantics, and Ontology"; Nelson Goodman, *Ways of Worldmaking*.

11 Ferdinand de Saussure, *Course in General Linguistics*.

12 Gilles Deleuze, *Negotiations*; Osborne, "On Mediators."

13 Osborne, "On Mediators," 441. Osborne cites Gregory Bateson, *Steps to an Ecology of Mind*, 381.

14 Reference to Osborne's claim that his conceptualization of the mediator as relatively 'value-neutral' when compared to Deleuze's conception is taken from Osborne, "On Mediators," note 9 on p. 446. The quotation appears on p. 441.

15 Anderson, *Imagined Communities*; Said, *Orientalism*.
16 Chomsky, "The Responsibility of Intellectuals"; Arendt, "Truth and Politics."
17 Kurzman and Owens, "The Sociology of Intellectuals."
18 Mannheim, "The Sociological Problem of the 'Intelligentsia'"; Chomsky, "The Responsibility of Intellectuals"; Talcott Parsons, "'The intellectual': a social role category"; Edward Shils, *The Intellectual Between Tradition and Modernity: The Indian Situation*; Christopher Hitchens, "The Plight of the Public Intellectual."
19 Mannheim, "The Sociological Problem of the 'Intelligentsia,'" 153–64.
20 Ibid., 161–62.
21 Ibid., 156.
22 Chomsky, "The Responsibility of Intellectuals," paragraph 2.
23 Mannheim, "The Problem of the 'Intelligentsia,'" 166.
24 Parsons, "'The intellectual': a social role category"; Hitchens, "The Plight of the Public Intellectual."
25 Hitchens, "The Plight of the Public Intellectual," paragraph 3.
26 Ibid., paragraph 1.
27 Ibid., paragraph 10.
28 Ibid., paragraph 4.
29 Ibid., paragraph 10.
30 Ibid.
31 Shils, *The Intellectual Between Tradition and Modernity*, 8–9.
32 Cited in Nils Gilam, *Mandarins of the Future: Modernization Theory in Cold War America*, 142.
33 Cited in Hemant Shah, "Race, Mass Communication, and Modernization: Intellectual Networks and the Flow of Ideas," 25.
34 Julien Benda, *The Treason of the Intellectuals*; George Orwell, "Writers and Leviathan"; Leszek Kolakowski, *Marxism and Beyond: On Historical Understanding and Individual Responsibility*; Vaclav Havel, *Disturbing the Peace: A Conversation with Karel Hvizdala*.
35 Robert Levy, *Intellectuals, unissez-vous!*, 164.
36 Hitchens, "The Plight of the Public Intellectual," 63.
37 Benda, *The Treason of the Intellectuals*, 43.
38 Ibid.
39 Ibid., 57.
40 Ignazio Silone, speech delivered at the International PEN Club Conference at Basel titled, "On the place of intellect and pretension of the intellectual."
41 Havel, *Disturbing the Peace*, 167.
42 George Orwell, *The Lion and the Unicorn: Socialism and the English Genius*; Joyce Carey, *African Freedom*, 1.
43 Christopher Hitchens provides a good example of Orwell's "power of facing," where he constantly circumvented surveillance and interference during his time working at the BBC in India to disseminate banned works

and ideas like those that were critical of fascism. See Christopher Hitchens, *Why Orwell Matters*, 23–26.

44 Ibid., 29.

45 For an understanding of the roles played by the Dreyfusian intellectuals during France in the 1890s, including the prominent role played by Zola in organizing the intellectuals, see Lewis A. Coser, *Men of Ideas: A Sociologist's View*, 215–25; Kolakowski, *Marxism and Beyond*; Said, *Representations of the Intellectual*, 85–102.

46 Jerome Karabel advocates for a 'realist' tradition of intellectuals rooted in classical contemporary sociology. See Jerome Karabel, "Towards a theory of intellectuals and politics," 205–07.

47 Antonio Gramsci, "Croce and Julien Benda," 470.

48 Ibid., 5.

49 William Domhoff, *Who Rules America?*

50 Kurzman and Owens, "The Sociology of Intellectuals," 74.

51 Derek Gregory, *The Colonial Present*; Hobsbawm, *Nations and Nationalism*; Smith, *Theories of Nationalism*; Suny and Kennedy, *Intellectuals and the Articulation of the Nation*; Anderson, *Imagined Communities*; Eyerman, *Between Culture and Politics*.

52 Eyerman, *Between Culture and Politics*, 198.

53 Ibid.

54 Anderson, *Imagined Communities*; Suny and Kennedy, *Intellectuals and the Articulation of the Nation*; Smith, *Theories of Nationalism*; Hobsbawm, *Nations and Nationalism*.

55 Lorenz Khazaleh, "Benedict Anderson: 'I like nationalism's utopian elements.'"

56 Gregory, *The Colonial Present*.

57 Bacchi, *What's the Problem Represented to Be?*

58 Derek Gregory, *The Colonial Present*, 11.

59 Benda, *The Treason of the Intellectuals*.

60 Chomsky, "The Responsibility of Intellectuals." See also Noam Chomsky, *American Power and the New Mandarins*. Chomsky is extremely critical of the liberal intellectuals, the new mandarins, who provided the necessary ideological cover for the atrocities committed by American forces against the Vietnamese.

61 Russell distinguishes between two kinds of knowledge of truths. One is direct, intuitive, certain, and infallible. The other is indirect, derivative, uncertain, and open to error. See "1905: On Denoting," in Bertrand Russell, *Mind, Logic and Knowledge*, 32–56. Alfred Jules holds a logical positivist understanding of truth. See Alfred Jules Ayer, *Language, Truth, and Logic*. Rudolf Carnap holds a logical empiricist conception of truth. See Rudolf Carnap, "Testability and Meaning." Susan Haack holds a naturalist position. See Susan Haack, *Evidence and Inquiry: Towards Reconstruction in Episte-*

mology. Alston defends a realist conception of truth. See William P. Alston, *A Realist Conception of Truth*.

62 Richard Rorty, *Objectivity, Relativism, and Truth: Philosophical Papers*; Jacques Derrida, "Force of Law," in *Deconstruction and the Possibility of Justice*; Jacques Derrida, *Positions*; Hans-Georg Gadamer, "The Problem of Historical Consciousness"; Heidegger, *Being and Time*; Toulmin, *Human Understanding*; Caputo, *Truth*; Arendt, "Truth and Politics."

63 Toulmin, *Human Understanding*; Caputo, *Truth*.

64 Caputo, *Truth*, 3.

65 Heidegger, *Being and Time*.

66 Hubert Dreyfus, *Being-in-the-World: A Commentary on Heidegger's Being and time, Division 1*.

67 Gadamer, "The Problem of Historical Consciousness."

68 Millard Clements, "Theory and Education," 124.

69 Gadamer, "The Problem of Historical Consciousness," 155.

70 Heidegger, *Being and Time*.

71 Hans-Georg Gadamer, *Truth and Method*.

72 Ibid., 277.

73 See Arendt, *Was Ist Politik?*, 19.

74 Arendt, "Truth and Politics," 231.

3. Dialectics, Ideal Types, Fuzzy Categories, and Analyzing Language

1 Roslyn Bologh, *Dialectical Phenomenology: Marx's Method*, 3.

2 V.I. Lenin, "The Marx-Engels Correspondence," paragraph 8.

3 Ollman and Smith, "Dialectics: The New Frontier," 333.

4 Ibid., 333–34.

5 Bertell Ollman, "Why Dialectics? Why Now?," 340.

6 See Ollman, *Dance of the Dialectic*, 39–40.

7 Georg Wilhelm Friedrich Hegel, *The Science of Logic*, 734–53.

8 Ollman, *Dance of the Dialectic*, 42.

9 Cited in Ibid., 45.

10 Ibid., 341.

11 Lotfi A. Zadeh, "Fuzzy Sets," 338.

12 Ibid.

13 Charles C. Ragin, *Fuzzy-Set Social Science*.

14 Zadeh, "Fuzzy Sets"; Lotfi. A Zadeh, "A Fuzzy-Set-Theoretic Interpretation of Linguistic Hedges"; Lotfi A. Zadeh, "A Note on Prototype Theory and Fuzzy Sets."

15 Ragin, *Fuzzy-Set Social Science*, 2.

16 Ibid., 5–7.

17 Ibid., 5.

18 Ibid., 6–7.

19 Ibid., 7.

20 Max Weber, "'Objectivity' in Social Science and Social Policy," 90.
21 Ibid.
22 Susan J. Heckman, "Weber's Ideal Type: A Contemporary Reassessment," 121.
23 Weber, "'Objectivity,' in Social Science and Social Policy," 81.
24 Ibid., 90–91.
25 Ibid., 66.
26 Muhammad Idrees Ahmad provides one of the better studies charting the neoconservative network in his book, *The Road to Iraq: The Making of a Neoconservative War*.
27 Cited in Joshua Rust, *John Searle and the Construction of Social Reality*, 110.
28 Hofstadter and Sandel, *Surfaces and Essences*, 296.
29 Ibid., 89.
30 Ibid., 79.
31 Ibid., 90.
32 Ibid., 92.
33 Ibid., 93.
34 Deleuze, *Negotiations*; Osborne, "On mediators: intellectuals and the ideas trade in the knowledge society."
35 Lakoff and Johnson, *Metaphors We Live By*.
36 Lakoff, "The Conceptual Metaphor," 185–238.
37 Midgley, *The Myths We Live By*.
38 Ibid., 1.
39 S.v.Simile, *The Cambridge Guide to Literature in English*, 1028.
40 George A. Miller, "Images and Models, Simile and Metaphors."
41 H. Smith Richmond and J.V. Brogan, "Simile," in *The Princeton Encyclopedia of Poetry and Poetics*.
42 S.v.Allegory, *The Cambridge Guide to Literature in English*, 9.
43 Midori Shibata et al., "Does simile comprehension differ from metaphor comprehension? A functional MRI study," 254.
44 Ibid.
45 Aristotle, *The Art of Rhetoric*, 367.
46 Shibata et al., "Does simile comprehension differ from metaphor comprehension?"
47 Sam Glucksberg, "The psycholinguistics of metaphor"; Sam Glucksberg and Boaz Keysar, "Understanding Metaphorical Comparisons: Beyond Similarity."
48 Shibata et al., "Does simile comprehension differ from metaphor comprehension?", 254.
49 See Dan Chiappe and John Kennedy, "Are metaphors elliptical similes?"; Dan Chiappe and John Kennedy, "Literal bases for metaphor and simile"; Dan Chiappe, John Kennedy, and Tim Smykowski, "Reversibility, aptness, and the conventionality of metaphors and similes."

50 Paul Bartha, "Analogy and Analogical Reasoning," paragraph 1.
51 John Algeo and Adele Algeo, *Fifty Years Among the New Words: A Dictionary of neologisms 1941–1991*, 1.
52 John Algeo, "Vocabulary"; John Algeo, "Where do all the new words come from?"; David Crystal, *The Cambridge Encyclopedia of the English language*; John Ayto, *Twentieth Century Words*.
53 Christopher Hitchens, "Defending Islamofascism: It's a valid term. Here's why," paragraph 3.
54 Ibid., paragraph 3.
55 Gaffney Jr., "Seeing the threat for what it is," paragraph 1.
56 "Neologism," *The American Heritage Medical Dictionary*.
57 Cerulo, *Deciphering Violence*.
58 Pirjo Nikander, "Constructionism and Discourse Analysis," 413.
59 James Paul Gee, *An Introduction to Discourse Analysis*, 11.
60 Norman Fairclough, *Discourse and Social Change*, 64.
61 Norman Fairclough defines critical discourse analysis as "discourse analysis which aims to systematically explore often opaque relationships of causality and determination between (a) discursive practices, events, and texts, and (b) wider social and cultural structures, relations and processes; to investigate how such practices, events, and texts arise out of and are ideologically shaped by relations of power and struggles over power; and to explore how the opacity of these relationships between discourse and society is itself a factor securing power and hegemony." See Fairclough and Holes, *Critical Discourse Analysis*, 135.
62 Norman Fairclough, *Analysing Discourse: Textual Analysis for Social Research*, 218.
63 Edward Said, *Culture and Imperialism*, 14.
64 Marianne Jørgensen and Louise Phillips, *Discourse Analysis as Theory and Method*, 64.
65 Ruth Wodak, "Aspects of Critical Discourse Analysis."
66 Ruth Wodak and Michael Meyer, "Critical Discourse Analysis: History, Agenda, Theory and Methodology," 8.
67 Fairclough, *Analysing Discourse*, 21–39.

4. Spreading the Rule of Reason: Liberal Imaginings of Wahhabism

1 Bacchi, *What's the Problem Represented to Be?*
2 Maureen Dowd, "Loosey Goosey Saudi."
3 See, for example, Amnesty International, "Saudi Arabia: Threats and cyber attack will not deter women from driving."
4 R. Jeffrey Lustig, *Corporate Liberalism: The Origins of Modern American Political Theory, 1890–1920*, 6.
5 Isaiah Berlin, "The Pursuit of the Ideal."
6 Cited in Joshua Cherniss and Henry Hardy, "Isaiah Berlin."
7 Isaiah Berlin, "The Pursuit of the Ideal," 28.

8 Ibid., 13.
9 For a basic understanding of some of the changes implemented by Morsi's government, collusion between his party and other ultraconservative Islamist parties and some of the implications of these actions, see BBC, "Profile: Egypt's Muslim Brotherhood."
10 Gray, *Black Mass*. See chapter "Armed Missionaries," 146–83.
11 Maurice Cranston, "Liberalism," 458.
12 John Locke cited in Karl Olivecrona, "Appropriation in the State of Nature: Locke on the Origin of Property," 217.
13 John Stuart Mill, *Collected Works of John Stuart Mill*, 262.
14 Gerald Gaus and Shane D. Courtland, "Liberalism."
15 Ibid.
16 Mill, *Collected Works*, 267.
17 Gaus and Courtland, "Liberalism."
18 Mill describes this principle in the first chapter of *Liberty*: "The object of this essay is to assert one very simple principle, as entitled to govern absolutely the dealings of society with the individual in the way of compulsion and control, whether the means used be physical force in the form of legal penalties, or the moral coercion of public opinion. That principle is, that the sole end for which mankind are warranted, individually or collectively, in interfering with the liberty of action of any of their number, is self-protection. That the only purpose for which power can be rightfully exercised over any member of a civilized community, against his will, is to prevent harm to others. His own good, either physical or moral, is not a sufficient warrant. He cannot rightfully be compelled to do or forbear because it will be better for him to do so, because it will make him happier, because, in the opinion of others, to do so would be wise, or even right. . . . The only part of the conduct of anyone, for which he is amenable to society, is that which concerns others. In the part which merely concerns himself, his independence, is, of right, absolute. Over himself, over his own body and mind, the individual is sovereign." See John Stuart Mill, *Liberty*, 72–73.
19 Ibid., 179.
20 Gaus and Courtland, "Liberalism."
21 Paul Starr cited in Stanley Fish, "Liberalism and Secularism: One and the Same," paragraph 8.
22 Ibid., paragraph 10.
23 Ibid., paragraph 2.
24 Ibid., paragraph 13.
25 Zadeh, "A Note on Prototype Theory and Fuzzy Sets," 291–95.
26 See Margaret Meek Lange, "Progress."
27 Ibid.
28 Anne-Robert-Jacques Turgot, "A Philosophical Review of the Successive Advances of the Human Mind"; Anne-Robert-Jacques Turgot, " On

University History"; Immanuel Kant, "Idea for a Universal History with a Cosmopolitan Purpose"; Marquis de Condorcet, *Outlines of an Historical View of the Progress of the Human Mind*; John Rawls, *A Theory of Justice*; John Rawls, *Political Liberalism*; John Stuart Mill, *On Liberty, Utilitarianism, and Other Essays*.

29 Rawls, *A Theory of Justice*, 4.
30 Ibid., 131.
31 John Rawls, "An Idea of Overlapping Consensus," 11.
32 Lange, "Progress."
33 Turgot, "On Universal History," 88.
34 Condorcet, *Outlines of an Historical View of the Progress of the Human Mind*, 123–24.
35 Kant, "Idea for a Universal History with a Cosmopolitan Purpose," 42–44.
36 Immanuel Kant, "Toward Perpetual Peace: A Philosophical Sketch," 98ff.
37 Thomas Farr, "Obama administration sidelines religious freedom policy."
38 Ibid., 8, paragraphs 4–5.
39 Lakoff, *Moral Politics*, 109.
40 Ibid., 109–10.
41 Ibid., 117.
42 Ibid., 204.
43 Doug Bandow, "Befriending Saudi Princes: A High Price for a Dubious Alliance," *USA Today*, 22.
44 Bandow, "Befriending Saudi Princes," Cato Institute, 2–3.
45 John Rawls, *Law of Peoples*, 59–61.
46 Ibid., 81.
47 John Keats, "32. Endymion, Book 1."
48 Dowd, "Loosey Goosey Saudi."
49 Mark Lander, "Obama Seeks Reset in Arab World."
50 Fareed Zakaria, "The Saudi Trap," paragraphs 23–25.
51 Azeem Ibrahim, "Secretary Kerry Must Stop U.S. Support for Islamic Extremism."
52 Ibid., paragraphs 3–4.
53 Cerulo, *Deciphering Violence*, 24–26.
54 Ibid., 17–21.
55 Ibid.
56 Thomas L. Friedman, "The Chant Not Heard," 11, paragraphs 4–6.
57 Thomas L. Friedman, "An Islamic Reformation," paragraph 1.
58 Ibid., paragraph 1.
59 Fareed Zakaria, "U.S. fuel to the Middle East fire," paragraph 2.
60 Bandow, "Befriending Saudi Princes," Cato Institute, 3.
61 Thomas L. Friedman, "The Other Arab Awakening," paragraph 2.
62 Ibid., paragraph 9.
63 Charles Lyell, *Principles of Geology*.

64 Dowd, "Loosey Goosey Saudi," paragraphs 11–12.
65 This period in the United States is well known for its counter culture and revolutionary movements that included the US Civil Rights movement and the second wave of the feminist movement. The counter-culture movement played a major role in 'liberating' many aspects of US society, including sexual identity and relations, questioning of authority, the role of government, and the demanding of freedoms for women and minorities. See, for example, Gerd-Rainer Horn, "The Birth of Second-Wave Feminism," in *The Spirit of '68: Rebellion in Western Europe and North America, 1956–1976*, 217–19.
66 Farr, "Obama administration sidelines religious freedom policy," paragraphs 5, 13.
67 Zakaria, "U.S. fuel to the Middle East fire," paragraph 5.
68 Ibid.
69 Dan Bilefsky, "An Islamic Revival in Bosnia Tests a Fragile Nation's Secular Cast."
70 Ibid., paragraph 8.
71 Ibid., paragraph 22.
72 See, for example, Nicholas Kristof, "The Terrorists the Saudis Cultivate in Peaceful Countries"; Daria Sito-Sucic, "Bosnia's Muslims divided over inroads of Wahhabism."
73 Bilefsky, "An Islamic Revival in Bosnia Tests a Fragile Nation's Secular Cast," paragraphs 30–31.
74 Ibid., paragraphs 19–21, 32.
75 Thomas L. Friedman, "Caution, Curves Ahead."
76 Ibid., paragraph 3.
77 Ibid., paragraph 4.
78 Ibid., paragraph 6.
79 Ibid., paragraph 8.

5. Themata, Generative Metaphors, and Making Sense of Liberal Intellectuals' Representations of Wahhabism

1 Hannah Arendt, *Rahel Varnhagen: The Life of a Jewess*.
2 Holton, "The Role of Themata in Science"; Danziger, "Generative metaphor and the history of psychological discourse."
3 Robert Nisbet, *Sociology as an Art Form*.
4 Gerald Holton, *Thematic Origins of Scientific Thought: Kepler to Einstein*.
5 Holton, "The Role of Themata in Science," 456.
6 Ibid.
7 Ibid., 454.
8 Ibid., 455.
9 Nisbet, *Sociology as an Art Form*, 29.
10 Holton, "The Role of Themata in Science," 458; Stephen Thornton, "Karl

Popper."
11 Holton, "The Role of Themata in Science," 458.
12 Ibid.
13 Ibid., 454–55.
14 Ibid.
15 Ibid., 456.
16 Ibid., 458.
17 Ibid., 456.
18 Ibid., 461.
19 Ibid., 462.
20 Ibid., 461–62.
21 Nisbet, *Sociology as an Art Form*, 37.
22 Ibid., 40.
23 Danziger, "Generative metaphor and the history of psychological discourse."
24 Ibid., 332.
25 Ibid., 331–32.
26 Ibid., 332.
27 Ibid.
28 Ibid.
29 Nisbet, *Sociology as an Art Form*, 33.
30 Danziger, "Generative metaphor and the history of psychological discourse," 333.
31 Ibid., 351.
32 Zhenghuan Zhou, *Liberal Rights and Political Culture: Envisioning Democracy in China*, 125.
33 Friedman, "An Islamic Reformation," paragraph 1.
34 Zakaria, "U.S. fuel to the Middle East fire," paragraph 2.
35 Bandow, "Befriending Saudi Princes," Cato Institute, paragraph 9.
36 Friedman, "An Islamic Reformation," paragraph 11.
37 Herbert Spencer, "Progress: Its Law and Cause," 2.
38 Lange, "Progress."
39 Spencer, "Progress: Its Law and Cause," 9.
40 Mill, "On Liberty," 14–15.
41 Friedman, "The Other Arab Awakening," paragraph 9.
42 Ibid., paragraph 2.
43 Danziger, "Generative metaphor and the history of psychological discourse," 331–32.
44 Ibid., 333.
45 Dowd, "Loosey Goosey Saudi," paragraph 6.
46 Ibid., paragraph 12.
47 Farr, "Obama adminstration sidelines religious freedom policy," paragraph 12.
48 David Hume, *The Natural History of Religion*, §III6.

49 Terry Eagleton, *On Evil*, 47.
50 Alasdair McIntyre, *After Virtue*.

6. Those Evil and Violent Savages: The Neoconservative Assault on Wahhabism, Saudi Arabia, and the Palestinian Struggle for Self-Determination

1 George W. Bush, "Address to a joint session of Congress and the nation."
2 Grondin, "Mistaking Hegemony for Empire"; George, "Leo Strauss."
3 Ian Shapiro makes this point in his book *Containment: Rebuilding a Strategy Against Global Terror*, xii.
4 Samuel Huntington is most popular for his clash of civilizations theory, which is the idea that people's religious and cultural identities would be the primary source of conflict in the post-Cold War world. Daniel Patrick Moynihan was a Democratic senator popular for his controversial governmental report *The Negro Family: The Case for National Action*, which was widely criticized at the time for blaming poor black American families for their dire economic situations. Irving Kristol, who is widely understood to be the godfather of neoconservatism, has enjoyed recent fame for the key role he played in creating a political faction intimately associated with the Bush administration's war on terror and its invasion of Iraq. Jeane Kirkpatrick was the US ambassador to the UN under President Ronald Reagan. She was fiercely anticommunist and is perhaps best known for championing a US foreign policy approach that embraced 'friendly authoritarian regimes,' which created tension in the neoconservative movement. While this approach received support from prominent intellectuals in the movement like Kristol, the second wave of neoconservative intellectuals has moved away from this approach and instead adopted the promotion of democracy abroad as the modus operandi.
5 Shadia Drury is a key proponent of this interpretation. See Shadia Drury, *Leo Strauss and the American Right* and Shadia Drury, *The Political Ideas of Leo Strauss*. This point was also made in the BBC documentary "The Power of Nightmares," which equated Strauss with Islamic political theologian Sayyid Qutb, claiming Strauss was to neoconservatives what Qutb was to al-Qaeda. See BBC, "The power of nightmares," written and produced by Adam Curtis, first broadcast October–November 2004.
6 Michael Harrington, "The Welfare State and Its Neoconservative Critics."
7 Irving Kristol, "Confessions of a True, Self-Confessed—Perhaps the Only—'Neo-conservative.'"
8 Irving Kristol, *Two Cheers for Capitalism*.
9 Charles Hagel, *Our Next Chapter: Tough Questions, Straight Answers*, 50; Grondin, "Mistaking Hegemony for Empire," 227–28.
10 George, "Leo Strauss," 76; Piki Ish-Shalom, "'The Civilization of Clashes': Misapplying the Democratic Peace in the Middle East," 533.

11 Muhammad Idrees Ahmad, *The Road to Iraq*, 6–13.
12 Ibid.
13 Michael Dolny, "FAIR STUDY: Think Tank Spectrum 2012."
14 Ahmad makes the point that the Brookings Institute has become more welcoming of neoconservative opinion since the establishment of the Saban Center for Middle East Policy at the think tank. The Saban Center was set up by Israeli-American media mogul Haim Saban, who is well known for his hardline pro-Israeli political posture. See Ahmad, *The Road to Iraq*, 13.
15 Fred Barnes, "Can Ted Cruz Actually Win?," 11–12; Stephen F. Hayes, "Donald Trump, Policy Wonk?," 18–20; William Kristol, "Donald and Decadence," 7.
16 Kristol, "Donald and Decadence," 7; John McCormack, "Unfit to Serve," 9–10.
17 John Mearsheimer, "Hans Morgenthau and the Iraq War: realism versus neo-conservatism," paragraph 19.
18 Arthur A. Goldsmith, "Making the World Safe for Partial Democracy? Questioning the Premises of Democracy Promotion," 3.
19 Ibid., 1.
20 George W. Bush, "President Bush Delivers State of the Union Address."
21 Ibid.
22 Ibid.
23 Mearsheimer, "Hans Morgenthau and the Iraq War," paragraph 19.
24 Bush, "President Bush Delivers State of the Union Address."
25 Mearsheimer, "Hans Morgenthau and the Iraq War," paragraph 19.
26 Francis Fukuyama, The End of History and the Last Man.
27 Jacob Heilbrunn, *They Knew They Were Right: The Rise of the Neocons*, 11.
28 Ted Boettner traces the movement's modern pro-Israeli stance back to the formative role played by intellectuals like Richard Perle, Paul Wolfowitz, Douglas Feith, Abram Shulsky, and Elliot Abrams. According to Boettner, many of these neoconservative intellectuals were strongly influenced by their Jewish religious beliefs and had been personally affected by events like the Holocaust and anti-Jewish discriminatory practices in the United States. See Ted Boettner, "Neo-Conservatism and Foreign Policy." Brandon High emphasizes the influential roles played by Jewish Marxist intellectuals in the formation of the neoconservative movement in the 1960s and 1970s. See Brandon High, "The Recent Historiography of American Neoconservatism," 475–91. Jacob Heilbrunn claims that this modern 'pro-Israeli' political posture is related to Jewish neoconservative intellectuals' experiences with anti-Semitism in the United States, the Holocaust, and the treatment of Jews by totalitarian regimes like Stalinist Russia. See Jacob Heilbrunn, *They Knew They Were Right*, 11–14.
29 Joel Benin, Stephen Walt, and John Mearsheimer are among those to point out the similarities in foreign policy between 'right-wing' political

and religious elements in Israel such as the Likud Party and US foreign policy promoted by neoconservatives. These authors have also highlighted numerous instances when neoconservatives have promoted foreign policies that prioritize the interests of the state of Israel to the detriment of US interests. Benin, Walt, and Mearsheimer identify the US involvement in Iraq as an example. Walt and Mearsheimer write, "Within the United States, the main driving force behind the Iraq war was a small band of neoconservatives, many with close ties to Israel's Likud Party." See John Mearsheimer and Stephen Walt, "The Israel Lobby and U.S. Foreign Policy," 54; Joel Benin, "The Israelization of American Middle East Policy Discourse."

30 Gaffney Jr., "Seeing the threat for what it is," paragraph 11.

31 David G. Littman, "Teaching Hatred in Saudi Arabia and Egypt: The UN Response"; Raymond Ibrahim, "Saudi Hypocrisy At Its Best"; Robert Spencer, "The Swine are Christians and the Apes are Jews"; Joe Kaufman and Beila Rabinowitz, "Islamic Saudi Hate Academy."

32 Kaufman and Rabinowitz, "Islamic Saudi Hate Academy."

33 Spencer, "The Swine are Christians and the Apes are Jews."

34 Saudi Press Agency (Riyadh), "Deputy Crown Prince Chairs Cabinet's Session," cited in Christopher M. Blanchard, "Saudi Arabia: Background and U.S. Relations," 29.

35 Blanchard, "Saudi Arabia: Background and U.S. Relations," 29.

36 See, for example, Frank Gaffney Jr., "Saudi Friends and Foes: Duplicitous desert kingdom could turn U.S. weapons on us"; Rachel Abrams, "Peace Process"; Lee Smith, "Requiem for the Peace Process."

37 Nicholas Saidel, "Saudi Arabia, the Mediator Israelis and Palestinians Have Been Waiting For?"

38 Bret Stephens, "The Arab Invasion."

39 Ibid., paragraphs 1–2, 5–6.

40 J.M. Blaut, *The Colonizer's Model of the World: Geographical Diffusionism and Eurocentric History*; J.M. Blaut, *Eight Eurocentric Historians*.

41 Cerulo, *Deciphering Violence*, 21.

42 Ibid., 23.

43 Ibid.

44 Gustav Jahoda, *Images of Savages: Ancient Roots of Modern Prejudice in Western Culture*.

45 Nick Haslem, "Dehumanization: An Integrative Review," 252.

46 Reuel Marc Gerecht, "Radioactive Regime," paragraph 21.

47 Amnesty International reports, "Most executions [in Saudi Arabia] are by beheading. Many take place in public. In some cases, decapitated bodies are left hanging in public squares as a 'deterrent.'" See Amnesty International, "Saudi Arabia: Scheduled beheading reflects authorities' callous disregard to human rights." See also Human Rights Watch, "Saudi Arabia: Surge in Executions."

48 David Pryce-Jones, "The Saudi Revolution," paragraphs 3–4.

49 Ibid., paragraph 7.
50 Ibid., paragraphs 4–5.
51 Ibid., paragraph 1.
52 Susan George, *Hijacking America: How the Religious and Secular Right Changed What Americans Think*, 69.
53 Ibid.
54 Frank Gaffney Jr., "Saudi friends and foes."
55 Ibid., paragraph 1.
56 Ibid., paragraph 2.
57 Ibid., paragraph 4.
58 Frank Gaffney Jr., "Undesirable influence."
59 Ibid., paragraphs 5, 7, 10.
60 Ibid., paragraph 9.
61 Ibid., paragraph 5.
62 For an understanding of the influence the Israeli lobby has had on US foreign policy see Mearsheimer and Walt, "The Israel Lobby and U.S. Foreign Policy."
63 Gaffney Jr., "Seeing the threat for what it is."
64 Ibid., paragraph 7.
65 Ibid., paragraphs 10–11.
66 Ibid., paragraph 4.
67 For an understanding of this analogy see Hitchens, "Defending Islamofascism."
68 Wikileaks, "H: ISRAEL, COUPLE OF THINGS. SID," paragraph 1.
69 Clifford May, "No Peace While World War Rages."
70 Ibid., paragraphs 1, 5, 7.
71 Cerulo, *Deciphering Violence*, 20.
72 May, "No Peace While World War Rages," paragraph 8.
73 Michael Ledeen, "The Wider War," *Wall Street Journal*; Michael Ledeen, "The Wider War," American Enterprise Institute.
74 Ibid., paragraph 3.
75 Ibid., paragraphs 2, 6.
76 Ibid., paragraphs 8–9.
77 Ibid., paragraph 18.
78 Reuel Marc Gerecht, "What Hath Ju-Ju Wrought!," paragraph 18.
79 Holton, "The Role of Themata in Science," 455.
80 Many neoconservatives use the Biblical terms Judea and Samaria when referring to what others typically refer to as the West Bank. See, for example, Fred Barnes, "In Defense of Settlers," paragraphs 3, 6–7; Rachel Abrams, "Cut Off Your Israeli Nose to Spite Your Palestinian Face," paragraph 1.
81 Donald Schön, "Generative metaphor: A perspective on problem-setting in social policy."
82 Danziger, "Generative metaphor and the history of psychological discourse," 351.

83 Gaffney Jr., "Seeing the threat for what it is."
84 Walter Wink, "Facing the Myth of Redemptive Violence," 2007.
85 Walter Wink, "Facing the Myth of Redemptive Violence," 1999, 1.
86 "Irving Kristol (1920–2009)," Right Web, paragraph 3.
87 David Frum and Richard Perle, *An End to Evil: How to Win the War on Terror*, 43.
88 Timothy J. Lynch, "Kristol Balls: Neoconservative Visions of Islam and the Middle East," 193–94.
89 Frum and Perle, *An End to Evil*, 147.
90 Jahoda, *Images of Savages*.
91 See Frank Chalk and Kurt Jonassohn, *The History and Sociology of Genocide: Analyses and Case Studies*; Herbert C. Kelman, "Violence Without Restraint: Reflections on the dehumanization of victims and victimizers."
92 Gaffney Jr., "Saudi friends and foes," paragraph 1.
93 Ibid., paragraph 2.
94 Bret Stephens, "The Arab Invasion."
95 Ibid., paragraph 8.
96 Ibid.
97 Gerecht, "What Hath Ju-Ju Wrought!," paragraph 18.
98 Ibid.
99 Michael W. Schwartz, "Wahhabism and the First Amendment," paragraph 15.
100 Clifford D. May, "Terror in Saudi Arabia," paragraph 18; Clifford D. May, "Saudi Ride of Tiger Gets Riskier," paragraph 14.
101 May, "Terror in Saudi Arabia"; May, "Saudi Ride of Tiger Gets Riskier"; Michael Ledeen, *The War Against the Terror Masters: Why it Happened. Where Are We Now. How We'll Win*, 76.
102 Stephen Schwartz and Irfan al-Alawi, "Valentine's Day in Saudi Arabia," paragraph 2; Stephen Schwartz, "The Second Kosovo War," paragraph 7.
103 Jahoda, *Images of Savages*.
104 Haslem, "Dehumanization: An Integrative Review," 252.
105 Reuel Marc Gerecht, "Victory Without Soldiers," 34; Reuel Marc Gerecht, "Wither Jihad?," 10.
106 Daniel Pipes's Twitter account, December 9, 2014, https://twitter.com/danielpipes/status/542428582891380736; Stephens, "The Arab Invasion," paragraphs 1–2; Pryce-Jones, "The Saudi Revolution," paragraph 5.
107 Gerecht, "What Hath Ju-Ju Wrought!," paragraphs 2, 17.
108 Ibid., paragraph 2.
109 Ter Ellingson, *The Myth of the Noble Savage*, 291–97, 343–45.
110 Amelia Hill, "Racists Created the Noble Savage," paragraph 4.
111 Ibid., paragraphs 1, 8.
112 These ideas are commonly traced back to the works of Thomas Hobbes. For an understanding of this approach, see Sharon A. Lloyd and Susanne Sreedhar, "Hobbes's Moral and Political Philosophy."

Bibliography

Abrams, Rachel. "Cut Off Your Israeli Nose to Spite Your Palestinian Face." *The Weekly Standard*, January 5, 2010. http://www.weeklystandard.com/cut-off-your-israeli-nose-to-spite-your-palestinian-face/article/413721.

———. "Peace Process." *The Weekly Standard*, May 22, 2009. www.weeklystandard.com/peace-process/article/28979.

Adut, Ari. "A Theory of the Public Sphere." *Sociological Theory* 30, no. 4 (2012): 238–62. doi:10.1177/0735275112467012.

Ahmad, Muhammad Idrees. *The Road to Iraq: The Making of a Neoconservative War*. Edinburgh: Edinburgh University Press, 2014.

Algar, Hamid. *Wahhabism: A Critical Essay*. Oneonta: Islamic Publications International, 2002.

Algeo, John. "Vocabulary." In *The Cambridge History of the English Language, Volume 4: 1776–1997*. Edited by Suzanne Romaine, 57–91. Cambridge: Cambridge University Press, 1998.

———. "Where do all the new words come from?" *American Speech* 55, no. 4 (1980): 264–77. www.jstor.org/stable/454567.

Algeo, John, and Adele Algeo. *Fifty Years Among the New Words: A Dictionary of Neologisms 1941–1991*. Cambridge: Cambridge University Press, 1991.

Allen, Charles. *God's Terrorists: The Wahhabi Cult and The Hidden Roots of Modern Jihad*. Cambridge: Da Capo Press, 2006.

Alston, William P. *A Realist Conception of Truth*. Ithaca: Cornell University Press, 1997.

Althusser, Louis, ed. *Lenin and Philosophy and other essays*. New York: Monthly Review Press, 1971.

The American Heritage Medical Dictionary. "Neologism." Boston: Houghton Mifflin, 2007.

Amnesty International. "Saudi Arabia: Scheduled beheading reflects authorities' callous disregard to human rights." August 22, 2014. https://www.amnesty.org/en/latest/news/2014/08/saudi-arabia-scheduled-beheading-reflects-authorities-callous-disregard-human-rights/.

———. "Saudi Arabia: Threats and cyber attack will not deter women from driving." October 23, 2013. www.amnesty.org/en/news/saudi-arabia-threats-and-cyber-attack-will-not-deter-women-driving-2013-10-25.

Anderson, Benedict. *Imagined Communities: Reflections on the Origins and Spread of Nationalism*. 2nd ed. London: Verso, 1991.

Andreotti, Sebastiano. "The Ikhwan Movement and Its Role in Saudi Arabia's State-Building." In *State Formation and Identity in the Middle East and North Africa*, edited by Kenneth Christie and Mohammad Masad, 87–112. New York: Palgrave Macmillan, 2013.

Arendt, Hannah. *Rahel Varnhagen: The Life of a Jewess*, 1st ed. Edited by Liliane Weissberg. Translated by Richard and Clara Winston. Baltimore: John Hopkins University Press, 1997.

———. "Truth and Politics." In *Between Past and Future: Eight Exercises in Political Thought*, 227–64. New York: Penguin, 1993.

———. *Was Ist Politik?* Edited by Ursula Ludz. Munich: Piper Verlag, 1993.

Aristotle. *The Art of Rhetoric*. Translated by John Henry Freese. London: Willian Heinemann, 1926.

Armajani, Jon. "Saudi Arabia." In *Modern Islamist Movements: History, Religion, and Politics*, 122–63. Oxford: Wiley-Blackwell, 2011. doi:10.1002/9781444344394.ch4.

Armanios, Febe. *CRS Report for Congress: The Islamic Traditions of Wahhabism and Salafiyya*. Washington: Congressional Research Service, 2003. Order code RS21695.

Aron, Raymond. *The Opium of the Intellectuals*. New Brunswick: Transaction Publishers, 2000.

al-Atawneh, Muhammad. *Wahhabi Islam Facing the Challenges of Modernity: Dar Al-Ifta in the Modern Saudi State*. Studies in Islamic Law and Society, vol. 32. Leiden: E.J. Brill, 2010.

———. "Wahhabi Self-Examination Post-9/11: Rethinking the 'Other', 'Otherness' and Tolerance." *Middle Eastern Studies* 47, no. 2 (2011): 255–71. doi:10.1080/00263206.2011.544098.

Atkin, Muriel. "The Rhetoric of Islamophobia." *Central Asia and the Caucasus*, no. 1 (2000): 123–32. https://www.ca-c.org/journal/eng-01-2000/16.atkin.shtml.

Atkins, Stephen E. *Encyclopedia of Modern Worldwide Extremists and Extremist Groups*. Westport: Praeger, 2004. www.praeger.com.ezproxy.lib.rmit.edu.au.

Ayer, Alfred Jules. *Language, Truth, and Logic*. 2nd ed. London: Gollancz, 1946.

Ayto, John. *Twentieth Century Words*. Oxford: Oxford University Press, 1999.

Bacchi, Carol. *What's the Problem Represented to Be?* New Jersey: Pearson Education Australia, 2009.

Baert, Patrick, and Joel Isaac. "Intellectuals and Society: Sociological and Historical Perspectives." In *Routledge International Handbook of Contemporary Social and Political Theory*, edited by Gerard Delanty and Stephen P. Turner, 200–11. London: Routledge, 2011.

Bandow, Doug. "Befriending Saudi Princes: A High Price for a Dubious Alliance." *Cato Institute*. March 20, 2002. https://www.cato.org/publications/policy-analysis/befriending-saudi-princes-high-price-dubious-alliance.

———. "Befriending Saudi Princes: A High Price for a Dubious Alliance." *USA Today*. July 2002.

Barnes, Fred. "Can Ted Cruz Actually Win?" *The Weekly Standard*. December 28, 2015/January 4, 2016.

———. "In Defense of Settlers." *The Weekly Standard*. August 27, 2010. www.weeklystandard.com/blogs/defense-settlers.

Bartha, Paul. "Analogy and Analogical Reasoning." *The Stanford Encyclopedia of Philosophy* (Fall 2013 ed.). Edited by Edward N. Zalta. http://plato.stanford.edu/archives/fall2013/entries/reasoning-analogy.

Bateson, Gregory. *Steps to an Ecology of Mind*. London: Paladin, 1972.

BBC. "Iraq's Weapons of Mass Destruction." September 24, 2002. www.bbc.co.uk/turkish/iraqdossier.pdf.

———. "Profile: Egypt's Muslim Brotherhood." December 25, 2013. www.bbc.com/news/world-middle-east-12313405.

Beinin, Joel. "The Israelization of American Middle East Policy Discourse." *Social Text* 21, no. 2 (2003): 125–39. http://muse.jhu.edu.ezproxy.lib.rmit.edu.au/journals/social_text/v021/21.2beinin.html.

Benda, Julien. *The Treason of the Intellectuals*. New York: W.W. Norton and Company, 1969.

Berger, Peter. *Invitation to Sociology. A Humanistic Perspective*. New York: Doubleday, 1963.

Bergmann, Gustav. *Logic and Reality*. Wisconsin: University of Wisconsin Press, 1964.

Berlin, Isaiah. "The Pursuit of the Ideal." In *The Crooked Timber of Humanity: Chapters in the History of Ideas*, edited by Henry Hardy and John Banville, 1–20. Princeton: Princeton University Press, 2013.

Bilefsky, Dan. "An Islamic Revival in Bosnia Tests a Fragile Nation's Secular Cast." *New York Times*, December 27, 2008. www.nytimes.com/2008/12/27/world/europe/27islam.html.

Bisley, Nick. *Great Powers in the Changing International Order*. Boulder: Lynne Rienner, 2012.

Blake, William. "The Everlasting Gospel." In *The Oxford Book of English Mystical Verse*, edited by D.H.S. Nicholson and A.H.E. Lee, 58. Oxford: Clarendon Press, 1917.

Blanchard, Christopher M. *CRS Report for Congress: The Islamic Traditions of Wahhabism and Salafiyya.* January 24, 2008. Washington: Congressional Research Service. Order code RS21695.

———. "Saudi Arabia: Background and U.S. Relations." *Congressional Research Service.* April 22, 2016. www.fas.org/sgp/crs/mideast/RL33533.pdf.

Blaut, J.M. *The Colonizer's Model of the World: Geographical Diffusionism and Eurocentric History.* New York: Guilford Press, 2000.

———. *Eight Eurocentric Historians.* New York: Guilford Press, 2000.

Boettner, Ted. "Neo-Conservatism and Foreign Policy." Master's thesis, University of New Hampshire, 2002. ProQuest (UMI Number: 1472051).

Bologh, Roslyn. *Dialectical Phenomenology (Routledge Revivals): Marx's Method.* New York: Routledge, 2009.

Bowen, Innes. *Medina in Birmingham, Najaf in Brent: Inside British Islam.* London: Hurst & Co., 2014.

Burke, Edmund. *Philosophical Enquiry: Into the Origins of Our Ideas of the Sublime and the Beautiful.* Edited by J.T. Boulton. Oxford: Basil Blackwell, 1987.

Bush, George W. "Address to a joint session of Congress and the nation." *The Washington Post*, September 20, 2001. www.washingtonpost.com/wp-srv/nation/specials/attacked/transcripts/bushaddress_092001.html.

———. "President Bush Delivers State of the Union Address." January 21, 2006. Washington, DC: White House. https://georgewbush-whitehouse.archives.gov/news/releases/2002/01/20020129-11.html.

Butler, Judith, and Gayatri Chakravorty Spivak. *Who Sings the Nation State? Language, Politics, Belonging.* Calcutta: Seagull Books, 2007.

Caputo, John. *Truth.* London: Penguin, 2014.

Carey, Joyce. *African Freedom.* London: Secker & Warburg, 1941.

Carnap, Rudolf. "Empiricism, Semantics, and Ontology." *Revue internationale de philosophie* 4 (1950): 20–40. http://www.ditext.com/carnap/carnap.html.

———. "Testability and Meaning." *Philosophy of Science* 3, no. 4 (1936): 419–71, *Philosophy of Science* 4, no. 1 (1937): 1–40.

The Cambridge Guide to Literature in English. 3rd edition. Edited by Dominic Head. Cambridge: Cambridge University Press, 2006.

Cassirer, Ernst. *The Philosophy of Symbolic Forms. Volume One: Language.* Translated by Bruno Cassirer. New Haven: Yale University Press, 1955.

———. *The Philosophy of Symbolic Forms. Volume Two: Mythical Thought.* Translated by Bruno Cassirer. New Haven: Yale University Press, 1955.

———. *The Philosophy of Symbolic Forms. Volume Three: The Phenomenology of Knowledge.* Translated by Ralph Manheim. New Haven: Yale University Press, 1965.

———. *The Philosophy of Symbolic Forms. Volume Four: The Metaphysics of Symbolic Forms.* Edited by John Michael Krois and Donald Phillip Verene. Translated by John Michael Krois. New Haven: Yale University Press, 1998.

Cerulo, Karen. *Deciphering Violence: The Cognitive Structure of Right and Wrong*. New York: Routledge, 1998.
Chalk, Frank Robert, and Kurt Jonassohn. *The History and Sociology of Genocide: Analyses and Case Studies*. New Haven: Yale University Press, 1990.
Chehab, Zaki. *Inside Hamas: The Untold Story of Militants, Martyrs and Spies*. London: I.B.Tauris, 2007.
Cherniss, Joshua, and Henry Hardy. "Isaiah Berlin." *The Stanford Encyclopedia of Philosophy* (Winter 2014 ed.). Edited by Edward N. Zalta. http://plato.stanford.edu/archives/fall2014/entries/berlin.
Chiappe, Dan, and John Kennedy. "Are Metaphors Elliptical Similes?" *Journal of Psycholinguistic Research* 29, no. 4 (2000): 371–98. doi:10.1023/A:1005103211670.
———. "Literal Bases for Metaphor and Simile." *Metaphor and Symbol* 16, no. 3 (2001): 249–76. doi:10.1080/10926488.2001.9678897.
Chiappe, Dan, John Kennedy, and Tim Smykowski. "Reversibility, Aptness, and the Conventionality of Metaphors and Similes." *Metaphor and Symbol* 18, no. 2 (2003): 85–105. doi:10.1207/S15327868MS1802_2.
Chomsky, Noam. *American Power and the New Mandarins*. New York: Pantheon, 1969.
———. "The Responsibility of Intellectuals." *The New York Review of Books*, February 23, 1967. http://www.nybooks.com/articles/1967/02/23/a-special-supplement-the-responsibility-of-intelle/.
Cision. "Top 10 US Daily Newspapers." June 18, 2014. www.cision.com/us/2014/06/top-10-us-daily-newspapers.
Clements, Millard. "Theory and Education." *Educational Theory* 12, no. 2 (2007): 124–28. doi:10.1111/j.1741-5446.1962.tb00082.x.
Cole, Juan. *Engaging the Muslim World*. Palgrave Macmillan: New York, 2010.
Commins, David. *The Wahhabi Mission and Saudi Arabia*. London: I.B.Tauris, 2006.
Condorcet, Marquis de. *Outlines of an Historical View of the Progress of the Human Mind*. New York: H.M. Carey and P. Rice and Co., 1796.
Cook, Michael. "On the Origins of Wahhabism." *Journal of the Royal Asiatic Society*, 2, no. 2 (July, 1992): 191–202. www.jstor.org/stable/25182507.
Cooper, William Wager, and Piyu Yue. *Challenges of the Muslim World: Present, Future and Past*. Bingley: Emerald, 2008.
Coser, Lewis A. *Men of Ideas: A Sociologist's View*. New York: The Free Press, 1970.
Cranston, Maurice. "Liberalism." In *Encyclopedia of Philosophy*, vol. 4, edited by Paul Edwards, 458–61. New York: Collier-Macmillan, 1972.
Crick, Bernard. *In Defense of Politics*. Chicago: The University of Chicago Press, 1992.
Critchley, Simon. *Infinitely Demanding: Ethics of Commitment, Politics of Resistance*. London: Verso, 2013.

Crystal, David. *The Cambridge Encyclopedia of the English Language*, 2nd ed. Cambridge: Cambridge University Press, 2003.

Curtis, Adam. *The Power of Nightmares*. Documentary directed by Adam Curtis. London: BBC, 2004.

Dahlgren, Peter. "The Internet, Public Spheres, and Political Communication: Dispersion and Deliberation." *Political Communication* 22, no. 2 (2006): 147–62. doi:10.1080/10584600590933160.

al-Dakhil, Khalid S. "Social Origins of the Wahhabi Movement." PhD diss., University of California Los Angeles, 1998. ProQuest (UMI Number: 9906191).

Danziger, Kurt. "Generative metaphor and the history of psychological discourse." In *Metaphors in the History of Psychology*, edited by David Leary, 341–56. Cambridge: Cambridge University Press, 1994.

Deleuze, Gilles. *Negotiations*. New York: Columbia University Press, 1995.

DeLong-Bas, Natana. *Wahhabi Islam: From Revival and Reform to Global Jihad*. Oxford: Oxford University Press, 2004.

Derrida, Jacques. "Force of Law." In *Deconstruction and the Possibility of Justice*, edited by Drucilla Cornell, Michael Rosenfeld, and David Gray Carlson, 3–67. Translated by Mary Quaintance. New York: Routledge, 1992.

———. *Positions*. Translated by Alan Bass. Chicago: The University of Chicago Press, 1981.

de Saussure, Ferdinand. *Course in General Linguistics*. Edited by Charles Bally, Albert Sechehaye, and Albert Riedlinger. Translated by Wade Baskin. New York: McGraw-Hill, 1916.

———. "Signs and language." In *Culture and Society: Contemporary Debates*, edited by Jeffrey C. Alexander and Steven Seidman, 55–64. Cambridge: Cambridge University Press, 1990.

Dolny, Michael. "FAIR STUDY: Think Tank Spectrum 2012." Fairness and Accuracy in Reporting (FAIR), July 1, 2013. http://fair.org/extra/fair%E2%80%88study-think-tank-spectrum-2012.

Domhoff, William. *Who Rules America?* New York: Simon and Schuster, 1999.

Doumato, Eleanor Abdella. "Manning the Barricades: Islam According to Saudi Arabia's School Texts." *The Middle East Journal* 57, no. 2 (2003): 230–47. www.jstor.org/stable/4329879.

Dowd, Maureen. "Loosey Goosey Saudi." *New York Times*, March 2, 2010. www.nytimes.com/2010/03/03/opinion/03dowd.html.

Dreyfus, Hubert. *Being-in-the-World: A Commentary on Heidegger's Being and Time, Division 1*. Boston: MIT Press, 1991.

Drury, Shadia. *Leo Strauss and the American Right*. New York: St. Martin's Press, 1999.

———. *The Political Ideas of Leo Strauss*. New York: Palgrave Macmillan, 2005.

Eagleton, Terry. *On Evil*. New Haven: Yale University Press, 2010.

Eliot, T.S. *Four Quartets*. New York: Harcourt, 1943.

———. *Poems: 1909–1925*. London: Faber and Gwyer, 1925.

Ellingson, Ter. *The Myth of the Noble Savage*. Oakland: University of California Press, 2001.

Esteva, Gustavo, and Madhu Suri Prakash. *Grassroots Post-Modernism: Remaking the Soil of Cultures*. London: Zed, 1998.

Eyerman, Ron. *Between Culture and Politics: Intellectuals in Modern Society*. Cambridge: Polity, 1994.

El Fadl, Khaled Abou. "Islam and the Theology of Power." *Middle East Report*, no. 221 (2001): 28–33. www.jstor.org/stable/1559337.

———. *The Great Theft: Wrestling Islam from the Extremists*. HarperCollins: San Francisco, 2005.

al-Fahad, Abdulaziz H. "From Exclusivism to Accommodation: Doctrinal and Legal Evolution of Wahhabism." *New York University Law Review* 79, no. 2 (May 2004): 485–519. www.nyulawreview.org/sites/default/files/pdf/NYULawReview-79-2-Al-Fahad.pdf.

———. "The Imama vs. the 'Iqal: Hadari-Bedouin Conflict and the Formation of the Saudi State." European University Institute Working Paper, 2002.

Fairclough, Norman. *Analysing Discourse: Textual Analysis for Social Research*. London: Routledge, 2003.

———. *Discourse and Social Change*. Cambridge: Polity Press, 1992.

Fairclough, Norman, and Clive Holes. *Critical Discourse Analysis: The Critical Study of Language*. London: Longman, 1995.

Farr, Thomas F. "Obama administration sidelines religious freedom policy." *The Washington Post*, June 25, 2010. www.washingtonpost.com/wp-dyn/content/article/2010/06/24/AR2010062405069.html.

Fish, Stanley. "Liberalism and Secularism: One and the Same." *New York Times Blogs*, September 2, 2007. http://opinionator.blogs.nytimes.com/2007/09/02/liberalism-and-secularism-one-and-the-same.

Foucault, Michel, and Gilles Deleuze. "The Intellectuals and Power: A Discussion Between Gilles Deleuze and Michel Foucault." *Telos* 16, (1973): 103–109.

Friedman, Thomas L. "Caution, Curves Ahead." *New York Times*, March 27, 2013. www.nytimes.com/2013/03/27/opinion/friedman-cautions-curves-ahead.html.

———. "The Chant Not Heard." *New York Times*, November 30, 2003. www.nytimes.com/2003/11/30/opinion/30FRIE.html.

———. "An Islamic Reformation." *New York Times*, December 4, 2002. www.nytimes.com/2002/12/04/opinion/an-islamic-reformation.html.

———. "The Other Arab Awakening." *New York Times*, November 30, 2013. www.nytimes.com/2013/12/01/opinion/sunday/friedman-the-other-arab-awakening.html.

Frum, David, and Richard Perle. *An End to Evil: How to Win the War on Terror*. New York: Random House, 2003.

Fukuyama, Francis. *The End of History and the Last Man.* London: Penguin Books, 2012.

Gadamer, Hans-Georg. "The Problem of Historical Consciousness." In *Interpretive Social Science*, edited by Paul Rabinow and William M. Sullivan, 103–62. Berkley: University of California Press, 1979.

———. *Truth and Method.* Translated by Joel Weinsheimer and Donald G. Marshall. New York: Continuum, 1994.

Gaffney, Frank Jr. "Saudi friends and foes: Duplicitous desert kingdom could turn U.S. weapons on us." *Washington Times*, November 2, 2010.

———. "Seeing the threat for what it is." *Washington Times*, May 8, 2006.

———. "Undesirable influence." *Washington Times*, June 17, 2003.

Gaus, Gerald, and Shane D. Courtland. "Liberalism." *The Stanford Encyclopedia of Philosophy* (Spring 2011 ed.). Edited by Edward N. Zalta. http://plato.stanford.edu/archives/spr2011/entries/liberalism.

Gee, James Paul. *An Introduction to Discourse Analysis*. London: Routledge, 1999.

Genevieve Lloyd, ed. *Feminism and History of Philosophy (Oxford Readings in Feminism)*. Oxford: Oxford University Press, 2002.

George, Jim. "Leo Strauss, Neoconservatism and US Foreign Policy: Esoteric Nihilism and the Bush Doctrine." *International Politics* 42, no. 2 (2005): 174–202. doi:10.1057/palgrave.ip.8800106.

George, Susan. *Hijacking America: How the Religious and Secular Right Changed What Americans Think*. Cambridge: Polity Press, 2008.

Gerecht, Reuel Marc. "Radioactive Regime." *The Weekly Standard* 18, no. 34. May 20, 2013. www.weeklystandard.com/articles/radioactive-regime_722050.html.

———. "Victory Without Soldiers." *The Weekly Standard*, October 26, 2015.

———. "What Hath Ju-Ju Wrought!" *The Weekly Standard*, March 14, 2005. http://www.weeklystandard.com/what-hath-ju-ju-wrought/article/6534.

———. "Wither Jihad." *The Weekly Standard*, May 16, 2011.

Gilam, Nils. *Mandarins of the Future: Modernization Theory in Cold War America*. Baltimore: John Hopkins University Press, 2003.

Glick, Caroline B. "Brandeis' Jewish Problem." February 21, 2007. http://carolineglick.com/brandeiss_jewish_problem.

Glucksberg, Sam. "The psycholinguistics of metaphor." *Trends in Cognitive Sciences* 7, no. 2 (2003): 92–96. doi:10.1016/S1364-6613(02)00040-2.

Glucksberg, Sam, and Boaz Keysar. "Understanding Metaphorical Comparisons: Beyond Similarity." *Psychological Review* 97, no. 1 (1990): 3–18. http://dx.doi.org/10.1037/0033-295X.97.1.3.

Gold, Dore. *Hatred's Kingdom: How Saudi Arabia Supports the New Global Terrorism*. Regnery: Washington, DC, 2003.

Goldsmith, Arthur A. "Making the World Safe for Partial Democracy? Questioning the Premises of Democracy Promotion." *International Security* 33, no. 2 (2008): 120–47. doi:10.1162/isec.2008.33.2.120.

Gonzalez-Perez, Margaret. "The False Islamization of Female Suicide Bombers." *Gender Issues* 28, no. 1 (2011): 50–65. doi:10.1007/s12147-011-9097-0.

Goodman, Nelson. *Ways of Worldmaking*. Indianapolis: Hackett, 1978.

Gramsci, Antonio. *Further Selections from the Prison Notebooks*. Translated by Derek Boothman. Minneapolis: University of Minnesota Press, 1995.

———. *Selections from the Prison Notebooks*. Edited and translated by Quintin Hoare and Geoffrey Nowell Smith. New York: International Publishers, 1971.

Gray, John. *Black Mass: Apocalyptic Religion and the Death of Utopia*. New York: Farrar, Strauss and Giroux, 2007.

Gregory, Derek. *The Colonial Present*. Oxford: Blackwell, 2004.

Grondin, David. "Mistaking Hegemony for Empire: Neoconservatives, the Bush doctrine, and the Democratic empire." *International Journal* 61, no.1 (2005–2006): 227–41. doi:10.1177/002070200606100115.

Haack, Susan. *Evidence and Inquiry: Towards Reconstruction in Epistemology*. Oxford: Blackwell, 1993.

Habermas, Jürgen. "Heinrich Heine und die Rolle des Intellektuellen in Deutschland." *Merkur: Deutsche Zeitschrift für europäisches Denken* 6 (1986): 453–68.

———. *The Structural Transformation of the Public Sphere: An Inquiry into a Category of Bourgeois Society*. Cambridge: Polity, 1989.

Hacking, Ian. *Mad Travelers: Reflections on the Reality of Transient Mental Illnesses*. Charlottesville: University Press of Virginia, 1998.

———. *The Social Construction of What?* Cambridge: Harvard University Press, 1999.

Hagel, Charles. *Our Next Chapter: Tough Questions, Straight Answers*. New York: Ecco, 2008.

Hakim, Yahya. "The Hashemite-Umayyad Divide and its Impact on the Future of Islam." *The Muslim World: a quarterly review of history, culture, religions & the Christian mission in Islamdom* 106, no. 1 (2016): 83–96. doi: 10.1111/muwo.12125.

Harrington, Michael. "The Welfare State and Its Neoconservative Critics." *Dissent* 20, no. 4 (September 1973): 435–54.

Haslem, Nick. "Dehumanization: An Integrative Review." *Personality and Social Psychology Review* 10, no. 3 (2006): 252–64. doi:10.1207/s15327957pspr1003_4.

Havel, Vaclav. *Disturbing the Peace: A Conversation with Karel Hvizdala*. New York: Vintage Books, 1991.

Hayes, Stephen F. "Donald Trump, Policy Wonk?" *The Weekly Standard*. April 18, 2016. www.weeklystandard.com/donald-trump-policy-wonk/article/2001898.

Hegel, Georg Wilhelm Friedrich. *The Science of Logic*. Translated by George di Giovanni. Cambridge: Cambridge University Press, 2010.

Heidegger, Martin. *Being and Time*. Translated by Joan Stambaugh. Albany: State University of New York Press, 1996.

Heilbrunn, Jacob. *They Knew They Were Right: The Rise of the Neocons*. New York: Doubleday, 2008.

Heinze, Eric A. "The New Utopianism: Liberalism, American Foreign Policy, and the War in Iraq." *Journal of International Political Theory* 4, no.1 (2008): 105–25. doi:10.3366/E1755088208000116.

Hekman, Susan J. "Weber's Ideal Type: A Contemporary Reassessment." *Polity* 16, no. 1 (1983): 119–37. doi:10.2307/3234525.

High, Brandon. "The Recent Historiography Of American Neoconservatism." *The Historical Journal* 52, no. 5 (2009): 475–91. https://www.jstor.org/stable/40264180.

Hill, Amelia. "Racists Created the Noble Savage." *The Guardian*, April 15, 2001. www.theguardian.com/world/2001/apr/15/socialsciences.highereducation.

Hitchens, Christopher. "Defending Islamofascism: It's a valid term. Here's why." *Slate*, October 10, 2007. www.slate.com/articles/news_and_politics/fighting_words/2007/10/defending_islamofascism.html.

———. "The Plight of the Public Intellectual." *Foreign Policy*, April 10, 2008. http://foreignpolicy.com/2009/10/07/the-plight-of-the-public-intellectual/.

———. *Why Orwell Matters*. New York: Basic Books, 2002.

Hobsbawm, Eric. *Nations and Nationalism since 1780: Programme, Myth, Reality*. Cambridge: Cambridge University Press, 1990.

Hofstadter, Douglas, and Emmanuel Sander. *Surfaces and Essences: Analogy as the Fuel and Fire of Thinking*. New York: Basic, 2013.

Holton, Gerald. "The Role of Themata in Science." *Foundations of Physics* 26, no. 4 (1996): 453–65. doi:10.1007/BF02071215.

———. *Thematic Origins of Scientific Thought: Kepler to Einstein*. Cambridge: Harvard University Press, 1988.

Horn, Gerd-Rainer. *The Spirit of '68: Rebellion in Western Europe and North America, 1956–1976*. Oxford: Oxford University Press, 2007.

Hroub, Khaled. *Hamas: A Beginner's Guide*. London: Pluto Press, 2006.

Huffington Post. "Top 10 Newspapers By Circulation: Wall Street Journal Leads Weekday Circulation." April 30, 2013. www.huffingtonpost.com/2013/05/01/newspaper-circulation-top-10_n_3188612.html.

Human Rights Watch. "Saudi Arabia: Surge in Executions." August 21, 2014. www.hrw.org/news/2014/08/21/saudi-arabia-surge-executions.

Hume, David. *The Natural History of Religion*. 1757. Online. http://stoa.usp.br/briannaloch/files/2564/16389/The+Natural+History+of+Religion+-+David+Hume.pdf

Ibrahim, Azeem. "Secretary Kerry Must Stop U.S. Support for Islamic Extremism." *Huffington Post*, March 18, 2013. www.huffingtonpost.com/azeem-ibrahim/secretary-kerry-must-stop_b_2806010.html.

Ibrahim, Raymond. "Saudi Hypocrisy At Its Best." *FrontPageMag*, February 7, 2013. www.frontpagemag.com/fpm/176697/saudi-hypocrisy-its-best-raymond-ibrahim.

"Irving Kristol (1920–2009)." Right Web, September 28, 2009. www.rightweb.irc-online.org/profile/kristol_irving.

Ish-Shalom, Piki. "'The Civilization of Clashes': Misapplying the Democratic Peace in the Middle East." *Political Science Quarterly* 122, no. 4 (2007/2008): 533–54. http://onlinelibrary.wiley.com/doi/10.1002/j.1538-165X.2007.tb00608.x/abstract.

Jahoda, Gustav. *Images of Savages: Ancient Roots of Modern Prejudice in Western Culture*. London: Routledge & Kegan Paul, 1999.

Joffe, Alex. "Fabricating Palestinian History: The Rhetoric of Nonsense." *Middle East Quarterly* 19, no. 3 (2012): 15–22. http://www.meforum.org/3262/palestinian-history-nonsense.

Jørgensen, Marianne, and Louise Phillips. *Discourse Analysis as Theory and Method.* London: Sage, 2002.

Juvenal. *Satires.* Translated by Charles Badham. New York: Harper and Brothers, 1855.

Kant, Immanuel. "Idea for a Universal History with a Cosmopolitan Purpose." In *Political Writings*, edited by H. Reiss, translated by H.B Nisbet, 41–53. Cambridge: Cambridge University Press, 1970.

———. "Toward Perpetual Peace." In *Political Writings*, edited by H. Reiss, translated by H.B Nisbet, 93–130. Cambridge: Cambridge University Press, 1970.

Karabel, Jerome. "Towards a theory of intellectuals and politics." *Theory and Society* 25, no. 2 (1996): 205–23.

Kaufman, Joe, and Beila Rabinowitz. "Islamic Saudi Hate Academy." *FrontPageMag*, June 20, 2008. http://archive.frontpagemag.com/readArticle.aspx?ARTID=31404.

Keats, John. "32. Endymion, Book 1." *The Poetic Works of John Keats.* London: Macmillan, 1884.

Kechichian, Joseph A. "The Role of the Ulama in the Politics of an Islamic State: The Case of Saudi Arabia." *International Journal of Middle East Studies* 18, no. 1 (1986): 53–71. www.jstor.org/stable/162860.

Kelman, Herbert C. "Violence Without Restraint: Reflections on the dehumanization of victims and victimizers." In *Varieties of Psychohistory*, edited by G.M. Kren and L.H. Rappoport, 282–314. New York: Springer, 1976.

Kettler, David, and Volka Meja. *Karl Mannheim and the Crisis of Liberalism.* New Brunswick: Transaction Publishers, 1995.

Khazaleh, Lorenz. "Benedict Anderson: 'I like nationalism's utopian elements.'" May, 25, 2011. University of Oslo. www.uio.no/english/research/interfaculty-research-areas/culcom/news/2005/anderson.html.

Kline, Scott. "The Culture War Gone Global: 'Family Values' and the Shape of US Foreign Policy." *International Relations* 18, no. 4 (2004): 453–66. doi:10.1177/0047117804048489.

Knysh, Alexander. "A Clear and Present Danger: 'Wahhabism' as a Rhetorical Foil." *Die Welt des Islams* 44, no. 1 (2004): 3–26. doi:10.1163/1570060047737l2569.

Kolakowski, Leszek. *Marxism and Beyond: On Historical Understanding and Individual Responsibility*. London: Paladin, 1971.

Kostiner, Joseph. "On Instruments and Their Designers: The Ikhwan of the Najd and the Emergence of the Saudi State." *Middle Eastern Studies* 21, no. 3 (2006): 298–323. doi: 10.1080/00263208508700631.

Kristof, Nicholas. "The Terrorists the Saudis Cultivate in Peaceful Countries," *New York Times*, July 2, 2016. https://www.nytimes.com/2016/07/03/opinion/sunday/the-terrorists-the-saudis-cultivate-in-peaceful-countries.html.

Kristol, Irving. "Confessions of a True, Self-Confessed-Perhaps the Only—'Neo-conservative.'" In *Reflections of a Neoconservative*, edited by Irving Kristol, 73–77. New York: Basic Books, 1983.

———. *Two Cheers For Capitalism*. New York: Basic Books, 1978.

Kristol, William. "Donald and Decadence." *The Weekly Standard*, March 28–April 4, 2016. www.weeklystandard.com/donald-and-decadence/article/2001621.

Kurzman, Charles, and Lynn Owens. "The Sociology of Intellectuals." *Annual Review of Sociology* 28 (2002): 63–80. doi:10.1146/annurev.soc.28110601.140745.

Lacy, Robert. *Inside the Kingdom: Kings, Clerics, Modernists, Terrorists, and the Struggle for Saudi Arabia*. New York: Viking Press, 2009.

Lakoff, George. "The Conceptual Metaphor: The Contemporary Theory of Metaphor." In *Cognitive Linguistics: Basic Readings*, edited by Dirk Geeraerts, 185–238. Berlin: Mouton de Gruyter, 2006.

———. *Moral Politics: How Liberals and Conservatives Think*. 2nd ed. Chicago: The University of Chicago Press, 2002.

Lakoff, George, and Mark Johnson. *Metaphors We Live By*. Chicago: The University of Chicago Press, 1980.

Lakoff, George, and Mark Turner. *More Than Cool Reason: A Field Guide to Poetic Metaphor*. Chicago: The University of Chicago Press, 1989.

Lander, Mark. "Obama Seeks Reset in Arab World." *New York Times*, May 11, 2001. A12.

Lange, Margaret Meek. "Progress." *The Stanford Encyclopedia of Philosophy* (Spring 2011 ed.). Edited by Edward N. Zalta. http://plato.stanford.edu/archives/spr2011/entries/progress.

Ledeen, Michael. *The War Against the Terror Masters: Why it Happened. Where Are We Now. How We'll Win*. New York: Truman Talley Books, 2003.

———. "The Wider War." *Wall Street Journal*, March 3, 2007. www.wsj.com/articles/SB117289056115525687.

———. "The Wider War." *American Enterprise Institute*, March 3, 2007. www.aei.org/article/foreign-and-defense-policy/regional/india-pakistan-afghanistan/the-wider-war.

Lenin, V.I. "The Marx-Engels Correspondence." *Pravda* 19, no. 268 (1920): 552–58. www.marxists.org/archive/lenin/works/1913/dec/x01.htm.
Levy, Robert. *Intellectuals, unissez-vous!* Paris: Michel Riviere, 1931.
Lewis, Bernard. "Freedom and Justice in Islam." *Society* 44, no. 2 (2007): 66–70. doi:10.1007/BF02819929.
Littman, David G. "Teaching Hatred in Saudi Arabia and Egypt: The UN Response." *FrontPageMag*, October 1, 2004. http://archive.frontpagemag.com/readArticle.aspx?ARTID=11185.
Lloyd, Sharon A., and Susanne Sreedhar. "Hobbes's Moral and Political Philosophy." *The Stanford Encyclopedia of Philosophy* (Spring 2014 ed.). Edited by Edward N. Zalta. http://plato.stanford.edu/archives/spr2014/entries/hobbes-moral.
Lustig, R. Jeffrey. *Corporate Liberalism: The Origins of Modern American Political Theory, 1890–1920*. Berkeley: University of California Press, 1982.
Lyell, Charles. *Principles of Geology*, Volume 1. Chicago: The University of Chicago Press, 1990.
Lynch, Timothy J. "Kristol Balls: Neoconservative Visions of Islam and the Middle East." *International Politics* 45, no. 2 (2008): 182–211. doi:10.1057/palgrave.ip.8800227.
Mahdi, Wael. "There is no such thing as Wahabism, Saudi prince says." *The National*, March 18, 2010. www.thenational.ae/news/world/middle-east/there-is-no-such-thing-as-wahabism-saudi-prince-says?pageCount=0#ixzz3FsvFSvG.
Mannheim, Karl. *Freedom, Power, and Democratic Planning*. Oxford: Oxford University Press, 1950.
———. *Ideology and Utopia: An Introduction to the Sociology of Knowledge*. London: Routledge, 1936.
———. "The Problem of the Intelligentsia." In *Essays on the Sociology of Culture*, edited by Bryan S. Turner, 91–170. London: Routledge, 1956.
———. "The Sociological Problem of the 'Intelligentsia.'" *Ideology and Utopia: An Introduction to the Sociology of Knowledge*, translated by Louis Wirth and Edward Shils, 153–64. San Diego: Harcourt Brace Jovanovich, 1985.
———. "The Sociology of Intellectuals." *Theory, Culture and Society* 10, no. 3 (1993): 69–80. doi:10.1177/026327693010003004.
May, Clifford D. "No Peace While World War Rages." *Moment Magazine*, March 10, 2010. www.defenddemocracy.org/media-hit/no-peace-while-world-war-rages/#sthash.Xgj8Qw1P.dpuf.
———. "Saudi Ride of Tiger Gets Riskier." *Daily Breeze*, May 16, 2003, A17.
———. "Terror in Saudi Arabia." *Cincinnati Post*, May 15, 2003. A18.0.
Mayall, James, and Ricardo Soares de Oliveira, eds. *The New Protectorates: International Tutelage and the Making of Liberal States*. London: Hurst & Co., 2011.
McCormack, John. "Unfit to Serve." *The Weekly Standard*, May 16, 2016.
McIntyre, Alasdair. *After Virtue*. Notre Dame: University of Notre Dame Press, 1981.

Mearsheimer, John. "Hans Mogenthau and the Iraq war: realism versus neo-conservatism." *Open Democracy*, May 19, 2005. www.opendemocracy.net/democracy-americanpower/Morgenthau_2522.jsp.

Mearsheimer, John, and Stephen Walt. "The Israel Lobby and U.S. Foreign Policy." *Middle East Policy* XIII, no. 3 (2006): 29–87. http://mearsheimer.uchicago.edu/pdfs/IsraelLobby.pdf.

Meja, Volker, and Nico Stehr, eds. *Knowledge and Politics: The Sociology of Knowledge Dispute*. London: Routledge & Kegan Paul, 1990.

Middle East Media Research Institute. "Special Dispatch No. 2571, Liberal Saudi Columnist: With Wahhabism as State Religion, There's No Chance of Reform for Saudi Schools." September 30, 2009. https://www.memri.org/reports/liberal-saudi-columnist-wahhabism-state-religion-theres-no-chance-reform-saudi-schools.

———. "Special Dispatch No. 4345, Saudi Textbook: The Enmity between the Muslims and the Jews is Everlasting." December 8, 2011. www.memri.org/report/en/0/0/0/0/0/0/5896.htm.

Middle East Media Research Institute TV, "#5059, Saudi Education Ministry Textbooks Used in Remote Burkina Faso Village," video clip, 2:22, August 20, 2015, www.memritv.org/clip/en/5059.htm.

Midgley, Mary. *The Myths We Live By*. London: Routledge, 2003.

Mill, John Stuart. *Collected Works of John Stuart Mill*. Edited by J.M. Robson. Toronto: University of Toronto Press, 1963.

———. *Liberty*. London: Everyman, J.M. Dent and Sons, 1910.

———. "On Liberty." In *Collected Works of John Stuart Mill*, edited by J.M. Robson, 213–310. Toronto: University of Toronto Press, 1963.

———. *On Liberty, Utilitarianism and Other Essays*, edited by Mark Philp and Frederick Rosen. Oxford: Oxford University Press, 2015.

———. *A System of Logic, Ratiocinative and Inductive*. London: Longmans, Green and Co., 1843.

Miller, George A. "Images and Models, Simile and Metaphors." In *Metaphor and Thought*, 2nd ed., edited by Andrew Ortony, 357–400. Cambridge: Cambridge University Press, 1979.

Mitchell, W.J.T. "Representation." In *Critical Terms for Literary Study*, 2nd ed., edited by Frank Lentricchia and Thomas McLaughlin, 11–22. Chicago: The University of Chicago Press, 1995. http://search.credoreference.com/content/entry/uchicagols/representation/0.

Moniquet, Claude. "The involvement of Salafism/Wahhabism in the support and supply of arms to rebel groups around the world." Directorate-General for External Policies, European Parliament Brussels, 2013. EXPO/B/AFET/FWC/2009-01/LOT4/23.

Mouline, Nabil. *Les clercs de l'Islam: autorité religieuse et pouvoir politique en Arabie Saoudite, XVIIIe–XXIe siècle*. Paris: Presses Universitaires de France, 2011.

Müller, Martin. "What's in a Word? Problematizing Translation between Languages." *Area* 39, no. 2 (2007): 206–13. http://onlinelibrary.wiley.com/doi/10.1111/j.1475-4762.2007.00731.x/abstract.

Müller-Doohm, Stefan. "Two Ways of Being a Public Intellectual: Sociological Observations Concerning the Transformation of a Social Figure of Modernity." *European Journal of Social Theory* 8, no. 3 (2005): 269–80. doi:10.1177/1368431005054794.

Nazer, Hisham. *Power of a Third Kind: The Western Attempt to Colonize the Global Village.* Westport: Praeger, 1999.

Nettl, J.P. "Ideas, Intellectuals, and Structures of Dissent." In *On Intellectuals: Theoretical Case Studies*, edited by Philip Rieff, 53–122. New York: Doubleday, 1969.

Nevo, Joseph. "Religion and National Identity in Saudi Arabia." *Middle Eastern Studies* 34, no. 3 (1998): 34–53. www.jstor.org/stable/4283951.

Nikander, Pirjo. "Constructionism and Discourse Analysis." In *Handbook of Constructionist Research*, edited by James A. Holstein and Jaber F. Gubrium, 413–28. New York: Guilford, 2008.

Nisbet, Robert. *Sociology as an Art Form.* New York: Oxford University Press, 1976.

Olivecrona, Karl. "Appropriation in the State of Nature: Locke on the Origin of Property." *Journal of the History of Ideas* 35, no. 2 (1974): 211–30. www.jstor.org/stable/2708759.

Oliver, Haneef James. *The Wahhabi Myth: Dispelling Prevalent Fallacies and the Fictitious Link with Bin Laden.* Trafford: Victoria, 2002.

Ollman, Bertell. *Alienation: Marx's Conception of Man in Capitalist Society*, 2nd ed. Cambridge: Cambridge University Press, 1976.

———. *Dance of the Dialectic: Steps in Marx's Method.* Chicago: University of Illinois Press, 2003.

———. "Why Dialectics? Why Now?" *Science and Society* 62, no. 3 (1998): 338–57. ISSN: 00368237.

Ollman, Bertell, and Tony Smith. "Dialectics: The New Frontier." *Science and Society* 62, no. 3 (1998): 333–37. ISSN: 00368237.

Orwell, George. *The Lion and the Unicorn: Socialism and the English Genius.* London: Secker and Warburg, 1962.

———. "Writers and Leviathan." In *The Intellectuals: A Controversial Portrait*, edited by George B. de Huszar, 267–71. Glencoe: The Free Press, 1960.

Osborne, Thomas. "On Mediators: Intellectuals and the Ideas Trade in the Knowledge Society." *Economy and Society* 33, no. 4 (2004): 430–47. doi:10.1080/0308514042000285224.

Parsons, Talcott. "'The intellectual': a social role category." In *On Intellectuals: Theoretical Studies, Case Studies*, edited by Philip Rieff, 3–26. Garden City: Doubleday, 1969.

Phillips, H.P. "Problems of Translation and Menacing in Fieldwork." In *Human Organisation Research: Field Relations and Techniques*, edited by N. Adams and J.J. Preiss, 290–307. Dorsey Press: Homewood, 1960.

Plato. *Apology*. Translated by G.M.A. Grube. Indianapolis: Hackett Publishing Company, 1981.

Prokop, Michaela. "Saudi Arabia: The Politics of Education." *International affairs* 79, no. 1 (2003): 77–89. doi:10.1111/1468-2346.00296.

Pryce-Jones, David. "The Saudi Revolution." *Wall Street Journal*, November 12, 2003. https://www.wsj.com/articles/SB106859058223389500.

Rakic, Marko, and Dragisa Jurisic. "Wahhabism as a Militant Form of Islam on Europe's Doorstep." *Studies in Conflict and Terrorism* 35 (2012): 650–63. doi: 10.1080/1057610X.2012.702671.

Ragin, Charles C. *Fuzzy-Set Social Science*. Chicago: The University of Chicago Press, 2000.

al-Rasheed, Madawi. *A History of Saudi Arabia*. Cambridge: Cambridge University Press, 2010.

Rawls, John. "An Idea of Overlapping Consensus." *Oxford Journal of Legal Studies* 7, no. 1 (1987): 1–25.

———. *Law of Peoples*. Cambridge: Harvard University Press, 1999.

———. *Political Liberalism*. New York: Columbia University Press, 1996.

———. *A Theory of Justice*. Cambridge: Belknap, 1971.

Richmond, H. Smith, and J.V. Brogan. "Simile." In *The Princeton Encyclopedia of Poetry and Poetics*, 4th ed. Princeton: Princeton University Press, 2012.

Right Web. "Middle East Media Research Institute." November 9, 2011. http://rightweb.irc-online.org/profile/middle_east_media_research_institute.

Rorty, Richard. *Objectivity, Relativism, and Truth: Philosophical Papers*, vol. 1. Cambridge: Cambridge University Press, 1991.

Rubin, Barry M., ed. *Guide to Islamist Movements*, vol. 1. New York: M.E. Sharpe, 2010.

Russell, Bertrand. "On Denoting." In *Mind, Logic and Knowledge*, 41f. London: George Allen and Unwin, 1956.

Rust, Joshua. *John and the Construction of Social Reality*. London: Continuum, 2006.

Said, Edward. *Culture and Imperialism*. New York: Vintage, 1993.

———. *Orientalism*. London: Penguin, 1977.

———. "The Public Role of Writers and Intellectuals." In *The Public Intellectual*, edited by Helen Small, 19–39. Oxford: Blackwell, 2002.

———. *Representations of the Intellectual: The 1993 Reith Lectures*. London: Vintage, 1994.

Saidel, Nicholas. "Saudi Arabia, the Mediator Israelis and Palestinians Have Been Waiting For?" *Haaretz*, May 16, 2016. www.haaretz.com/opinion/.premium-1.719848.

Sartre, Jean-Paul. *Anti-Semite and Jew*. Translated by George G. Becker. New York: Schocken Books, 1948.

Al Saud, Mohammed bin Nawaf. "Saudi Arabia does not support Islamic State terrorists—or any others." *The Guardian*, August 18, 2014. www.theguardian.com/world/2014/aug/17/saudi-arabia-not-support-islamic-state-terrorists.

Schmitt, Carl. *The Concept of the Political*. Chicago: The University of Chicago Press, 1996.

Schön, Donald. "Generative metaphor: A perspective on problem-setting in social policy." In *Metaphor and Thought*, edited by A. Ortony, 137–63. Cambridge: Cambridge University Press, 1979.

Schutz, Alfred. "The Problem of Transcendental Intersubjectivity in Husserl." In *Collected Papers III: Studies in Phenomenological Philosophy*. The Hague: Martinus Nijhoff, 1970.

Schwartz, Michael W. "Wahhabism and the First Amendment." *Commentary Magazine*, January 13, 2010. www.commentarymagazine.com/articles/wahhabism-and-the-first-amendment.

Schwartz, Stephen. "Natana DeLong-Bas: American Professor, Wahhabi Apologist." *Real Clear Politics*, January 19, 2007. www.realclearpolitics.com/articles/2007/01/natana_delongbas_american_prof.html.

———. "The Second Kosovo War." *The Weekly Standard*, February 2, 2009. www.weeklystandard.com/the-second-kosovo-war/article/17182.

———. *The Two Faces of Islam: The House of Sa'ud from Tradition to Terror*. New York: Doubleday, 2002.

Schwartz, Stephen, and Irfan al-Alawi. "Valentine's Day in Saudi Arabia." *The Weekly Standard*, March 5, 2007. www.weeklystandard.com/valentines-day-in-saudi-arabia/article/14452.

Shah, Hemant. "Race, Mass Communication, and Modernization: Intellectual Networks and the Flow of Ideas." In *Anti-Racism and Multiculturalism: Studies in International Communication*, edited by Mark D. Alleyne, 21–54. New Jersey: Transaction, 2011.

Shapiro, Ian. *Containment: Rebuilding a Strategy Against Global Terror*. New Jersey: Princeton University Press, 2007.

Shavit, Uriya. "Raising *Salafi* Children in the West." *Islam and Christian-Muslim Relations* (2016): 1–22. http://dx.doi.org/10.1080/09596410.2016.1239920.

Shibata, Midori, Akira Toyomura, Hiroki Motoyama, Hiroaki Itoh, Yasuhiro Kawabata, and Jun-ichi Abe. "Does simile comprehension differ from metaphor comprehension? A functional MRI study." *Brain and Language* 121, no. 3 (2012): 254–60. doi:10.1016/j.bandl.2012.03.006.

Shils, Edward. *The Intellectual Between Tradition and Modernity: The Indian Situation*. The Hague: Mouton, 1961.

———. *The Intellectuals and the Powers and Other Essays*. Chicago: The University of Chicago Press, 1972.

Shurmer-Smith, Pamela, ed. *Doing Cultural Geography*. London: Sage, 2002.

Silone, Ignazio. "On the place of intellect and pretension of the intellectual." In *The Intellectuals: A Controversial Portrait*, edited by George B. de Huszar, 261–66. Glencoe: The Free Press, 1960.

Sito-Sucic, Daria. "Bosnia's Muslims divided over inroads of Wahhabism."

The Washington Post, December 29, 2006. http://www.washingtonpost.com/wpdyn/content/article/2006/12/29/AR2006122900325_pf.html.

Smalley, W.F. "The Wahhabis and Ibn Sa'ud." *The Muslim World* 22, no. 3 (July 1932): 227–46. doi: 10.1111/j.1478-1913.1932.tb02882.x.

Smith, Anthony. *Theories of Nationalism*. London: Duckworth, 1971.

Smith, Lee. "Requiem for the Peace Process." *The Weekly Standard*. July 31, 2013. www.weeklystandard.com/requiem-for-the-peace-process/article/742378.

Sorensen, Georg. *A Liberal Order in Crisis: Choosing between Imposition and Restraint*. Ithaca: Cornell University Press, 2011.

Spencer, Herbert. "Progress: Its Law and Cause." *Essays: Scientific, Political, and Speculative: Volume 1*, 1–54. London: D. Appleton and Company, 1858.

Spencer, Robert. "The Swine are Christians and the Apes are Jews." *FrontPageMag*, May 23, 2006. http://archive.frontpagemag.com/readArticle.aspx?ARTID=4320.

Stanley, Trevor. "Understanding the Origins of Wahhabism and Salafism." *Terrorism Monitor* 3, no. 14 (2005). Online. www.jamestown.org/programs/tm/single/?tx_ttnews%5Btt_news%5D=528&#.U-uIZtwxHlI.

Starr, Paul. *Freedom's Power: The True Force of Liberalism*. New York: Basic Books, 2007.

Stefon, Matt. *Islamic Beliefs and Practices*. New York: The Rosen Publishing Group, 2009.

Stephens, Bret. "The Arab Invasion." *Wall Street Journal*, April 17, 2007. www.wsj.com/articles/SB117677971027672274.

Suny, Ronald G., and Michael D. Kennedy, eds. *Intellectuals and the Articulation of the Nation*. Ann Arbor: University of Michigan Press, 1999.

Taylor, Charles. "The Politics of Recognition." In *Multiculturalism: Examining the Politics of Recognition*, edited by A. Gutmann, 25–73. Princeton: Princeton University Press, 1994.

Temple, Bogusia, and Alys Young. "Qualitative research and translation dilemmas." *Qualitative Research* 4, no. 2 (2004): 161–78. doi:10.1177/1468794104044430.

Thornton, Stephen. "Karl Popper." *The Stanford Encyclopedia of Philosophy* (Summer 2014 ed.). Edited by Edward N. Zalta. http://plato.stanford.edu/archives/sum2014/entries/popper.

Toulmin, Stephen. *Human Understanding: The Evolution of Concepts*, vol. 1. Oxford: Oxford University Press, 1982.

Turgot, Anne-Robert-Jacques. "A Philosophical Review of the Successive Advances of the Human Mind." In *Turgot on Progress, Sociology and Economics*, edited by R.L. Meek, 41–59. Cambridge: Cambridge University Press, 1973.

———. "On University History." In *Turgot on Progress, Sociology and Economics*, edited by R.L. Meek, 61–118. Cambridge: Cambridge University Press, 1973.

United States Government. "Terrorism Financing: Origination, Organization, and Prevention: Hearing before the Committee on Governmental Affairs United States Senate: One Hundred Eight Congress First Session." July 31, 2003. www.gpo.gov/fdsys/pkg/CHRG-108shrg89039/pdf/CHRG-108shrg89039.pdf.

U.S. Senate Select Committee on Intelligence. "Press Release of Intelligence Committee Senate Intelligence Committee Unveils Final Phase II Reports on Prewar Iraq Intelligence—Two Bipartisan Reports Detail Administration Misstatements on Prewar Iraq Intelligence, and Inappropriate Intelligence Activities by Pentagon Policy Office." www.intelligence.senate.gov/press/record.cfm?id=298775.

Vaïsse, Justin. *Neoconservatism: The Biography of a Movement*. Cambridge: Belknap, 2010.

Vlastos, Gregory. *Studies in Greek Philosophy*, vol. 2. Edited by Daniel W. Graham. New Jersey: Princeton University Press 1997.

Walzer, Michael. *The Company of Critics*. New York: Basic Books, 1988.

Watts, Rob. "Truth and Politics: Thinking About Evidence-Based Policy in the Age of Spin." *Australian Journal of Public Administration* 73, no. 1 (2014): 34–46. doi:10.111/1467-8500.12061.

Weber, Max. "'Objectivity' in Social Science and Social Policy." *The Methodology of the Social Sciences*, edited and translated by E.A. Shils and H.A. Finch, 49–112. New York: The Free Press, 1949.

———. "The Profession and Vocation of Politics." *Political Writings*, edited and translated by P. Lassman and R. Spiers, 309–69. Cambridge: Cambridge University Press, 1994.

Wikileaks. "H: ISRAEL, COUPLE OF THINGS. SID." March 16, 2010. https://wikileaks.org/clinton-emails/emailid/3251.

Wikipedia. "Wahhabi Movement." http://en.wikipedia.org/wiki/Wahhabi (accessed November 2, 2014).

Wiktorowicz, Quintan. "Anatomy of the Salafi Movement." *Studies in Conflict & Terrorism* 29, no. 3 (2006): 207–39. doi:10.1080/10576100500497004.

Wilson, James Q. ""Policy Intellectuals" and public policy." *The Public Interest*, no. 64 (Summer 1981): 31–46. https://www.nationalaffairs.com/public_interest/detail/policy-intellectuals-and-public-policy.

Wimborne, Brian. "The Tactical Myth of Palestinian Identity." *Quadrant Online*, June 7, 2014. http://quadrant.org.au/magazine/2014/06/tactical-myth-palestinian-identity.

Wink, Walter. "Facing the Myth of Redemptive Violence." *The Bible in Transmission* (Spring 1999). www2.goshen.edu/~joannab/women/wink99.pdf.

———. "Facing the Myth of Redemptive Violence." November 16, 2007. www.ekklesia.co.uk/content/cpt/article_060823wink.shtml.

Witt, Charlotte, and Lisa Shapiro. "Feminist History of Philosophy." *The Stanford Encyclopedia of Philosophy* (Winter 2014 ed.). Edited by

Edward N. Zalta. http://plato.stanford.edu/archives/win2014/entries/feminism-femhist.

Wittgenstein, Ludwig. *On Certainty*. Edited by G.E.M. Anscombe and G.H. von Wright. Translated by Denis Paul and G.E.M. Anscombe. New York: Harper and Row. 1969.

———. *Philosophical Investigations*. Edited by G.E.M. Anscombe and R. Rhees. Translated by G.E.M. Anscombe. Oxford: Blackwell, 1953.

Wodak, Ruth. "Aspects of Critical Discourse Analysis." http://userpages.uni-koblenz.de/~diekmann/zfal/zfalarchiv/zfal36_1.pdf.

Wodak, Ruth, and Michael Meyer. "Critical Discourse Analysis: History, Agenda, Theory and Methodology." In *Methods of Critical Discourse Analysis*, 2nd ed., edited by Ruth Wodak and Michael Meyer, 1–33. London: Sage, 2009.

———. "What CDA is About—A Summary of its History, Important Concepts and Its Development." In *Methods of Critical Discourse Analysis*, 1st ed., edited by Ruth Wodak and Michael Meyer, 1–13. London: Sage, 2001.

Zadeh, Lotfi A. "A Fuzzy-Set-Theoretic Interpretation of Linguistic Hedges." *Journal of Cybernetics* 2, no. 3 (1972): 4–34. doi:10.1080/01969727208542910.

———. "Fuzzy Sets." *Information Control* 8, no. 3 (1965): 338–53.

———. "A Note on Prototype Theory and Fuzzy Sets." *Cognition* 12, no. 3 (1982): 291–97. doi:10.1016/0010-0277(82)90036-1.

Zakaria, Fareed. "The Saudi Trap." *Newsweek*, June 27, 2004. www.newsweek.com/saudi-trap-128707.

———. "U.S. fuel to the Middle East fire." *Washington Post*, January 16, 2014. www.washingtonpost.com/opinions/fareed-zakaria-us-fuel-to-the-middle-east-fire/2014/01/16/489c2424-7ef1-11e3-95c6-0a7aa80874bc_story.html.

Zargar, Cameron. "The Hanbali and Wahhabi Schools of Thought: As Observed Through the Case of *Ziyarah*." Master's thesis, The Ohio State University, 2014. https://etd.ohiolink.edu/!etd.send_file?accession=osu1398829915&disposition=inline.

Zhou, Zhenghuan. *Liberal Rights and Political Culture: Envisioning Democracy in China*. New York: Routledge, 2005.

Index